REFLECTIONS

on a

RAVAGED

CENTURY

REFLECTIONS
on a
RAVAGED
CENTURY

Robert Conquest

W. W. Norton & Company
New York ◆ London

For information about permission to reproduce selections from this book, write to Permissions,
W. W. Norton & Company, Inc., 500 Fifth Avenue, New York, NY 10110

This book is composed in Centaur
Desktop composition by Tom Ernst
Manufacturing by Quebecor Printing, Fairfield, Inc.
Book design by BTDnyc

Library of Congress Cataloging-in-Publication-Data
Conquest, Robert.
Reflections on a ravaged century / by Robert Conquest.
p.   cm.
Includes bibliographical references and index.
ISBN 0-393-04818-7
I. History, Modern—20th Century. I. Title.
D421.C595   1999
909.08—dc21   99-31980
CIP

W. W. Norton & Company, Inc., 500 Fifth Avenue, New York, N.Y. 10110
www.wwnorton.com

W. W. Norton & Company Ltd., 10 Coptic Street, London WC1A 1PU

2 3 4 5 6 7 8 9 0

for
Helen

Contents

PART II
FACING THE CONSEQUENCES

◆

Preface

This book appears as the world lumberingly and indecisively turns back from the abysses which we were lucky to escape, and which still yawn. Its theme is that the main responsibility for the century's disasters lies not so much in the problems as in the solutions, not in impersonal forces but in human beings, thinking certain thoughts and as a result performing certain actions.

Acknowledgments are due to the Hoover Institution on War, Revolution and Peace, Stanford University; also to the United States Institute of Peace and the Institute of Contemporary Studies. Much gratitude goes to my editor Robert Weil, also to Grant McIntyre. And I am greatly indebted to Anatol Shmelev for indefatigable and invaluable research and other assistance; to Amy Desai, even more than usual, for her unmatched standard of secretarial work, in particularly difficult circumstances; and, as ever, to my wife.

Some of the material first appeared in the *New York Review of Books*, the *Times Literary Supplement*, the *Daily Telegraph*, the *New Criterion*, *Izvestiya*, *We and They* (1980) and my 1993 Jefferson Lecture in the Humanities.

ROBERT CONQUEST
Stanford 1999

Introduction

In a story by the science fiction writer Hal Clement, when an inter-stellar fugitive's miscalculation has led to his death, the comment is made, "Live and learn, they say . . . but the difficulty seems to lie in living while you learn." Over this century the human race has survived experiences that, to put it mildly, should have been instructive. Scores of millions have been slaughtered, and it cannot be said that the avoidance of the even worse catastrophe of nuclear war was foreordained. Have the lessons been learned? And if so, to what extent?

2.

Ideas that claimed to transcend all problems, but were defective or delu-sive, devastated minds, and movements, and whole countries, and looked like plausible contenders for world supremacy. In fact, humanity has been savaged and trampled by rogue ideologies.

The central aim of this book is therefore an investigation, and a demonstration, of how and why these disastrous mental distortions arose, how and why they came to motivate movements, parties and states. We trace their incubation, their nature and their results; and con-clude with suggestions for their future prevention.

Seventy years ago W. B. Yeats famously wrote that, then,

The best lack all conviction, while the worst
Are full of passionate intensity.

This has been true in the sense that obsessive attachment to these ideas has been a powerful characteristic of our century. But lack of obsessive "conviction" has not been a decisive disadvantage. I think of Richard Hillary, the Battle of Britain pilot eventually killed in the war, who wrote in his *The Last Enemy* of how one of his motives was to show that skeptics like himself could take on—and defeat—"the dogma-fed youth of the Luftwaffe."

And though the struggle with the forces of "dogma" has been long and hard, the open society has so far prevailed; there is no reason, in principle, why it should not do so in the future if the lessons have been truly learned, and when learned, not forgotten.

3.

In dealing with such themes, this book seeks to avoid what Orwell called "the lure of the profound." Though in a sense philosophical, it is not formal political philosophy. Though much research has, of course, gone into it, it is primarily a product not so much of "research" as of knowledge, judgment, thought and experience.

So if I support certain views and reject others, it is less from prejudice than from postjudice.

And then, the mind is a venue of thought, but also of feeling, not always rationally describable. Late in 1997 the Paris *Le Monde* interviewed me by phone. I was asked did I find the Holocaust "worse" than the Stalinist crimes. I answered yes, I did, but when the interviewer asked why, I could only answer honestly with "I feel so." Not a final judgment, let alone to suggest that the Holocaust was *much* "worse" than the Stalinist terrors, or to decry the view of the great Jewish Soviet writer Vasily Grossman, whose own mother was killed by the Nazis, that there is almost nothing to choose between the two systems. Still, this primary "feeling," based indeed on knowledge, has a validity of its own. I would argue, too, that, whatever view one takes, without feeling the Holocaust one cannot feel, or understand, Stalinism. The crux is nevertheless that such feelings are only acceptable when based on, or conjoined with, sound knowledge and careful thought. And, on the other side of our concern, our problems have been due not to fallacious ideas in the abstract but to the extreme, uncontrolled, emotional charge they carry.

4.

Much of the knowledge and thought deployed here comes from a wide range of observers and thinkers, and these are given full credit. I have quoted them when, as Montaigne wrote, they do better "what I cannot so well express"; or when their authority gives weight to an argument (or, on the other hand, when a passage is a striking illustration of what I conceive to be an absurdity).

Nor, over most of what follows, have I sought to "prove" this or that thesis by an accumulation of evidence. The instances given, sometimes from personal experience, are intended as illustrations or clarifications.

On a subsidiary point, I have not used references except where this appears to be unavoidable, or where the original may be hard to find. This is not because of any hostility to notes, as such: fifty and more pages of these are to be found in other books of mine.* I trust that few will mind their absence here.

The present book is not a holy text, and those persuaded by its main thrust will not necessarily agree with every point. Some of the opinions advanced will be contested in good faith and with respectable argument—though it would be naïve to expect this of every critic. G. K. Chesterton once complained that a reviewer of his *The Man Who Was Thursday* had failed to read the book's subtitle, *A Dream*. One of the present writer's works was reviewed some years ago by a critic who failed not quite so ostentatiously, having only omitted to read the second paragraph of the short preface acknowledging my academic sponsors. Many writers must have had similar experiences.

It may be rather more cogently argued that my account of the culture of the rule of law and political liberty does not give proportionate space to all the blemishes, the incompetence, the fallings off from its promise. My concern was in no way to deny these, but to present the strengths and virtues more central to that culture which, to the extent that they have deteriorated, or been undermined, are yet viable and capable of revival; and that it is in any case our, and the world's, only resource in the struggle with truly homicidal obsessions.

It is impossible to have any understanding of the present without some perspective on humanity's past, and on its unpredictable but conceivable futures. The present writer can plead that he is a long-standing member of the Society for the Promotion of Roman Studies and has written on various ancient, medieval and nineteenth-century themes; and at the same time

---

*See *The Great Terror: A Reassessment* (New York: Oxford University Press; London: Century Hutchinson, 1990), pp. 491–544; *The Harvest of Sorrow* (same publishers, 1986), pp. 348–93.

is a Fellow—from pre-*Sputnik* days—of the British Interplanetary Society and author of a science fiction novel and stories in *Analog* and *Galaxy*. Indeed, I have suggested elsewhere that it is more helpful to think of conceptions hostile to our own not as good or bad but as alien. Imagination is certainly required in considering those temporally or culturally remote from us. It was imaginative novelists like Orwell and Koestler, rather than Professors Webb or Laski, who understood and transmitted the realities of Stalinism. This is no more than to claim a certain breadth of outlook, perhaps a necessary, though not itself an adequate, qualification for writing on some of the key questions of this century.

5.

The book's general theme, then, is that any concept given anything like absolute status becomes not a guide to action but an abstraction whose imposition on reality reveals an incompatibility, as engineers say of parts that do not fit, and that can only be made to fit by main force, and even then ineffectively or ruinously.

Nor, as we describe such phenomena in action, is this to examine a dead past, but rather a still living past, where we can trace the primitive but still powerful notion that any political or other objective can be achieved by mere force.

The world still faces a legacy of dangers fueled by the fatal ideas to which this attitude gives rise. Far from history having come to an end with global acceptance of market economies and pluralist politics, we face a long and dangerous struggle to bring a highly refractory planet into a peaceable, let alone democratic, condition. The technology of power developed over the past century is still at the disposal of a variety of dangerous rulers. The overwhelmingly destructive weaponry now available remains an appalling threat. Archaic hatreds, ideologically modernized and totalitarianized, flourish.

We should not take a very short view of our problems, nor should we take a very long view. For we can only be reasonably clear about possibilities over a decade or two at most. To fail to face comparatively urgent danger, as generally speaking the West long failed to face the threat of Nazism, can lead to catastrophe. But we should also avoid the temptation of policies supposed to solve all problems and determine the whole future, as has been seen with the disasters of the despotic-utopian regimes.

The survival of civilization in the twentieth century was a near thing.

And the perils were greatly exacerbated by unreal thinking within the democratic culture itself. Kierkegaard once said that the most dangerous mental faults are laziness and impatience. Laziness of mind meant unwillingness to face unfamiliar, complex and refractory realities. Impatience led to infatuation with supposedly all-explanatory theories in lieu of thought and judgment.

Democratic muddleheadedness, or a resurgence of fanaticism, could destroy the present opportunity.

And part of the reason the totalitarian ideologies achieved such a measure of success was that they were misunderstood by too many in the democratic countries. We have to examine the ways in which these, or variants, have to one degree or another, in one guise or another, affected our intellectual atmosphere—in part because of misconceptions based on what Dostoevsky called "being in bondage to advanced ideas." There are other relevant Western weaknesses we also have to consider.

Above all, we must insist, as against the utopian concepts, that a tolerable order of things is one of a proper balance between the social and the individual: that a human being is neither an ant nor a shark.

On such issues, this book is less a rebuke than a warning, and in most cases it should be no more resented than a sleepwalker should resent being stopped walking off a cliff or than a child should resent being given nasty medicine. But of course, on the record, it would be vain to be too sanguine about this.

6.

We face threats, but also opportunities. A ship aims both to avoid rocks and to keep heading towards its destination. In such a context, this book amounts to an overview, an attempt to present in a coherent way the crucial causes of past disaster, and so of the problems still facing us in our hopes for a reasonably peaceful and consensual world.

Part I

MINDSLAUGHTER

CHAPTER I

◆

History's Battleground

I.

The huge catastrophes of our era have been inflicted by human beings driven by certain thoughts. And so history's essential questions must be:

How do we account for what has been called the "ideological frenzy" of the twentieth century? How did these mental aberrations gain a purchase? What was the sort and condition of people affected? Who were the Typhoid Marys who spread the infection?

We need to develop the history and the nature of the various destructive ideologies in action. We need to consider the history and traditions of the culture that stood in opposition to them.

But before we turn to these broader themes, we need to examine the history and background of the mental arena in which the battle of ideas was fought.

2.

Both scarcely formulated fanaticisms and closed systems of ideas are, of course, to be found throughout the past. These historical phenomena are full of lessons for our time (indeed ignorance of history is one of the most negative attributes of modern man). The basic characteristic and attraction was and is the archaic idea that utopia can be constructed on earth; the offer of a millenarian solution to all human problems. This central trend has been, at least in vocabulary, modernized. The aspirations which in the sixteenth and seventeenth centuries spoke in the dialect of Theology, in the eighteenth century took up that of Reason, and in the nineteenth century that of Science.

With the two last, we get the delusion that our knowledge of human society is so complete that we have the power to reinvent it according to the formulae so obtained, that human affairs are in principle fully understandable and fully manipulable: a fetishism of whatever happens, or happened, to be the supposed current state of knowledge about social, economic, psychological and other phenomena.

The origin of the modern era's ideologies lay in John Locke's derivation of scholastic generalities from traditional English understandings of liberty, thus excessively rationalizing and at the same time limiting, or in a sense desiccating, the more complex reality.

At any rate, this, and the success of the physical and other sciences in England in the seventeenth century, gave the French intelligentsia the idea that everything could now be determined by Reason—in whose name the Revolution was made—with the "Romantic" input from Rousseau as part of the meld. The often argued "contradiction" between them may appear valid in a formal way, but in practice they went well together, the perfection sought being both intellectual and emotional. This unfortunate combination persisted. The "Ideas" in this sense were in any case mental, but not primarily intellectual, phenomena. Insofar as one can make the distinction, they seem, rather, to have been the verbalizations of largely emotional content.

As Alexander Yakovlev, the former Politburo member who became a stout proponent of democracy, noted in a speech on the two hundredth anniversary of the French Revolution, "The morbid faith in the possibility of forcing through social and historical development, and the idealisation of violence, traces back to the very sources of the European revolutionary tradition."

Marx himself said that he combined German philosophical, English economic and French political ideas. And it is indeed in France that we first find Revolution in the sense of the complete destruction of the existing order, and its replacement by abstract concepts—these latter formulated by, and dictatorially enforced by, theorists with no experience of real politics. The Revolution Idea then spread over half the world.

It is sometimes argued that the social strains on the fabric of human culture, of human minds, since the Industrial Revolution have been so intense that all this has been a natural "objective" result. Since the main centers of that revolution—in particular Britain and the United States—escaped the frenzy, this cannot stand up.

Not that the advocates of free-market industrialization were exempt from a different, and less total, form of excess ideation: an extreme anti-regulatory economic theory was widely held and inflicted. In the mid-nineteenth century in Britain, it was a loose coalition of traditionalists and social reformers who brought in the legislation which curbed the excesses of the first decades of the Industrial Revolution (though the dramatic fall in the death rate was also due to such works as the vast new London sewage system).

3.

Revolutionaries, and some reformers, spoke and still speak of "radical" change. It is worth remembering that such change is not necessarily *greater* than that associated with the gradualist approach. Cutting the taproot is in one sense a *lesser* operation than lopping off a number of dead branches. To pursue the metaphor further, it is much easier to kill a tree, and requires considerably less knowledge of dendrology, than to prune it effectively. The English Revolution of 1688 and the American Revolution in 1776, both of them undertaken in protection of the legal and civic order, had no connotation of total and utopian change—though Marxists and others have sometimes implied the opposite.

As to the Jacobin claim to absolute democracy (with Marat as l'Ami du Peuple!), Sunil Khilnani writes of its legacy in his *Arguing Revolution:*

> But the Revolution—and the left it created—proved to be the . . . worst enemy of these values. Democracy in its constitutional representative form—the only form in which inhabitants of the modern political world are ever likely to be durably acquainted with it—remained in quite fundamental respects unpracticed, untheorised and unloved in France. To the intellectual left, constitutional representative democracy, "bourgeois" or "formal" democracy, was a contemptible and mystifying illusion.

And, he adds, "only beginning in the late 1970s did it gradually come to be accepted [in France] as a political form in its own right, and not merely an illicit simulation of 'true,' direct or revolutionary democracy."

Edmund Burke, in a famous passage (written, moreover, before the worst excesses), pointed out that the French revolutionaries' delusion that force could solve all problems was above all a "slothful" attempt to ignore the complexity of reality.

A century and a half later Orwell similarly remarked on the "mental coarseness" of revolutionaries, who "imagine that everything can be put right by altering the shape of society." He might have added that there is something infantile or childish in the whole revolutionary-despotic approach, which is, in effect, based on the simpleminded attitude "If I were King . . . ," that it only needs well-intentioned people in power to solve everything by mere decree. Rémy de Gourmont calls the excesses of the French Revolution "nothing but the anger of a disappointed child."

I find that high school students, imbued with or attracted to it, can easily follow the central objection (more than can be said for some at higher, or further, levels of education): How is equality to be attained? Answer: By being enforced. Who is to do the enforcing, and how can the enforcer remain "equal" to the rest? . . . And to assume the best of motives even for the initial commitment to an Idea is to be charitable: for in most humans a component of hatred for the designated oppressor has usually been quite as motivating as sympathy for the oppressed. But many, the world over, thought and still think in terms of social revolution, of a judgment against the rich and powerful which will be followed by "liberation"—another slippery general term.

"Revolution" has long been a powerful mantra. In her memoirs, *Hope against Hope*, Nadezhda Mandelshtam, the widow of the great poet murdered by the Stalinists, takes the view that a generation of Russian intellectuals was ruined by the word, which none of them could give up, and which prevented them from opposing the dictatorship. For what the Bolsheviks had effected was undoubtedly a "revolution," and not to be resisted.

4.

There are men who are revolutionaries by temperament, to whom in fact bloodshed is natural. Pushkin had understood the dangers: "Those in our midst who plan impossible revolutions are either young men who do not know our people, or cruel-hearted men who place a low value on their own necks, and an even lower value on the necks of others." There were those who came to it entrapped by the Idea, and prepared to destroy "enemies of the people." Even intellectuals who are not strictly speaking revolutionaries, but who claim to speak in the interests of "humanity" as a whole, have taken sinister stands. For example, Bertrand Russell is quoted as accepting "that if it could be shown that humanity would live happily ever after if the Jews were exterminated, there could be no good reason not to proceed with their extermination" (Frederic Raphael, *Prospect*, May 1996).

The revolutionary believed it to be in the nature of things that dictatorship and terror are needed if the good of humanity is to be served, just as the Aztec priests believed themselves to be entirely justified in ripping the hearts out of thousands of victims, since had they not done so, the sun would have gone out, a far worse catastrophe for mankind. In either case, the means are acceptable, being inevitable—that is, *if* the theory is correct. . . .

Like all paranoiacs, revolutionists legitimized hatred, which they practiced effectively. They claimed to legitimize it in the interests of humanity: in this they were deceived. Or, to put it another way, the primitive search for certainty, of mental submission to revelation, of which we have spoken is melded with the primitive submergence of the individual mind into a supposed mass mind. Something of the sort may also be said of an addict's acceptance of not only terror but also lies—those two characteristics of the absolutist Idea, like Sin and Death in an earlier literature. And when it came to the Soviet Union there was what amounted to an acceptance of the old Russian distinction between transcendent Truth (*pravda*) and mere factual truth (*istina*). It was Pushkin, again, who wrote sardonically, "The lie that uplifts us is dearer to me than the mass of petty *istinas*."

Another great Russian writer, Dostoevsky, points out, in *The Possessed*, that "causes" are attractive for another reason, because they provide an excuse for behaving badly, giving "the right to dishonor," which, as he puts it, is endlessly fascinating. One of the things that gave even Stalinism its prestige in the West, even (or especially) among those who recognized that its methods were immensely ruthless, was the abstract, utopian notion that there was a certain horrible grandeur in what was going on. Men of ideas, who had profoundly considered the laws of history, were creating a new society and taking upon themselves the guilt of the necessary merciless action. Such an attitude is to be seen even in the interrogators in Arthur Koestler's *Darkness at Noon,* and Koestler has recorded that a young Frenchman once wrote to tell him that he had become converted to Communism by that very book.

As its lowest method of justification, the excuse was, in effect, that "you can't make borscht without cutting up beets"—to adapt a remark about omelettes attributed earlier to Robespierre.

The point, surely, is to discourage the combination of a vague and self-congratulatory general goodwill towards humanity with an acceptance of systems and, resulting from that, the (often gradual) acceptance of extreme inhumanity—and falsification—if done in the name of the supposedly humanitarian concepts.

For as that great historian Norman Cohn has remarked (in his *Warrant for Genocide*):

> There exists a subterranean world, where pathological fantasies disguised as ideas are churned out by crooks and half-educated fanatics for the benefit of the ignorant and superstitious. There are times when that underworld emerges from the depths and suddenly fascinates, captures, and dominates multitudes of usually sane and responsible people. . . . And it occasionally happens that this subterranean world becomes a political power and changes the course of history.

But the world can no longer afford the rise of revolutionary-ideologues, any more than it can afford nuclear war—in part *because* the takeover of states by ideolaters *must* lead to gross inhumanity, and *may* lead to nuclear confrontations.

5.

What, then, is the mental material into which they insert their ideas, like certain wasps into certain grubs?

Dostoevsky writes of a human type "whom any strong idea strikes all of a sudden and annihilates his will, sometimes forever." The true Idea addict is usually something roughly describable as an "intellectual." The British writer A. Alvarez has (and meaning it favorably) defined an intellectual as one who is "excited by ideas." Ideas can indeed be exciting, but the use of the intellect might be thought to be primarily one of subjecting them to knowledge and judgment—especially on the record of our century.

Intelligence alone is thus far from being a defense against the plague. Students, in particular, have traditionally been a reservoir of infection. The Nazis won the German students before they won the German state, and there are many similar examples. In much the same way, a leading scholar of Russian affairs (Ronald Hingley of Oxford) noted during the Soviet period that basic misapprehensions about it in the West were rare among truly serious scholars, and also among ordinary people, being confined to those of fair intelligence. He commented, "For it is surely true, if not generally recognised, that real prowess in wrong-headedness, as in most other fields of human endeavour, presupposes considerable education, character, sophistication, knowledge, and will to succeed."

Eric Hoffer suggests that those who become possessed by exciting Ideas and identification with causes are often "selfish people who were forced by innate shortcomings or external circumstances to lose faith in their own selves." It might be argued that, whether through temperament or accident, some who are simply *bored* with the quotidian turn to Ideas as stimuli. We are told of hostesses in Berlin in the early 1930s to whom National Socialism gave "meaning to their empty lives."

Boredom is indeed a pitiable condition. And the feeling of meaninglessness, of accidie, can be devastating. Still, to compensate by abandoning reason for ideology is a desperate remedy.

6.

Political opinion seems in fact to be largely a matter of temperament. This is implicitly admitted by Marx himself in that passage in the *Communist Manifesto* in which, having insisted that in general people act according to their class economic interest, he makes an exception for— Marxist intellectuals! "A portion of the bourgeoisie goes over to the proletariat, and, in particular, a portion of the bourgeois ideologists, who have raised themselves to the level of comprehending theoretically the historical movement as a whole." As we know, most Marxist and Communist leaders have been of bourgeois origin. Marx is here admitting that their motivations are not those normally provided for by Marxism. What are they, then? Marx himself would have been the last to say that any of his followers were the intellectual superiors of Darwin or Clerk Maxwell; nor is it likely that a Communist in this century would have claimed that Molotov was the intellectual superior of Ivan Pavlov or Anton Chekhov, or Louis Aragon of Louis de Broglie or Albert Camus. But if not intellect or interest, we are left with temperament.

Even the philosopher, William James remarks, is really much motivated by temperament:

Temperament is no conventionally recognised reason; so he argues impersonal reasons for his conclusions. Yet his temperament really gives him a

stronger bias than any of his more strictly objective premises. . . .
Wanting a universe that suits it, he believes any representation of the universe that does suit it.

Pavel Akselrod, one of the leaders of the Russian revolutionary Marxists in the struggle against Eduard Bernstein and "revisionism," remarked (privately, to be sure) that "the whole thing is a matter of temperament," adding that the real objection to peaceful revolution, whatever its advantages, is that it "would be exceedingly boring"—once again that dreadful prospect. Similarly, Simone de Beauvoir, in a revealing passage in *The Prime of Life*, wrote that she and Sartre were "temperamentally opposed to the idea of reform."

Times of stress have produced both revolutionaries and mystics, Zealots and Christians. It would be hard to define precisely the psychological differences between the types. And indeed, there is usually a good deal of movement from one view to the other; even in the United States, one notes some of the political activists of the sixties later becoming involved in strange religious quietisms. Such changes are explicable psychologically, but hardly sociologically.

For a useful, almost classical demonstration of the revolutionary mind-warp, the motivation behind acceptance of a totalitarian Idea, we turn to an interview given by the Marxist historian Eric Hobsbawm on "The Late Show," 24 October 1994 (see *TLS*, 28 October 1994). When Michael Ignatieff asked him to justify his long membership of the Communist Party, he replied: "You didn't have the option. You see, either there was going to be a future or there wasn't going to be a future and this was the only thing that offered an acceptable future."

Ignatieff then asked: "In 1934, millions of people are dying in the Soviet experiment. If you had known that, would it have made a difference to you at that time? To your commitment? To being a Communist?"

Hobsbawm answered: "This is a sort of academic question to which an answer is simply not possible. Erm . . . I don't actually know that it has any bearing on the history that I have written. If I were to give you a retrospective answer which is not the answer of a historian, I would have said, 'Probably not.'"

Ignatieff asked: "Why?"

Hobsbawm explained: "Because in a period in which, as you might say, mass murder and mass suffering are absolutely universal, the chance of a new world being born in great suffering would still have been worth backing. Now the point is, looking back as an historian, I would say that the sacrifices made by the Russian people were probably only marginally worthwhile. The sacrifices were enormous, they were excessive by almost any standard and excessively great. But I'm looking back at it now and I'm saying that because it turns out that the Soviet Union was not the beginning of the world revolution. Had it been, I'm not sure."

Ignatieff then said: "What that comes down to is saying that had the radiant tomorrow actually been created, the loss of fifteen, twenty million people might have been justified?"

Hobsbawm immediately said: "Yes."

It will be seen that, first, Hobsbawm accepted the Soviet project not merely on the emotional ground of "hope" but on the transcendental one of its being the "only" hope. Then, that he was justified because, although it turned out wrong, it might have turned out right (and it was not only a matter of deaths, but also of mass torture, falsification, slave labor). Finally, that he believes this style of chiliastic, absolutist approach to reality is valid in principle.

It might be added that addiction to a historico-social analysis which admittedly proved defective could be taken to cast some doubt on the method, and hence the conclusions, of Hobsbawm's historical work—some of which, on the Bolsheviks, we shall consider in its context in a later chapter.

7.

Again, cultures—an inadequate word—have doubtless produced, or at least selected, personalities with overall results different from those of other cultures. It is not easy to get into another man's skin, let alone that of another culture. In seventeenth-century France the great Condé once remarked to the Cardinal de Retz that the reason why historians got things wrong was that *"Ces coquins nous font parler et agir comme ils auroient fait eux-mêmes à notre place."* He noted, in fact, that intellectuals of his own culture would not make, or at any rate had not made, the effort adequately.

It is not as if Condé himself was an intellectually muscle-bound thug of a professional soldier. Those who frequented his château when he was in disgrace—Molière, Racine, Boileau, La Fontaine, Bossuet—make almost a roll call of the genius of the Grande Epoque. But if academics fail to understand the temperaments of the generals of their own culture, they are all the more unlikely to grasp the temperaments producing and produced by other traditions. When it comes to alien cultures, the immodesty of some anthropologists and social historians, who believe that they have got into the essence of a society, is a constant trap.

Louis MacNeice, the poet, who was also a Professor of Greek and deeply versed in ancient Athens, could nevertheless write:

> And how one can imagine oneself among them
> I do not know.
> It was all so unimaginably different,
> And all so long ago.

And this is Athens! Incomparably closer to us, in many ways, than most of the other ancient cultures and many modern ones.

And yet the effort must be made. And when it comes to modern alien cultures, no understanding, and so no policy, is worth anything unless academics, statesmen and all others concerned make that effort, to the degree that unreal assumptions are driven even from their almost unconscious first thoughts on affairs. After that they need, it may be suggested, to master the idea that these deep-set historical forces of motivation are not merely very strange to us but cannot easily be changed by argument or manipulation.

The true criticism of Neville Chamberlain is that he could not really imagine a man like Hitler or a party like the Nazis. "He's a good fellow and 'twill all be well," whatever may be said of it as theology, is a parochial and limited attitude when it comes to foreign politics. It is not only on the left—and, of course, many on the left are exempt—that one finds this inability to grasp the totalist mentality imaginatively. The notion that people who raised the alarm about Hitler in the 1930s were being immoderate and unreasonable was found in the *Times* and at All Souls, in all the blinkered and complacent crannies of the Establishment. The concept of a quite different set of motivations, based on a different political psychology, was absent.

We are still faced with the absolutely crucial problem of making the intellectual and imaginative effort *not* to project our ideas of common sense or natural motivation onto the products of totally different cultures. The central point is less that people misunderstand other people, or that cultures misunderstand other cultures, than that they have no notion that this may be the case. They assume that the light of their own parochial common sense is enough. And they frame policies based on illusions. Yet how profound is this difference between political psychologies and between the motivations of different political traditions, and how deep-set and how persistent these attitudes are!

8.

On the confused and complicated mental battlefield where all these issues are being fought out, we must now turn to examine our own record and prospects. What are the resources available to us? What are our strategic and moral advantages? What are our weaknesses and how (and to what extent) have they been overcome?

To repudiate or at least deplore Ideas is not to favor the shortsightedness, the narrow establishmentarian or *immobiliste* attitudes which are almost as common now as they have been over recent centuries.

The "Western" culture has always implied the absence of absolutes, disbelief in perfect political wisdom, in readily predictable futures. But the avoidance of the extreme, ideologized way of thinking does not in itself save the political entity concerned from a milder, but still potentially dangerous, form of the affliction. And these less malignant varieties have to some extent taken hold—with uncritical devotion to various quick-fix solutions by humans and their states to the problems facing them. As in medical usage we speak of "-itis" in a real ailment and "-osis" in merely a morbid condition, we might speak of "ideitis" in the totalitarian countries and "ideosis" in certain Western cases.

To look at it from a different angle, we may consider if packages of lesser "ideas" are a unity based on reason or a temperamental one. None other than Hobsbawm once penetratingly noted the causes pursued by the typical progressive figure a hundred or more years ago: "natural philosophy, phrenology, free thought, spiritualism, temperance, unorthodox medicine, social reform, and the transformation of the family" (*New Statesman*, 4 April 1970)—each supported with just as much righteousness and certainty as the partially different batch now so much heard of. The point is once again, clearly, that what comes out of the package is not intellectual coherence, or the pursuit of interests, but a cast of mind. There is no logical connection, no overriding ideological connection, between the views noted, but only the accidental one of novelty and unorthodoxy, and the temperamental one of the *odium theo-*

logicum. (It is hard to exaggerate the element of sheer lunacy in some of the "progressive" thinkers who are still highly regarded. Fourier sincerely believed that under socialism the sea could be turned into lemonade.)

Now, modern men, though they might not agree on every point, would certainly grant that some of the opinions in that earlier package were totally crackpot and that others were not. The difficulty is that one cannot yet distinguish easily between what may prove to be a possibly useful contribution to social or other progress and what will in a century be regarded with amusement as the strangest of aberrations.

Obsessions can cover the whole of society, or can be concentrated on minor points—such as the theory that Bacon wrote Shakespeare, or even such lesser matters as the pseudo-Anastasia's claim to be the Tsar's daughter. Concerning the point on which their obsessions concentrate, believers are often very well informed, with a mass of detail not readily available to their critics, though in fact either distorted or meaningless.

It would seem to follow (since political decisions are of more immediate consequence than literary ones) that certain temperaments are unfitted for action or advice in a pluralist order. But in most cases, no doubt, minds are not so rigidly set in their ways as to make them immune to experience and argument. The problem is in their breathing an atmosphere of thought containing at least a trace of noxious fumes. Indeed, in controversies of this sort, and more generally, one seems to see a certain degeneration. Except in admittedly extreme cases, it was usual even among those "committed" to certain opinions to preserve at least the appearance of rationality, balance, objectivity. Even this is often now abandoned.

Even when full-scale ideologies have not possessed human minds, less complete but still dangerously obsessive ideas have thus distorted our societies. Certainty on matters in which our knowledge is inevitably imperfect is the enemy of good understanding and good policy.

We must indeed distinguish between the aim or actuality of the total state, on the one hand, and what are no more than partial, and often hardly intentional, tendencies distorting normal states or systems of states. But even when totalist programs are not in question, the principle of state control and the actuality of bureaucratic power have become excessive even in the West—including excessive legislation, excessive regulation, and excessive litigation, often for aims based more on conviction than on knowledge. Misleading general views that perfuse the political class at any given time, whether in the West or elsewhere, are not for that reason sound, or durable. They gain momentum by involvement in state, or international, negotiations and administrations, until they appear unstoppable. But eventually, as often as not, they burn out.

What has suffered in all these cases is a sense of balance, between the proper rights of the individual and the necessary rights of the state, between personal aims and mutual obligations, between the often conflicting claims of liberty and of equity.

9.

General ideas, general concepts, general principles, interpreted as absolutes rather than approximations, are mere kindling wood for a new conflagration. But of course we must use general ideas and general concepts. General words are necessary and natural—as long as those who use them understand that their generality is a convenience, bringing together certain phenomena for certain purposes, but not a monolith. We must keep a balance, and not allow these to get out of hand and take over. They must be our servants, and not our masters. In fact, as in all our arrangements, we must once again seek a balance. We must learn from experience, yet not believe we can see far into the future. We must take short views, but not too short. We must allow the state a role in social affairs, but not a dominance. We must grant the legitimate claims of nationality, but reject its extreme manifestations. This undogmatic type of approach has been among the essentials of the civic and pluralist culture.

There is no formula that can give us infallible answers to political, social, economic, ecological and other human problems. There is no simple concept which will answer such questions as how much the state can do (though we have learned that to give it too much power is disastrous), or how far market forces can give positive results (though we have learned that their abolition is disastrous). Nor is there a simple guide to the conduct of foreign policy.

What does not need to be done needs not to be done—though, of course, there are things that need to be done, and situations so dangerous that quick and major action is required. But it is not enough to show that a situation is bad; it is also necessary to be reasonably certain that the problem has been properly described, fairly certain that the proposed remedy will improve it, and virtually certain that it will not make it worse.

This requires thought, common sense, careful judgment, and above all no untested, or ill-tested, all-purpose solutions. All that sounds obvious and indisputable. It has not been the usual practice in the twentieth century.

In part this is because, as we have suggested, many cannot admit that the condition of humankind in all its vast complexity is not to be understood by formula, and that in any but the short run its developments cannot be predicted by theory, or otherwise. The future appears to us neither as impenetrable darkness nor as broad daylight, but rather in a half-light, in which we can descry the rough form of the nearest objects, and vague outlines farther off. We cannot do without ideas: but we should not make ideas into Ideas. We should note the catastrophes due to fascination with fantasy, addiction to absolutes.

10.

Generally speaking, the political virtues of free discussion, political compromise, plural societies, piecemeal practicality, change without chaos, and market economics have triumphed. But it was a near thing, and we are still beset by a whole array of great dangers.

What we call "democracy" is far less a matter of institutions than of habits of mind. It is vulnerable to various weaknesses and always needs adjustments and improvements—but if these are to be helpful, they need to go with the grain of, and be within, the established order. The stresses and strains that affect the democracies and the minds of their citizens today need not be overestimated, but they must be taken into account in any survey of the world as it is, and as it may be.

It is in this context that we must emphasize the measure of success totalitarian ideas had in the minds of citizens of the pluralist countries. Many in the West gave their full allegiance to these alien beliefs. Many others were at any rate not ill disposed towards them. And beyond that there was, as we have said, a sort of secondary infection of the mental atmosphere of the West which still to some degree persists, distorting thought in countries that escaped the more wholesale disasters of our time.

For example, we still find, even in the West, especially in parts of academe, the idea that everything is a struggle for power, or hegemony, or oppression; and that all competition is a zero-sum game. This is no more than repetition of Lenin's destructive doctrine—Who-Whom? Intellectually, it is reductionism; politically, it is fanaticism. Then again,

much policy-determining "research" is based on supposedly indisputable statistical data, which economists at least are now beginning to abandon but which are widely used in other contexts—the *nombre fixe* being almost as hard to uproot as the *idée fixe.*

It was basically common sense that kept the mass of the people in Britain and America less liable than the intelligentsia to delusion about the Stalinists. As Orwell said, they were at once too sane and too stupid to accept the sophistical in place of the obvious. But common sense by itself has its vices, or inadequacies. First, it can go with parochialism. Chamberlain was not alone in failing to understand that Hitler was capable of acts incredible to his Birmingham City Council or other "plain, shrewd Britons." Similarly, this philistine "shrewdness" inclines to the view that there is "something to be said on both sides" in international disputes. (In the Nazi case, the Germans of the Sudetenland had a legitimate wish to join Germany; but to put this in the scale was to unjustifiably counterbalance the essentials of National Socialism.) And then, common sense can decline into muddleheadedness if it is not well integrated with the critical faculty, with an open-ended fund of knowledge and with a breadth of imagination adequate to unfamiliar phenomena.

It was, in fact, what might be called imaginative realism.

On these matters, as we have said, the inexplicit habits of mind of the public are often more sensible than the prescriptions elaborated in the minds of the intelligentsia. Understanding of the complications and contradictions in life implies that all ideas, but particularly those carrying a high emotional charge, should be critically examined in the main areas where they are generated and transmitted—that is, at a superficial level in the media, and at a more responsible level in education.

We may here take note of what we may call Ismology. It has long, though not all that long, been a custom to use the termination "-ism" to validate one's own opinion or to demonize another's.

In the latter case, a crude effect is obtained by the use of the grab-bag term "fascism" not to specify a form of state or of state theory, but, often enough, to object to the use of any form of authority or discipline. Indeed George Orwell noted (as early as 1944) that he had heard the word "Fascist" applied to a list of targets including farmers, shopkeepers, Social Credit, corporal punishment, fox hunting, bullfighting, Kipling, Gandhi, Chiang Kai-shek, homosexuality, Youth Hostels, astrology, women, dogs. . . . He also pointed out that at a more serious level, "conscription and a professional army are both denounced as Fascist phenomena." But more usually (and less absurdly) ism-ing brings together under one term a complexity of examples, or a variety of phenomena, phraseologically obliterating the often crucial contexts or differences, as with "capitalism" or "imperialism" (see Chapter XIII).

Using the termination positively, though equally concretizing a fluidity, we find such concepts, or banners, as "feminism" and "environmentalism" where long-standing and broadly accepted attitudes take on—or often take on—a good deal of the intensity and lack of proportion of ideologies proper, and some of the viral qualities of an Idea. Nor should we perhaps forget the strange usage "activism," almost always a favorable word, though the Nazis (for example) were at least as "active" as their betters—indeed deserving of the label "hyperactivist."

Though only peripherally within the scope of this book, we must also note that acceptance of Freudian and other more or less deterministic psychological theories was also an example of the attractions of a pseudoscience, with enough intellectual complexity and a mission in human life. The result was a culture of, or tendency toward, *tout comprendre c'est tout pardonner*—and, in conjunction with social determinism, of distorting the legitimate claims of social order.

Nevertheless, as J. A. C. Brown remarks at the end of his book *Freud and the Post-Freudians,* "The explanation of the irrational is a special task of the twentieth century." We shall not attempt an explanation properly speaking, but a mere examination of the phenomenon may be helpful in understanding and avoiding it.

As we have said, intellectual errors in general are often due to ignoring the fact that the human being is both social and individual. To conceive him as solely, or preponderantly, one or the other leads to distortions of policy. The normal human being is motivated both by a desire to improve his own lot and a desire to conform to certain social or moral principles; and in normal life there is mutual adjustment of these urges, sometimes in makeshift fashion.

Hypostatized ideas lead to a lack of balance in this and other respects. In fact, we may see the essential of the civic society in its preservation of balance—between the individual and the community, between the desirable and the possible, between our knowledge and our imagination.

The balance implies that we should neither accept solutions, however fashionable, however much supported by narrow-gauge experts, nor deny or minimize the problems. What one might call the nonideology of moderation.

Our purpose is not so much to condemn as to understand the negative phenomena, and especially in the context of helping to prevent such misconceptions in future—not as matters of mere mental improvement in the abstract, but more importantly in warning against the huge disasters lying in wait for the unaware.

We have developed what is often left implicit, the positive characteristics, though also the weaknesses, that have arisen in our own social and political order. We should now consider how such orders have emerged.

CHAPTER II

◆

The Culture of Sanity

I.

The only reason we are able to examine our own and other history in an open way is that the culture which makes such thinking possible has, so far, survived and prevailed.

People forget what a remarkable thing it is that in our countries we have such rights and liberties. Civilizations have existed for thousands of years in which there was no trace of the mere idea of criticizing the government, of being secure from arbitrary arrest, of having a fair trial (or even a fairish trial, or even a trial at all), of printing almost anything one likes, of voting for one of a number of candidates for public office.

We need to consider the origins and development of our social and political order. What follows, therefore, is an examination of our history in that context, and an appraisal of its present heritage. That is to say, we are not concerned with the blemishes it shares with all cultures, nor with the triumphs in literary and other spheres which it also shares with many, or most. We seek, rather, the essential developments that marked the emergence of the Open Society.

2.

In England a consensual tradition was maintained, with occasional lurches and recoveries, through Anglo-Saxon times and, presumably, from the prehistoric originals. Of necessity, a consensual relationship existed in primitive society. The more or less egalitarian order could not be maintained after the population of a given community rose above a fairly small number. Anthropologists have estimated that a maximum figure seems to be around four or five hundred. Common sense and the experience of schools, army units and so forth would suggest the same. The reasons for change were thus strictly those associated with the impossibility of maintaining purely personal relations with larger numbers, together with the fact that specialization could begin to emerge when numbers were large enough. At this point a "chiefdom" type of organization arose.

Engels was right in finding a cooperative type of order in the general prehistoric condition of man. But the economic reductionism that makes such cooperation primarily an economic matter distorts this primitive communalism to the hard category of "primitive communism," seeing the situation as in essence the mere absence of economic classes. In fact, the economic side, even in primitive society, where the pressure of need might be thought greatest, clearly did not play this supposedly dominating role in human relationships, where family, magic and general cultural attitudes were if anything predominant. If it comes to that, even the "social" organization of the higher apes does not seem to be dominated solely by feeding habits. Perhaps Marxism comes into its own somewhere lower down the evolutionary scale.

It is true that the great civilizations of Asia could not have emerged without a centralized despotic state, usually to control the large-scale irrigation systems beyond the scope of smaller units. Much was therefore gained, but much was also lost. The hopeful direction of democratic culture is to combine the tradition of consensual tribalism with the centralization of those complex civilizations.

For the rise in the West and elsewhere of "chiefdoms," and later of a variety of legal and political forms, did not of necessity mean the end of the older communalism and consensualism, but rather its rise to a more "civic" level. To the natural articulation between individuals or families was added a more complex articulation between local communities. Thus, as the social order became more complex, and larger, we may again agree with the Marxists and others that formal law and central organization became necessary. From this time on we may trace in every civil order the struggle between the civic and the state elements.

Naturally, the machinery of power attracted, to put it at its simplest, those who like power. In many areas, as we have said, the older relations gave way to despotism. This depended on local circumstances. But it was not a matter of economic or cultural level: Egypt and later Mongolia became despotisms; Attica and later Jutland retained an articulation of citizenry.

As is indeed obvious, there are elites in all orders, including democracy itself. Outside very small groups, any political formation involves some form of leadership, with either a large or a negligible element of consent. Power is always, to some degree, in the hands of minorities. And all political organizations have a tendency to fall into the hands of oligarchical bureaucracies (a tendency that Robert Michel asserts as a law). Nor is it just a matter of bureaucracy. We find a still broader and more troublesome tendency: the merger of various political and economic as well as bureaucratic interests, based on mutual accommodation in sharing the political and economic control, and the political and economic profits. If democracies have been far less corrupt, or less unchallengedly corrupt, than their equivalents in the old totalitarian regimes (or in some of the new economies of, in particular, Asia), this is due precisely to the liberties and the pluralism of our societies. Thus, in the consensual order these are obstacles that can be overcome, the community as a whole possessing the means to exert the necessary pressures, if in an untidy, belated and incomplete way.

3.

In its most important aspect, the civic order is that which has created a strong state while still maintaining the earlier principle of consensus. It was the Western European nation-state which provided the possibility—no more—of political society on a scale which was neither too small (as with the Greek city-states) nor too large (as with the Eurasian empires). This was partly a matter of geographical luck.

Primitive consensuality was rarely able to survive for long the evolution of highly organized, larger state forms; yet at a very advanced state of chiefdom, among the Saxons and other sophisticated "tribal" societies, a type of civic relationship persisted. There is, of course, nothing new in the idea that our liberties derive from early times. Montesquieu saw the origins of the English Constitution in the woods of Saxony. Bancroft even traced the early American institutions to the forest Teutons, calling the early Virginians "Anglo-Saxons in the woods again."

It has often been pointed out that appeals to past tradition, which have always marked English history in particular, have usually been appeals to bogus history. This is true, but only in a rather superficial sense. Seventeenth-century parliamentarians appealing to Saxon liberties against the Norman oppressor are easy to laugh at. Yet they had the nub of the matter. The memory is blurred, idealized, wrong in a number of respects; but it contains in this slightly distorted form the idea of the rights of Englishmen, and the truth that these rights in a general sense are rooted in the remembered tradition. Since the collapse of Rome there has never been any significant period in Britain when the state was strong enough to enforce its will without considerable concessions to the rights and liberties of important sections of its subjects and without reliance upon consent. By later standards, the early rights and liberties were defective and incomplete. But their continuity proved a solid foundation for their extension century by century.

The special characteristic that gave rise to an English society different from those on the Continent seems to be that the English conquest of (most of) Britain was piecemeal. It was not a question, as in France or Spain, of united barbarian armies under their acknowledged kings simply taking over a country. The piecemeal progress of the English meant that individual settlements sprang up, of varying origins, incorporating the indigenous populations, having the same or similar laws and customs and (eventually) acknowledging one or another small king. The groupings on a fairly small scale remained the traditional basis of the nation, which was thus created from below rather than from above.

The Germanic nations that came to Britain had various political customs. While the Anglos had had "kings" for several centuries, the Saxons had not. All the Saxon "townships" judged important legal cases and agreed upon the plans that would guide them in peace or war during the coming year.

The effect on the American political culture of the special circumstances of its Frontier has, of course, been much discussed since the end of the last century. The idea of the determining effect of small communities owing a general allegiance to government on the coast, but beyond its effective protection and compelled to rely on their own common initiative, clearly has much to be said for it in accounting for the special circumstances of American democracy. This was in a sense a reenactment of the original spread of the English settlers in Britain.

In both the English and the American cases, it was not, of course, a matter of traditionless man evolving administrative forms to suit the circumstances. Both Americans and Saxons built their new communities on the basis of traditional laws and rights as they remembered them.

Of course, it is ridiculous to claim any special merit for the Anglo-

Saxon culture because it was the first to develop, or rather to maintain, a civic level of state. If ours were to succumb, there are other sources of a consensus civilization from which it could again emerge. It is not necessary for us to be overbearing about the heritage; it is a matter of luck that we are born into it. (All the same, why should we not repeat the words of Naboth, "Jehovah forbid that I should give unto thee the inheritance of my forefathers"?)

4.

This flexible articulation had thus evolved from earliest English times. But a further, associated characteristic of English society, long misunderstood, was socioeconomic in that as far back as can be documented, that is, into the twelfth century, there seems to have been no English "peasantry" in the European sense. It had long been assumed by historians that—perhaps as late as the seventeenth century—something like the situation in France had prevailed in the English countryside: insulated, introspective village communities, with little migration and little economic contact outside, and little social mobility, all living on an "extended family" basis. All this now appears to be untrue. There was much mobility, personal rather than family ownership, much trade and nonagricultural production, much sale and transfer of lands—even by villeins (the tenure of villeinage was only abolished in 1926). Thus, it is now felt, what may be seen as a market economy was long in existence and largely prevalent, and was the basis from which the Anglo–Industrial Revolution could emerge.

The product of the higher form of political order was variety in unity. As W. H. Auden put it (summarizing Whitehead, in *The Portable Greek Reader*):

> Civilisation is a precarious balance between barbaric vagueness and trivial order. Barbarism is unified but undifferentiated; triviality is differentiated but lacking in any central unity; the ideal of civilisation is the integration into a complete whole and with the minimum strain, of the maximum number of distinct activities.

In its most important aspect, the civic order is that which created a strong state while still maintaining the principle of consensus that existed in primitive society. Such an aim involves the articulation of a complex political and social order in which strains cannot be eliminated but can be continually adjusted.

The civic culture, though containing the possibility of democracy, is thus not necessarily "democratic." And though containing the potentiality of the "Open Society," it is not in itself, or necessarily, definable as such. It is a society in which various elements can express themselves politically, in which an articulation exists between these elements at the political level: not a perfect social order, which is in any case unobtainable, but a society that hears, considers and reforms grievances.

In England liberty and the rule of law long preceded "democracy." And indeed, it could be argued that only those who already practice consensual politics are equipped to make democracy work; or, to put it another way, that democracy cannot spring fully formed and viable out of the depths of despotism. (The confusion of liberty with democracy is a strange one. When one hears, as one not seldom does, an Englishman in a pub saying indignantly, "It's a free country, isn't it?" he is in no way referring to his right to elect the government, but merely to his right to say what he wants—and he knows it. There seems to be no reason why more sophisticated folk should not also see this.)

The civic order thus includes the "future": that is, it is open to it. As Macaulay acutely remarked, the 1689 Declaration of Rights, though it did not in itself establish a number of the liberties later won by the English people, did not give dissenters full equality, prohibit the slave trade, reform the representative system, or secure the liberty of the press, nevertheless contained the "germ" of all these good laws, and also "of every good law which may hereafter, in the course of ages, be found necessary to promote the public weal, and to satisfy the demands of public opinion." In fact, it established an open-ended system under which "the means of effecting every improvement which the constitution requires may be found within the constitution itself." Macaulay has, of course, been crimed for his Whig Interpretation of History. Insofar as he suggests that the progress after 1689 was almost unimpeded, that it was almost complete by the time he wrote, and that it had a certain inevitability, this criticism is obvious. But it does not really affect the broader concept. So, to put it slightly differently, the general principles then established, or rather reaffirmed, were imperfectly realized in the then state of affairs, for the practical reason that the political nation was not ready to approve of them; but their future development, barring the overthrow of the system, was guaranteed, by the fact that their lack was progressively felt in each case to be an anomaly rather than a legitimate and natural result of English principles. The reformer—the corrector of wrongs—was always to feel at a moral advantage, and his opponent to plead merely practical difficulties and the unripe state of public opinion—pleas not without their force, but all the same admittedly limited and temporary.

There was, in fact, a built-in tendency in the civic order to extend itself to those originally excluded from it, whether because of their belief, like the Catholics, or for economic class reasons, like the bulk of the working class, or for reason of sex, i.e., women. The history of British constitutional progress has been that of making these extensions. These groups were, it is true, assimilated piecemeal into the system against considerable inertia. It may be argued that gradualness ensured the thoroughness of the assimilation.

But it is also the case that, partly owing to the anomalies resulting from the very archaism in the system, the working class were not by any means totally excluded even before the Reform Bills of the nineteenth century. In the London and Middlesex constituencies, and in Preston in Lancashire, the franchise was already wide, and it was generally understood that these constituencies indicated the feeling of that section of the people not elsewhere represented. Moreover, the more general civil liberties enabled a good deal of pressure to be brought to bear on voters by the nonvoting sectors of the community. Both the threatening aspect of the "mob" and the kisses of the Duchess of Devonshire played their part. Again, the fact that the premier duke of England was a Roman Catholic was only one of the various ways in which that particular minority could exert its influence. Such things may be thought to be among the advantages arising from the inconsistencies inherent in a nondogmatic system.

In fact, we cannot ignore the mere idiosyncrasies, as they may appear to be, in the history of the cultures of various countries; these apparently superficial and sentimental matters are often of great influence, usually in reinforcing the traditional consensus (or otherwise) of the country in question.

5.

One peculiarity distinguished the English Parliament, almost from the medieval start, from most of its then equivalents on the Continent: the representatives of the shires and cities sat together as a single chamber.

The merchants and the knights were thrown into collaboration. For there were two partially separate civic trends. In the newly developing towns specific liberties and independences were needed for the development of trade; in the countryside the traditional desire for consultation and order remained.

One of the few other areas where the civic order prevailed almost uninterruptedly was Switzerland, another example of the pragmatically born nation-state. As has been pointed out, on the face of it the country had none of the qualifications for statehood, let alone for a stable civic order. It lacked ethnic, cultural, economic and, later, religious unity. It was a strange alliance of small communities of farmers, cities, minor feudal lordlings, each generally supporting the others, in a network of rights and obligations built up piecemeal.

Elsewhere it is particularly striking to see the Iceland of the saga period, a country with no state machinery whatsoever, nevertheless forming into a community of settlements scattered over a huge area under the shield of a traditional Law, often broken but eventually prevailing—until the culture decayed for other reasons.

John Morris, the (left-wing) historian of the Dark Ages, has put it of England that "custom has expected that men of suitable standing should be heard before decision is reached; society has frequently disagreed about which men should be heard but when it has reached agreement, governments that ignored agreed opinion have been denied obedience and revenue." Local tenures and local institutions "trained English society to respect governments that co-ordinate and to discipline governments that rule by command."

These attitudes maintained the flexibility of English society, with an easier movement of ideas and smoother social change than was possible in most of Europe. Above all, it became possible to correct a powerful central government, which was still obliged to observe the restraints of custom: "Time and effort shaped a tradition of firm leadership and light rule."

Generally speaking, great and successful rulers in England were those, like Edward I and Edward III, who worked within the laws and customs and sought cooperation rather than submission from the representatives of the cities and counties. In turn, from Magna Carta on, the community rarely called into question the essential powers of the executive, though particular kings might be, and were, removed. These were those monarchs, like Edward II, Richard III and James II, who sought to extend the power of the state at the expense of the community. And the balance in each case was restored by a constitutionalist counterrevolution.

For the civic tradition of Britain has fairly often in the past been faced by more dynamic, more modern "waves of the future." In Yorkist times in the fourteenth century, the attempt was made to install in England a streamlined, Renaissance-style despotism (complete with the torture and treachery of the Sforzas and the Borgias). In Stuart times in the seventeenth century came the attempt to turn England into one of the new Divine Right monarchies, again to the accompaniment of illegality and torture. In fact, like the more successful despotisms in France and elsewhere, to use the power of the executive to destroy the civic nature of English society. This was finally defeated by the Revolution of 1688, just as George III's attempt to do the same thing in his American territories was destroyed by the Revolution of 1776.

The medieval style of civic order, with its system of rights and obligations, was powerful in many parts of Europe where it was later crushed—for example, in Aragon. But as Karl Mannheim points out, the "democratization" of the late Middle Ages was followed by a retrograde tendency in which European society became "refeudalized." The condition of the peasantry in the France of the thirteenth century was better than in the France of the eighteenth century, just as in the Russia of 1910 it was better than in the Russia of 1980. Until Philip II, or Louis XIV, the civic element was still putting up a struggle, just as in England, until William III, the despotic element in Britain still seemed capable of victory. The general effect of the victory of "absolutism" in France from Louis XIV's time was to prevent political and economic evolution.

6.

As we have noted, the French Enlightenment originated as a side effect of the British Enlightenment, and its originators from Montesquieu to Voltaire were quite clear about this. Over the next couple of generations, detached from much real political experience or inheritance, their movement had diverged into abstract Reason and abstract Romanticism— illustrated in the celebration by the two almost equally extreme sects in the Revolution, of the Goddess of Reason and the Supreme Being, respectively. The contrast between this sort of thing and the British Enlightenment is well expressed by Lytton Strachey, who saw the latter's essence in the "profound, sceptical and yet essentially conservative genius of Hume." The French Revolution can be seen, from the constructive point of view, as the release of tensions, like a sudden slip in the San Andreas Fault, so that the long overdue emergence of the market economy in the countryside could eventuate. It could be and has been argued that the excesses were in some sense unavoidable, and that by the time of the Third Republic France had gradually settled down to a situation already achieved in Britain. According to this view, the 1871 Commune was the last temblor of the catastrophe. Unfortunately, the mere fact that a civic tradition had been so largely destroyed, and a revolutionary-messianic tradition had had such a run for its money, left the latter powerfully embedded in the French consciousness even a hundred years later, though now being seen in a skeptical perspective.

Our cultures, our histories, grasp us with a thousand invisible fingers. The characteristics of individual countries, even, are of an enormous complexity; the details that give them savor and body, that pull them into one, are often not merely fantastic but also contradictory. They resemble, rather than a monolith, a conglomerate rock that has been pressed together from a variety of minerals into a tough solidity. Again, each country is inhabited not only by its citizens but also by ghosts from the past and by phantasms from imaginary futures or saints from lands outside time. Even as to the details, Boswell remarked truly of English history that if it were not so well attested, no one could believe it.

Cultures have had, as they still have, great intrinsic momenta, and they cannot be rapidly turned in new directions. The processes involved are often long ones; it may take generations for a civic culture to emerge from a despotic environment and, equally, generations to destroy previously existing civic attitudes. In his great chapter on the English Revolution of 1688, Macaulay writes of the French Revolution that "had six generations of Englishmen passed away without a single session of Parliament," then we too would have needed years of blood and confusion "to learn the very rudiments of political science," and been equally duped by childish theories; and have equally "sought refuge from anarchy in despotism, and been again driven from despotism into anarchy." Six generations: even though France had started not too far from the English style and had by no means become *totally* uncivic. At any rate, we must avoid being too sanguine about the early blossoming of new cultural styles in areas where history has rooted others.

7.

As against the absolutist attitudes of its rivals, it is a condition of the "Western" or "democratic" or "pluralist" culture that it makes no claim to perfection and is always in a process of adjustment and argument, and often of indecision and muddleheadedness. Nor is "democracy" in the abstract a sound definition of these societies.

At worst, it may lead to a fetishizing of elections, of popular voting, as such. This has so often—as with the German election of 1933—led to disaster that it is now not seriously urged. At a rather higher level, we find the view that the crux is institutional. It is true that without the various institutions we think of as democratic, democracy can hardly subsist. But here again there are enough states with institutions that are admirable in form, but that are deficient in some essential intrinsicality.

The first questioning of the existing state by the pre-Socratics and the eventual rise of a variety of Greek regimes which gave Aristotle the material for his empirically comparative work—all this is deep in our background; but it had little directly to do with the emergence of the pluralist order in the West, with which we are here concerned, where "democracy" in principle opposes the rights of a majority to, in Madison's words, act in a way "adverse to the rights of other citizens or to the permanent and aggregate interests of the community." Other founders or refounders of the American system, like Jefferson, were equally clear about the danger of the "tyranny of the majority."

Above all, it is no part of its culture that a government elected by a bare majority, or even by a fairly large majority, is thereby empowered to totally reconstruct the social and political order by sacrificing the minority. That great political philosopher Michael Oakeshott notes that for some people government is "an instrument of passion; the art of politics is to inflame and direct desire." For others, which is to say, in general, for those who have a traditional regard for the unity and continuity of a culture, the business of government is something different: "to restrain, to deflate, to pacify, and to reconcile; not to stoke the fires of desire, but to damp them down," on the grounds that, as Oakeshott puts it, "the conjunction of dreaming and ruling generates tyranny." For it is a basic principle of true, as against despotic, politics that it is more important for the civic system as such to be unshaken than for particular measures to be opposed or insisted on to the limit. A democratic community enjoying political liberty is only possible when the attachment of the majority of the citizens to political liberty is stronger than their attachment to specific political doctrines. And this is to say that on many controversial issues a certain comparative apathy must prevail among a large part of the population. But apathy cannot appear a virtue to the man who has committed himself to an intellectually elaborated scheme or policy.

In a famous investigation of the politics of the small town of Elmira, New York, in the 1950s, the scholars concerned (Paul Lazarfeld, Bernard Berelson and William McPhee) were at first surprised by the results. The democratic processes had worked very satisfactorily in the town for a very long period. So, on theoretical principles, the researchers expected to find the citizenry well informed about political issues, with firm and clear-cut opinions. They found, on the contrary, that the majority were fairly ill informed and fairly apathetic. They concluded, after admirable heart-searching on their own part, that this was the condition for a working democracy. On the other hand, it may be urged that the instability of many of the Greek states was due to the devotion to politics of all concerned and that, to a lesser degree, this has been the cause of many of the difficulties met with in France in the last fifty years (though it has been suggested that the ideological enthusiasm of the French electorate was to some extent compensated for by the cynicism and apathy of the deputies themselves).

At any rate, all the major troubles the world has had in our era have been caused by people who have let politics become a mania. The politician should be a servant and should play a limited role. For what our political culture has stood for (as against the principles of total theorists and abstractionists) is the view of society as a developing and broadening of established liberties and responsibilities, and the belief, founded in experience, that in political and social matters long-term predictions, however exciting and visionary, seldom work out.

Reviewing James Scott's *Seeing Like a State* in the *New Republic* of 18 May 1998, Cass R. Sunstein sums up one of Scott's main points: "States should take small steps rather than large ones. Policies are apt to be more successful if they can be reversed once they start to go awry, and so good planners ensure reversibility." The point, obvious enough but not available to many enthusiasts, is what one might have thought the well-established conclusion that actions have unexpected results. Or, to put it another way, that in the human context we cannot predict on the basis of theory.

Meanwhile, we can again stress that it is part of the heritage of sanity, or of political adulthood, to admit that any real order cannot be perfect. But this does not mean that we can ignore, or fail to combat, tendencies to degeneration of the civic order—in part due to penetration of its intellectual atmosphere by the direct, or dilute, effects of the totalitarian ideas.

Nor is abstract "libertarian" principle of much use in real life. Since a political order of the consensual type depends on the maintenance of a strong mediating state, since liberty and law are mutually dependent, it follows that when state and law are threatened by immediate danger they have the duty to defend themselves, even at the cost of a temporary suspension of particular rights.

The maintenance of liberties, the principle of the accommodation of various interests, the preserving of balances, imply totally different aims and attitudes in the civic politician from those prevailing among revolutionaries and despots. It would be impossible for a representative of *their* cultures to see that the highest praise possible to confer on a statesman in an advanced society would be in the nature of what was said (by Macaulay) about Halifax: that he was "the foremost champion of order in the turbulent Parliament of 1680, and the foremost champion of liberty in the servile Parliament of 1685."

8.

By the Western "democratic" culture we primarily mean that of the English-speaking countries. In most other Western countries it took hold, flickered, faded, failed and much later revived.

Mature democracy as we know it developed not on the basis of theory but from earlier times, in which something like consensus or balance had to be reached between various limited groups in society, and it was only long after these conventions had been established that the principle gradually extended to the entire adult population. That is to say, democracy is the latest and in principle highest development of a long process. Or, to put it another way, it depends for its arrival and survival on long-established foundations, both institutional and mental.

"Civil society" has been much spoken of as a condition of modern democracy, since de Tocqueville noted the networks of private and voluntary organizations that permeated British and American society. This habit of spontaneous legal, public activity is clearly an adjunct, if not a condition, of the Anglo-Celtic culture. "Civil society" is often heard both in the ex-Communist countries and in the West as the order to which those areas seek to evolve. "Civil society" was the formulation of the Scottish eighteenth-century philosophers, and implied, as Michael Ignatieff puts it, one that allows "individuals to associate with each other in bewilderingly complex rituals—friendships, sports teams, work groups, and amateur and professional associations of all kinds"— adding that they "form a pattern of life absolutely distinct from the kinship ties of tribal society or the party ties of the totalitarian state." Indeed this type of association is implicitly condemned by Rousseau as disruptive of the General Will.

But in covering the interaction of politics and society, the interaction between the state and its citizens, and between the various political groupings of those citizens, "civil society" only takes us so far.

After all, "civil society" in this definition applied not only to England but also to France of the *ancien régime.* That is to say, it only goes part of the way in achieving the higher level of a civic or consensual order. Thus the concept of civil society, true and important though it is, covers only the nonpolitical, or unofficial, side. To comprehend our order as a whole, we need a broader view.

Concepts better suited to these phenomena are, indeed, "civic" and "consensual." A civic society can be seen as one in which the state and its citizens are in balance, with the state prevented from exercising excessive power. A consensual society is one in which the various political elements among the population accept systematic methods of compromise, and so avoid anything like majoritarian despotism.

Thus the mere creation of democratic institutions and electoral processes is nothing like enough to guarantee the survival of democracy unless and until an evolution of political attitudes, and an acceptance of consensual principles, really permeate the society in question, and above all the Rule of Law that represents and realizes these principles.

More broadly, confusion in some minds over the whole relationship between liberty and democracy can lead to dangerous political results.

CHAPTER III

◆

The Marxist Irruption:
How and Why

I.

Of the various challenges the civic and democratic order has faced, the most pervasive and most tenacious has been Marxism.

The year 1998 marked the 150th anniversary of the *Communist Manifesto.* The odd respectable journal suggested that the thought of its authors, Marx and Engels, was still of much relevance, since they had predicted a world market. In this they were not unique: and other and more distinctive predictions they made proved, to put it mildly, to be dangerous will-o'-the-wisps. In fact, the ideas promulgated in the *Manifesto,* and elaborated by the authors until their deaths in 1883 and 1895, respectively, have been a major source of trouble in the world over five generations.

Other manifestations of revolutionary-utopian fantasies—anarchism, syndicalism and their offshoots—survived, but for a variety of reasons, which we shall examine, Marxism was the overwhelmingly dominant form in which this mind-set has presented itself.

Some discussion of its particular fallacies must naturally emerge in any treatment of it; but for our purposes the questions are: how did it arise? how did it develop? and what were the characteristics which enabled it (and to a lesser degree still enable it) to affect so many minds? What follows is thus neither a full examination nor a full critique of Marxism. Marxism is here considered in the way it gained acceptance—allegiance, in fact—as a human mental phenomenon.

2.

Norman Cohn points out in his classical study of apocalyptic movements in medieval and postmedieval Europe, *The Pursuit of the Millennium*, that modern revolutionaries picture the coming society much as their predecessors did: "as a state of total community, a society wholly unanimous in its beliefs and wholly free from inner conflicts." To envisage a unanimous social order is to envisage the absence of individuality. Utopia amounts to the inflation of the "community" into an entity in its own right, rather than a coherence of individual social human beings.

The late great historian and humanist Leonard Schapiro has shown in a striking passage that what Marx envisaged

> was the disappearance, or transcendence (Aufhebung), of the state as a result of the social revolution, with a consequent end to the alienation to which man is subject. One class by coming to power abolishes all classes forever. How does "a class" (if there is such a thing) take power, except through commissars? And, even if the state should disappear, this does not entail the disappearance of all forms of rule, and certainly does not do away with the alienation of man. It may be the case that Marx's utopia of the disappearance of the state was the most dangerous utopia of all times. For the end of the state means the end of legal order—but it does not mean the end of rule. What survives when the state goes is therefore naked rule, unrestrained by law, constitution or convention.

Marxists argued that in a stateless society any surviving crime would be put down by the citizenry—that is, a sort of revival of the Old West's lynch law. But as even Lenin also pointed out in *State and Revolution* (on the authority of Engels): "Take a factory, a railway, a vessel on the high seas . . . is it not clear that not one of these complex technical units, based on the use of machines and the cooperation of many people, could function without a certain amount of subordination, without some authority or power?" Marx assumed that in the homogeneous society of the future such power would be voluntarily accepted. More generally, this supposed human unanimity means abandoning criticism of society, that is to say, abandoning our reasoning powers.

The hazy notion that all problems will be solved, or at least that all tragedies will be acceptable or transcended, is also absurd. André Malraux asked a Communist who was describing the perfect life of the future, "What about the man who is run over by a tram?" The answer

was, "In the perfect tramway system of the future there will be no accidents." An absurd example, but even less extreme ebullitions of this sort
of utopian mind-set imply, in T. S. Eliot's words (in *The Rock*), seeking
"systems so perfect that no man could ever be good."

And among these happy Eloi we are also to have an efflorescence of
"creativity." Why, it is hard to say, except on the principle that the Good
Society must have everything. As we know, genius is often, perhaps
always, the product of tensions and struggles. Yet one is often told in this
sort of literature that once cleansed from the pressures of class society,
every man may be a Shakespeare or a Beethoven-and-Shakespeare. How
can there be several billion ways of being gigantically original? And these
results are supposed to emerge from extreme homogenization!

Of course all real life is caught up in parochial or shortsighted
motives; of course all organizations are inefficient; of course selfishness
and corruption occur in all societies. The civilized response is indignation, revulsion, political action; but it is also a sense of proportion, a
rejection of the idea of utopian alternatives.

Finally, all such militant dogmas and allegiances and enthusiasms
denouncing implacable, destructive, even satanic opponents appeal to a
human emotion in presupposing the "enemy"—a scapegoat, an object of
hate: in the Marxist case the class or ideological enemy—the bourgeois,
both in themselves and as part of the system (Hitler, too, was to urge his
followers not only against Jews or plutocrats, but also against *das System*).

3.

Marx was seen, and saw himself, as "the Darwin of society": as the
originator of a historical science to match Darwin's biological science.
He provided his certainties in terms of proven theory. The contrast
between his own and Darwin's methods is very striking, and indeed,
Marx saw this himself—referring rather patronizingly to Darwin's
"crude English empiricism." By this he meant no more than the perfectly true circumstance that Darwin accumulated facts before developing
his theory, as against the supposedly superior method Marx derived
from his German academic background, of inventing the theory first
and then finding the facts to support it. His appeal to Darwinism was
in accord with the victorious advances in every other field, which predis-
posed audiences to the idea that the same could be done for the study
of humanity. In fact, Marxism's most persistent fault, and the hardest to

be rid of, was one much more widely believed and one which was to have other incarnations: that our knowledge of the workings of human behavior is now so scientific that we can shape society according to scientific, or rational, blueprints. It is clear, on the contrary, that even now we do not know enough about the endlessly complex affairs of the human mind or of human society to predict, plan and manipulate.

Marx's new scientific wording was, above all, modern. A Russian revolutionist around the turn of the century tells how this aspect of Marxism struck him and his fellows:

> We seized on Marxism because we were attracted by its logical and economic optimism, its strong belief, buttressed by facts and figures, that the development of the economy, the development of capitalism (this was why we were so interested in it), by demoralising and eroding the foundations of the old society, was creating new social forces (including us) which would certainly sweep away the autocratic regime together with all its abominations. With the optimism of youth we had been searching for a formula that offered hope, and we found it in Marxism. We were also attracted by its European nature. Marxism came from Europe. It did not smell and taste of home-grown mould and provincialism, but was new, and fresh and exciting.

This modernity still clung to the image of the "scientifically socialist" Soviet Union well into the twentieth century.

Marx's (then) modernity consisted also in its basing itself on what were new phenomena—heavy industry and the industrial proletariat—seeing the latter as the class destined to bring history to its appointed climax.

The "proletarian" element in Marxism carries much of its weight, both morally and messianically. Nothing better illustrates the temporally parochial set of the whole of its social philosophy. The rise of "heavy" industry had indeed, in a general sense, brought together a worker stratum concentrated in enterprises where solidarity of interests could easily be organized. The existence, and role, of this new phenomenon struck other students of the social scene besides Marx. But Marx erected on it the theory that this was the last exploited class—faced by the "capitalist" owner as the last exploiting class—and would inherit the earth after the (scientifically proven) collapse of the capitalist economy.

Marx came to his conclusions about the mystic historical nature of the new proletarian class before he had even seen an actual proletarian—as, indeed, was true of Lenin in the 1880s. But come to that, Marx seems to have had a very odd idea of the bourgeoisie. Who can read without laughter those paragraphs of the *Communist Manifesto*, which are solemnly printed year after year, about bourgeois sex life in Victorian times?

> The Communists have no need to introduce community of women; it has existed almost from time immemorial. Our bourgeois, not content with having the wives and daughters of their proletarians at their disposal, not to speak of common prostitutes, take the greatest pleasure in seducing each other's wives. Bourgeois marriage is in reality a system of wives in common.

Apart from the notion of the Victorian bourgeoisie sharing each other's wives on this grand scale, there is something a little unreal, is there not, about the idea of the factory owner passing around the slums that house his employees, debauching a wife here, a daughter there? Particularly, perhaps, during the period of which Marx was writing. It is true that Marx himself seduced, and had a child by, his maid—who might perhaps be regarded in this context as a proletarian employee.

Marx did not consider that the proletariat might not be the last "New Class"—a term Milovan Djilas coined for the Soviet priviligentsia. Nor did he contemplate the possibility that the then new style of heavy industry itself, with its horny-handed toilers, might also not be permanent. Indeed, the failure of the Soviet Union in the later technological, and military-technological, contest with the West may in part be seen as the defeat of archaic heavy industry by newer automated and sophisticated conditions of production: a defeat of Magnitogorsk by Silicon Valley.

In any case, those who nominate themselves as "representatives" of a given economic class are usually not really so in any rational sense: they represent, that is to say, not what will benefit those to whom they are supposedly devoted, but an ideological future in which not the real interests of the group in question but the theoretical and messianic notion of its historical role prevails. In much the same way, extreme nationalists (for example, the Nazis) set themselves up as the "representatives" of their nation. The Nazis did indeed messianize or idolize the German nation. In their theory the nation played a far more sublime role than it did in the minds of many members of moderate parties in the German state. But few, I think, would argue that the Nazis' unrivaled devotion to nationality in fact operated in the real interests of the German people as against a less extreme view.

In fact, such parties do not necessarily act so much in the real interests of the stratum they purportedly serve as for some Idea of those interests in which they have wrongly been led to believe. It was always a conscious strategy of the Marxists to inculcate into the more or less spontaneous movements of the industrial working class the idea that socialism was its main, long-term interest. It is an ironic commentary on this that the great workers' risings took place in countries where capitalism had been overthrown, in cities like East Berlin, Poznan, Budapest, Gdansk. Adam Ulam, in his book *Communism*, notes that in the 1970 events in Gdansk, "the Lenin Shipyard was finally cleared of its sit-in strikers after they had been threatened with an artillery bombardment," "the Paris Commune Shipyard was stormed by government forces," and "Karl Marx Street witnessed a confrontation between a defiant mob and army tanks."

One principle basic to all these regimes is that the parties concerned came to power while concealing from their rank-and-file supporters the inevitable sacrifices that would be asked of them. As Lenin put it: "The victory of the workers is impossible without sacrifices, without a temporary worsening of their situation." Continuing the tradition, Che Guevara says the same thing in his *Man and Socialism in Cuba*:

> The vanguard group is ideologically more advanced than the mass; the latter is acquainted with the new values, but insufficiently. While in the former a qualitative change takes place which permits them to makes sacrifices as a function of their vanguard character, the latter see only by halves and must be subjected to incentives and pressures of some intensity; it is the dictatorship of the proletariat being exercised not only upon the defeated class but also individually upon the victorious class.

The result of "proletarian" revolutions has, at any rate, always been a lowering of the standard of living of the working class, together with the removal of their right to defend themselves against this in traditional fashion.

Marx's own attitude to the working class was already that it had its duty to support him. When industrial workers voted Conservative in the British election of 1867, Engels wrote to his colleague, "Once again the English working class has disgraced itself." It is hard to imagine what he would have thought of the elections of the 1970s and

1980s, when the skilled proletariat voted heavily Conservative—many years after Capitalism, Conservatism and suchlike were destined to have disappeared.

4.

The acceptance of sectarian doctrine on trust is always notable among the less intelligent adherents of one or another totalist party. The mobs of Byzantium and Alexandria who supported the homoousion, the strange fanatics of seventeenth-century London who interpreted Revelation, obviously have much in common with the rank-and-file Nazis or Communists. I remember being told by the late Jacques Katel, once prominent in French Communist circles, of how he attended a meeting of the Party branch at the Renault works in 1934. A somewhat supercilious representative of the Central Committee was putting forward the new line of the "United Front" with the Socialist Party. When he finished, one of the huge, loyal *militants* on whom the French Communist Party so strongly based itself got up and said *"Camarade! Il y a une chose que je n'ai pas bien compris. Comment se peut-il que les Socialistes hier étaient des fascistes, et aujourd'hui ils sont des camarades?"* The representative of the Central Committee answered shortly, *"Camarade, c'est la dialectique."* Upon which, somewhat to Katel's surprise, the militant said, *"Ah, oui, bien sûr . . . ah, vous avez raison . . . oui, c'est ça, la dialectique . . ."* and sat down perfectly satisfied.

The Marxist appeal was not simply the attraction of utopia and of dogma. It was also a matter of becoming one with the masses—the proletariat—or with the movement itself. This sort of renunciation of individuality has been interpreted as arising, in many cases, in a weak personality using others as support; in some cases in a strong, power-seeking personality projecting itself. It is not our purpose here to develop a psychology of the phenomenon, which has been pursued by others, but to stress its practical importance.

Nor did the Marxist elites, when in power, have much respect for the masses. The Yugoslav Communist Anton Ciliga tells of how in the early 1930s the Soviet Communist intelligentsia and apparat already saw the masses, as under Fascism, as merely the raw material of the party. Joseph Berger, the veteran secretary of the Palestine Communist Party, was told, when in postwar Poland: "As a Party member you have no business to talk about what the masses want. They will want what we want." In fact, this was put in even more authoritarian fashion by the

Hungarian Communist leader János Kádár, in his address to the Hungarian National Assembly in 1957:

> The task of the leaders is not to put into effect the wishes and will of the masses. The task of the leaders is to accomplish the interests of the masses. Why do I differentiate between the will and the interests of the masses? In the recent past we have encountered the phenomenon of certain categories of workers acting against their interests.

Only when envisaged in the abstract, as verbal icons, did the proletariat or the masses figure positively.

Identification with masses and movements is not, of course, unique to Marxism. The nation, or the race, provided masses just as plausible as the proletariat, and movements just as dogmatically overpowering as the Communists.

5.

Marxism's appeal had the advantages of both simplicity and complexity. It was not so simple as to sound naïve, like Proudhon's "Property is theft." Its main themes were simple enough to be apprehended without much strain, but at the same time it was convoluted enough to require what amounted to a caste of interpreters. It may be thought that such conceptual deviousness would be a disadvantage rather than an advantage. And it may be asked how such a work as *Capital*, very difficult reading in its economic sections proper, had such a wide repute.

As the late Hugh Gaitskell (later leader of the Labour Party) explained, the ideas of economic heretics

> are frequently vague or complicated and not as a rule expressed in the clearest possible manner. How is it that, in spite of this, they achieve such fame and popularity? As we have suggested above, vagueness and complexity are not really limitations, but, on the contrary, advantages. For they make the task of criticism tedious and difficult and enable the heretic to say with perfect truth that his views have never been refuted. At the same time the support of the plain man is not any way forfeited. For the most part he will not bother his head with the complicated details. He will be content to accept the broad conclusions largely on irrational grounds.

Thus, as David Simmons puts it (in his *Ideals and Dogma*), "It is possible that the faults of Marxism stem from an inability to express things clearly;

it is equally likely that the lack of clarity is sometimes a device to mask the fact that the conclusions sought could not be arrived at by logical means."

A further advantage of Marxism lay in its irrefutability, even apart from its critics' inherent disqualification. For it was sufficiently vague and flexible to be adjusted to fit any subject matter, at least to the satisfaction of its practitioners. As Gibbon noted of the Neoplatonists, "This free-dom of interpretation . . . exposed the vanity of their art . . . the solemn trifling and the impenetrable obscurity of these sages who pro-fessed to reveal the system of the universe. As they translated an arbitrary cipher they could extract . . . any sense that was adapted to their favourite system."

Discussion in Marxist terms reminds me of Peter de Vries's remark about someone being profound only on the surface, while deep down remaining superficial. Nadezhda Mandelshtam, the widow of the doomed poet, tells of her husband's conversations with a dedicated Marxist:

> I was irritated by the debate between them. To Chechanovski it was self-evident that M.'s view of the world was quite outmoded, and that he was unable to reform, poor fellow. M., on the other hand, was just wasting his breath by disputing Chechanovski's not very sophisticated dialectical con-structions, which were food neither for the mind nor for the heart. If Marxism had not been the official ideology, binding everybody who wanted to earn his daily bread, M. would scarcely have allowed himself to get seriously involved in a discussion of the "basis" and the "superstruc-ture," or the theory of "leaps." . . . In arguing against Marxism, its oppo-nents were forced to use the same language, and by the very nature of the subject, any discussion of it inevitably led to a drop in the intellectual level. But M. was so desperate to have someone to talk with that he was only too glad of these conversations even with such an ill-matched (but on the whole innocuous) companion as Chechanovski. There really was no one to talk with, and the level was being systematically lowered all the time. Marxists and non-Marxists were becoming equally dreary.

A former professor, the nephew of the reformer of Alexander II's time, Loris-Melikov was even more dismissive. He mentioned to a fellow camp inmate that at his institute he had given lessons in dialectical materialism. Asked if he knew the subject, he replied, "What is there to know about such rubbish except the patter?"

To be fair, serious Soviet scholars having to work within, or present their work as if within, these categories, sometimes contrived to make sense, especially in spheres of no great sensitivity. But by the end of the 1980s, as discipline relaxed, even the central Party ideological bodies held discussions in which Marx was hardly mentioned, and the names heard were Westerners like Durkheim and Weber. An editor of the Party's theoretical journal, *Kommunist*, approached me in my office for a contribution. When I asked him how the journal was doing, he answered that it was selling very poorly—"What do you expect with a title like that?" he added. The title was later changed, though not before my contribution had been published (*Kommunist*, no. 17, 1990). The head of the Department of Scientific Communism at a Soviet universi-ty told me how he proposed to handle his staff of thirty academics: ten could be fired, ten were old enough to be given retirement, and the remaining ten he felt were retrainable.

The sophistication or complexity even of a true scientific theory have little bearing on its correctness, though they do appeal to some intellec-tual temperaments. The Ptolemaic geocentric apparatus was, for a mil-lennium and a half, the victor over the truer heliocentric view largely because of the greater intricacy of its epicycles, its glow of cleverness. Though incorrect, it remained at least coherent. Marxism was not only erroneous—it was self-contradictory.

6.

Marxism was also attractive in that it provided (like other ideologies) automatic refutation of its critics.

Marx and Marxists spoke much of the "false consciousness" of people whose arguments are only superficially intellectual, being (though they themselves are unaware of it) mere projections of class prejudice, and who thus believe themselves to be acting from religious or other motives while really driven by economic interests. Translated into the terms of the later-established Marxist regimes, this confirmed that all opposition was due to malignant class enmity, with which rational argument was in any case impossible or inadequate, and to which the only effective reply was force.

The same concealment, or unconsciousness, of real motive postulat-ed by Marx can of course be applied to Marxism itself. Orwell coun-tered that Communists "pretended, perhaps . . . even believed," that they had taken power unwillingly and temporarily to bring in very soon a free human paradise—but that their *real* motive was power.

Since Marxists took their theory to be science, the science of society, including history, sociology and economics, when this became the official view of the state it implied, and in fact resulted in, the substitution of Marxism for the prescientific gropings that had hitherto prevailed. In all the Marxist states, alternative views were suppressed, in academe as well as in society as a whole. And this led, of course, to a mental enslavement and degeneration of thought. Nor did this apply only to the subjects of Marxist dictatorship. It equally affected many others accepting the doctrine. As Lewis S. Feuer noted in his *Ideology and the Ideologists,* "Under no conditions whatever will the ideologist renounce his ideology. Thus the master of European Marxism, Georg Lukács, declared in 1967 that even if every empirical prediction of Marxism were invalidated, he would still hold Marxism to be true."

There was yet another level of defense for Marxism—one much employed by Marx and Engels and still often put forward: criticism was deflected by the claim that it dealt only with "vulgar Marxism," while its more sophisticated proponents had provided a variety of subtle reservations, or, if not quite reservations, at least nuances.

7.

The Anarchist Bakunin suggested at the time that Marxists' real aim was a "pedantocracy": that is to say, a regime in which theoreticians—their own type of theoreticians—would be in charge: or, to put it another way, in which a political intelligentsia, unemployable in normal circumstances, took the positions of power. And indeed, in many countries there is still a large overproduction of people educated to be lawyers and administrators. The intellectual have-nots can only take the power posts by removing the haves, so the incentive to revolution is obvious (their "false consciousness" as to such motives is equally understandable).

But then, why be Marxists in particular? An important reason since 1917 seems to have been that in most cases a Communist organization was in existence, well funded, ready for recruitment, and apparently possessing a viable road to power. This is not to say that such recruitment was *merely* a vehicle to power. On the contrary. The young revolutionists truly accepted the Marxist-Leninist dogmas. Ethiopia might easily have in any case been taken over by brutal revolutionary officers, but the way they ruined the country's agriculture was the result of the complete acceptance of poisonous doctrine.

8.

The "science" was embodied, however, in Marx's economic and historical theory. The former is basic, in the sense that he viewed even consciousness as determined by the means of production. But apart from this supposedly scientific demonstration of the fundamentals of exploitation, his historico-political thought has provided the main momentum.

Marx's work made specific deductions; in *Das Kapital* he speaks of having discovered the "Natural Laws" of capitalist production, adding that "these laws worked things out with iron necessity towards inevitable results." And Marx's Marxism was indeed a scientific theory, in the sense that it made predictions which were falsifiable: that as the proportion of capital to labor in production increased, profit must (obviously) fall and wages decrease; that capitalism would operate as a constraint on production; that the industrial countries must become increasingly polarized between a small group of capitalists and a huge and increasingly impoverished proletariat; and that the latter must overthrow the former in a revolution. These predictions of Marx's were not random suggestions, but were rigorously deduced from his whole analysis of the workings of the capitalist system.

The Marxian theory of value is, in fact, not an abstraction. He seriously urged on many occasions that price fluctuated round "value" as determined by labor theory. For Marx, in the end, presented himself above all as an economist. And he himself would have conceded that without the supposedly "objective" support of his economic researchers, his social theories would have lacked all verification and intellectual respectability and would have been mere rhetoric. He proved, to his own satisfaction, that the class rift in modern times is rooted in the fact that all profit is extracted from the workers.

The crux of Marxism in fact was this theory of "surplus value." It has no evidential basis—argued at this level, profit can just as easily be defined as produced by capital, or by a conjunction of capital and labor. When in the late 1920s an attempt was made among Italian Communists to debate the theory, their leader Palmiro Togliatti (as one of his colleagues tells us) could not be brought to show any interest— the theory, he explained, was for the masses, not for economists.

It is, indeed, no more than a way to give an apparently scientific and doctrinal form to the simple notion that the rich rob the poor. Now a German *Doktor* had proved it.

Marx derived all the evils of "capitalism"—alienation, exploitation, crises, etc.—from "commodity" production, that is, from the market system. In fact, the whole history of the USSR testifies to a refusal to face the fact that a complex modern economy cannot operate without a market mechanism. Why (even leaving aside economic common sense) Marx thought that a bureaucrat's decision was less alienating than the "unplanned" play of market forces is not clear.

"Capitalism" is an economic term and can only be used to describe a whole social or political order on the assumption that such orders are thoroughly determined by their economic structures, as they are not. Similarly, the "capitalist" motivations are by definition the economic, not the moral or cultural or legal, ones. Of course, except among embezzlers and psychopaths, the individual "capitalist" is never motivated solely by economic considerations. "Total" economics (that is, capitalism pure and simple) has failed to prevail in Western economies. The "free market" is, for some reason, an image of economic anarchy. But it has never been free in the sense of not being bound by laws—laws against fraud and forgery, laws enforcing contracts—for such laws form the necessary framework of a properly operating market economy. It is a condition of the free market that trust must prevail between those engaged in commerce: they cannot be "cutthroat" in any usual sense.

In fact, the really exploitative element in market capitalism emerges under two conditions. The first is when there is no law at all, as in trade with savage areas. The risk is then so great that profits are both high and unreliable, and the inducements to improve the margin by any means soon make trade barely distinguishable from piracy. The second is the situation in which capitalism is overregulated, where the state is able to divert the natural benefits of the market to its own monopolist nominees or even into its own pockets. Again, the margin is minimal and the inducement to fraud is greater. In the extreme case where capitalism was actively illegal, as in the old Soviet Union, so that no mechanism existed to regulate (as against destroy) the market, trade was inevitably beset with bribery and blackmail.

But Marxism's greatest success has been the demonizing of "capitalism." No one is likely to raise barricades under the flag of "capitalism"—presumably the skull and crossbones. And its evils are constantly attacked, not only by conscious Marxists. No one, for example, would suggest South Korea as a messianic utopia. But when softhearted anticapitalist academics of my acquaintance are faced with the question of why South Korea's infant death rate is so astonishingly lower than that of socialist North Korea, they are at a great loss to grant any credit to the systemic economic difference. An extreme example of this sort of thing was a letter in the *Washington Post* (5 November 1996) from John Le Carré, saying that though Communism didn't work, capitalism is in much of the world "a wrecking, terrible force," displacing people and ruining lifestyles "with the same recklessness as Communism."

Indeed, the changes that are taking place the world over are in many ways disruptive (as Marx noted while accepting that such changes were "progressive"). But as ever the parallelism of these two "systems" is a fallacy. To make the best of, or to improve, the operation of the market is a genuine challenge, but it cannot be effected under un-sane categorization.

If "capitalism" is preferable to some other economic forms, it is not because it is just, but because the injustices inherent in any real system are, in its case, understood to be such; that the exercisers of economic power never win anyone's blind trust. When the economic rulers are nominees of "the people" and claim to be seen not as bureaucrats but as democracy incarnate, who can query them?

Even at the level of Marxism itself, accepting its socioeconomic propositions, Marx has long since been refuted in practice on his own terms. As Engels wrote of the sixteenth-century revolutionist Thomas Münzer: "The social transformation that he pictured in his fantasy was so little grounded in the then existing economic conditions, that the latter were a preparation for a social system diametrically opposed to that of which he dreamt." Marxism, in fact, fails under its own critique.

9.

In the circumstances, it may not seem surprising that Marx's pronouncements are neither encompassing nor coherent; and that they are often self-contradictory, self-refuting, with his theory of historical development—slave-feudal-capitalist-socialist—being in effect, as has often been pointed out, negated by his later view of an "Asiatic" society outside the scheme. Indeed, Marxism does not have, and does not even pretend to have, any mechanism to explain the internal development of the social system it describes as "Asiatic." In these areas of traditionalist despotism, under which the larger part of the world's population lived for thousands of years, Marx quite explicitly and admittedly found no class conflict, in the absence of opposing groups categorizable as economic classes. (Change only came, as he puts it, when Western culture burst in on them: an unconscious illustration of Marx's Eurocentrism). But this is an extraordinary state of things. There is no law of geography which dictates that it would be impossible for all the inhabitable areas of the earth to lie in latitudes, and be subject to physical conditions, of the type that produced the Asian empires. But a theory of history that even pretends to be comprehensive becomes absurd once such a point is admitted. (Indeed, how can any "rigorous" theory account for Britain's being an island, a fact that has certainly contributed most importantly to the world's social and political development. Its insulation was the merest accident on any rational time scale, dating from some ten thousand years ago, a geological instant.)

At best, the Marxist view accepts that all institutional and economic developments in the various countries of the world can meaningfully be ascribed to the four or five Marxist categories. The variety within societies described as "feudal," for example, are in reality far more striking than the points they have in common, as is the case with any study when particulars become more widely known. A whale may be called a fish only by an inadequately informed categorizer.

The extent to which these Marxist notions penetrated our thought is remarkable. His division into slave, feudal and capitalist epochs in the West is commonly used, though feudalism in particular is a shaky enough concept. Marxist class analyses of England in the seventeenth century are still met with, though seldom among historians of the period. These have shown class analysis to be thoroughly defective with respect to James I's reign. On a slightly different note, a recent book on the English Civil War notes that ten cavalier colonels had brothers or sons on the other side. As a recent historian puts it, the allegiances "arose from inclination, temperaments and other humours that will ever defy precise analysis" (P. R. Newman, in his *The Old Service*). Similar points might be made about the American Revolution, with such well-known cases as Edmund Randolph's father, Benjamin Franklin's son and Gouverneur Morris's brother.

In many periods it has been shown that class struggle in the Marxian sense has hardly existed. For example, it is clear that in French villages in the early sixteenth century, though there were small elites of rich peasants, a mass of ordinary "plowmen" and a small set of manual laborers, the confrontations and struggles were those uniting the village against outside groups (the error is not a minor one, since it was almost exactly paralleled in Lenin's, and later Stalin's, positing a "class struggle" in the Russian village, which was a major element in their justification of terror in the countryside).

At a different level, historians like Emmanuel Le Roy Ladurie have long since pointed out that the French Revolution was not in any comprehensible sense one of capitalism against feudalism. As he says, the "feudal" and "capitalist" modes of production, "far from being antagonistic, were moving together during the eighteenth century and putting up a united front against the peasant-smallholder family-farm economy," which defeated both of them in the Revolution. In the towns it was, of course, different—but here it was not "the bourgeoisie" in general but a "legal" bourgeoisie, for some time far more important than the industrial and commercial, or "economic," bourgeoisie. In fact, "class struggle" was not an adequate concept even where some such confrontation did indeed play a role. Thus Marxism and its offshoots' attempt to reduce the whole broad scope of interhuman relations to matters of hostility is defective. As Matthew Arnold wrote: "Culture is the eternal opponent of the two things which are the signal marks of Jacobinism—its fierceness and its addiction to an abstract system."

Research more profoundly damaging to the class concept has included analyses (both "left" and "right") which show that anything like a specifically working-class "culture" differentiated from the general culture only began to come into being in Britain in the early 1920s, and faded away within a few decades.

What remains today of Marxism, once a large and ambitious structure, is little more than this basic dogma that our society (and all others) is driven by unappeasable strife, in which one contestant must inevitably destroy the other. It was back in the 1840s that Marx announced this discovery, though the search for the supposed evidence for it took decades. His great point was that people had previously made all sorts of political, philosophical and other moves without realizing that their motive was class struggle, but that at last the truth was out.

The Marxian attitude to this was odd. It might be thought that when unconscious causes of strife are brought to light the natural thing would be to subject them to conscious control and abate them. When

Christianity identified Original Sin as a source of trouble, it did not say, "Well, now we know what's wrong, go ahead and indulge it." Marx, on the other hand, sought none of the benefits of his supposed new knowledge; he merely urged the side he put his money on to do its worst.

10.

It is still occasionally said (e.g., by Eric Hobsbawm) that all serious approaches to history must be based on Marxism's breakthrough in understanding, on the grounds that Marxism provided a historical perspective in the study of humanity (as if previous theories had uniformly failed to do so). But is a false perspective better than no perspective? Are highly distorting glasses better than short sight? At any rate, Hobsbawm's addiction to Marxism led him into many years of, if not unqualified approval of, then undisguised preference for, the Communist regimes. But the notion is false to the point of absurdity on several counts. First, the idea of political conflict among economic-interest groups was very far from new and was taken for granted by Thucydides. Second, conflict occurs between "interest" groups where the mutual uncongeniality cannot be called economic, except by fiddling with the evidence or exaggerating minimals. Third, cooperation or regulated competition among both economic and other interest groups has been as common as—more common than—irreconcilable conflict (particularly in the more advanced countries).

It may be remarked that Marx and Engels wrote at a time when economic forces were unprecedentedly powerful and political ones very weak, at least in the countries they were chiefly concerned with. Since then political mechanisms more powerful than the social forces have been invented, and the wills of powerful dictatorships have been enforced against all the real wishes of society and in opposition to the needs of the economy. The epoch of Stalin, Mao and Hitler is the very last one to which a materialist conception of history, as the product of economic trends, could possibly be applied.

The way in which Marxist or other schematic assumptions afflict all of us may be seen in the view (which I ignorantly shared) that in Roman times slavery inhibited technological development—machines being unnecessary when an unlimited source of human energy was available. Peter Salway, in his new Roman volume of *The Cambridge History of England*, points out that sophisticated mill and mine machinery driven by waterpower was common in those times, and that the Romans were well aware of the poor productivity of slaves. He concludes:

> I see no reason to suppose that the Romans would not have used cheap mechanical power if it had been available nor any evidence to suggest that the failure to put to practical use the power of steam, of which the ancient world was aware, was due to anything more than the lack of those crucial inventions in the eighteenth century that made commercial steam engines a viable proposition.

II.

Marxism, and generally all theories stressing conflict as the center of historical development, also create their evidence by inflating anything resembling a riot or revolt into the central event of the period. Professor Toru Haga, mentioning a few peasant risings in eighteenth-century Japan, was asked why they hardly entered into his general account of the period. He replied that they were peripheral and atypical and were only widely bruited at present because of a doctrinally motivated Marxist search for events suited to that theory. The same, of course, could be said of English history. To read some writers, one would think that the nineteenth century consisted largely of the Peterloo Massacre, the Tolpuddle Martyrs and Bloody Sunday. All were exceptional rather than typical events, and even if they were not, they would contrast pretty markedly with experience in, for example, France. Six were killed in the Peterloo rioting; none of the Tolpuddle Martyrs, though they were all disgracefully victimized and "transported," was actually martyred in the normal sense; while Bloody Sunday produced precisely one death, an accidental one. Indeed, the use of such a term for such an event shows a remarkable scraping of the barrel by those determined to find British parallels to Continental shenanigans. The total death toll in civil disturbances in Britain over a century and a half can hardly be much over a hundred, or, to put it another way, the equivalent of a single busy afternoon on a Paris barricade. This search for, and exaltation of, armed clashes seems no more than a weak version of that patriotic romanticism about battles so much sneered at by people perfectly happy with this left-wing equivalent.

Possession of, or by, the idea that one has final answers to all the problems of history and of society seems to lead to "final answer" dogmas in other fields. There was and is a strong tendency among Marxists to accept pseudosciences. The mechanism seems to be related to the desire for complete solutions—which are, of course, more commonly found in the pseudosciences than in the sciences proper.

Wilhelm Liebknecht, one of Marx's most trusted followers after Engels himself, tells in his memoirs that Marx examined his skull with his fingers on their first meeting. Though not "as zealous a devotee" of phrenology as revolutionaries like Gustav Struve, "he believed in it to some extent," even having "the phrenologist of the party" (that is, of the Communist League), Karl Pfaender, give Liebknecht a further and more professional check later. Fortunately, Pfaender did not find "anything which would have prevented my admission" into the League. Again, in 1866 Marx became enthusiastic about the theories of the adventurer Pierre Trémaux, who held that the distinctions between the races were attributable to the different soils on which they lived.

An extraordinary array of officially endorsed pseudosciences attended triumphant Marxism in the USSR, as we shall see. And in the early sixties the Maoists reverted to various ancient but implausible devices, such as the swallowing of tadpoles as a means of contraception. During the Cultural Revolution "bourgeois" acupuncture specialists were driven out in favor of inexperienced enthusiasts. A team of these used previously "forbidden points" for sticking the needles in so effectively that a high proportion of deaf-mutes treated by this method were heard to shout "Long live Chairman Mao" (New China News Agency, 3 November 1968).

Not all Marxists would have been capable of such powerful idiocy. But to some degree Marxism itself may be blamed. First of all, the principle of accommodating science to a particular metaphysic rather than leaving it to act autonomously seems bound to produce distortion. Second, the notion that Marxism is a basic universal science leads to the condition in which many people professing it feel that they are already fully educated and, in effect, capable of judging any subsidiary studies without adequate humility or effort. Hence, perhaps, part of its attraction.

These notions may also tend to show that those who seek cure-all formulae for reconstructing society are temperamentally inclined towards "unorthodox" fads in other fields. This in turn may tend to cast doubt on the validity of their political-economic analyses.

It was Jonathan Swift who said that the most positive men are the most credulous. There are temperaments that will always seek absolutes, and no argument could persuade them otherwise. The practical problem is to see that their notions do not get too widely accepted.

12.

Marxism thus, as was noted even at the time, had two different, even contradictory aspects. It was science, predicting the way things were objectively bound to turn out (and this gave credibility to Marxists who called for patience and maneuver). It was also revolutionism, subjectively urging the militant to fight.

By the end of the nineteenth century, the Marxist predictions of a capitalist failure to expand production, of a fall in the rate of profit, a decrease in wages, of increasing proletarian impoverishment and the resulting approach of revolutionary crisis in the industrial countries had all proved false.

But Marxism had already become the accepted doctrine of a number of key working-class parties. Rather than abandon it, the more realistic social democrats "revised" it. Eduard Bernstein and others in effect accepted both that the "laws" had failed and that "revolution" was unnecessary, but still called the residue Marxism. This was enough for the practical members, in particular for the workers as such; and the residual claim to Marxist philosophy appeased at least some of the intellectuals. Though the "socialist" and *étatiste* element in Marxist (and pre-Marxist) thought still resulted in imprudent social policies, the larger Idea had been to an important degree tamed.

A large section of those under Marxist influence was thus reclaimed for nonrevolutionary civic society. Even they, it is true, stood to varying degrees for the principle of class struggle—in any case vaguely implicit in representing workers' interests. More doctrinally, though less inevitably, the idea of socialism became a mark of the working-class movement in Europe (though only peripherally and briefly in the United States). In their inspirational aspect, the words "socialism" and "communism" convey an economy without sin. In the old days, and partly through Marxist jargon, the active definition was easy—a society without capitalists. Unfortunately, since then a number of societies without capitalists have been created in various countries, and it would take a word fetishist of terrific obstinacy to maintain that these were indeed without sin.

The command economy got confused with the idea of a just and democratic social order when the concept of the "nationalisation of the means of production, distribution and exchange" was adopted as the official aim of the Labour Party (though the Trade Unions only included it to please their nonworker intellectual groups like the Fabians). Different ideas about providing social control—such as guild socialism or syndicalism—became unfashionable. It was later realized that nationalization is quite compatible with private ownership of the state itself, by a single entrepreneur (e.g., Stalin) or a small board of directors (e.g., Brezhnev and company).

Such programmatic socialist ideas had already been tried out, unsuccessfully, in the first months of the 1848 Revolution in France. When Robert Owen asked Lord Brougham to put before Queen Victoria, through the Prince Consort, a proposal for a commission on the theory of Socialism, Albert replied to Brougham:

> I have felt that I could with safety lay Mr Owen's memorial before the Queen as by so doing I commit neither Her Majesty nor myself to any expression of opinion upon the subject matter. I think you could, as from yourself, tell your old friend, that it is hardly by the appointment of a Commission to enquire into the Theory of Socialism that we can hope to arrive at a satisfactory result, but that the value of its principles could alone be tested by their practical adaptation. Such practical experiments have unfortunately hitherto been found to be exceedingly expensive to the Nation which tried them. However, one upon a large scale is now being carried on in France, which I think might be considered as a "Monster Commission" for the instruction of the rest of Europe.

We have had more experience since.

13.

It is clear that Lenin, who naturally attacked Bernstein's revision of Marx with some virulence, did so not because he felt Bernstein to be wrong but because he feared he might be right. Lenin concluded that the working-class movement, unless guarded by a "socialist vanguard," would become petty bourgeois. And he defined the vanguard as full-time professional revolutionaries.

In effect, Lenin saw that history was not behaving in accordance with Marxist theory, so he decided to force it to do so by subjective effort, like some phrenologist finding one of his subjects lacking the right bumps and producing them by clouting him on the head.

But though Lenin in practice gave up the "scientific" context of Marxism, he still maintained that it was an infallible doctrine. He even, in his *Marxism and Empiriocriticism,* undertook philosophical polemics over its most metaphysical content. That is, the Idea was still his motive force.

The Communist acceptance of Marxism as dogma, with sacred texts, led to such oddities as the official Stalinist printing and distribution in the West, as elsewhere, of Engels's *Germany: Revolution and Counterrevolution* (checked on by Marx, too). In citing it here, we are not so much concerned with the general aberrations to which Marxist analysis was and remained prone, as with a particular and crucial blind spot—the question of nationality. In it we read that "Poles and Czechs are essentially an agricultural race"; that in East European cities manufacturers are Germans and traders Jews—whom he accounts as more German than otherwise, their native tongue being "a horribly corrupted German"; that German culture, too, was now prevailing and, together with diplomatic and military pressure, ensuring "the slow but sure advance of denationalisation by social developments." "The dying Czech nationality," even if continuing to speak their own tongue, "could only exist henceforth as part of Germany."

It is not only the sponsorship of this and similar material by the regime of a—Slavic—Moscow that makes it worth quoting. Indeed, that would be no more than a demonstration of the idolatry of texts common to communities of closed minds. The excerpt also gives us other insights. First, the shallow quality of thought is revealed, but even more, its complete, and by now one would have thought embarrassing, misevaluation of major historical processes—the area in which Marxism submits itself for judgment. Furthermore, its thoughts well illustrate the overlap between socialist and nationalist ideas which, in another context, contributed to the National Socialist experience.

By the test of serious *intellectual* persuasiveness, Marx was hardly a "great thinker," though he often appears as such in low-level Western academic curricula. This is hard to reconcile with the fact that outside his sect few serious philosophers accepted his philosophy; few economists accepted his economics; few historians accepted his theories of history. We are here speaking, in doctrinal terms, of Marxism proper.

As such observers as Raymond Aron and Ernest Gellner have pointed out, there are fashions in what is still called Marxism in the West which are, in the latter's words, "neo-Hegelian, existentialist, phenomenological, structuralistic, etc.," and "unintelligible." Here the claim to Marxism is little more than verbal—a dash of garlic in the casserole. We can note in France, even in the early stages when the dogma still to some extent clung, such variations on it as Simone de Beauvoir's argument that the Marquis de Sade was "a great moralist" because he "passionately exposes the bourgeois hoax which consists in erecting class interests into universal principles."

The intellectual and practical failure of Marxism is by now reasonably well understood in a general way, and contrary views are mainly explainable in terms of the—much precedented—persistence of obsolete notions. Still, that persistence remains a dangerous and destructive element in many minds, from Pyongyang to Peru. Moreover, it still affects the mental atmosphere even in circles that repudiate it at a conscious level.

◆

CHAPTER IV

The Nation:
Hope and Hysteria

(Nationality, Nationalism, Fascism, National Socialism)

I.

Revolutionary Marxism was not the only absolutist ideology to poison the minds of the twentieth century. The concept or feeling of nation and nationality has had, and still has, good as well as bad manifestations. These latter have been, and to a great extent still are, dangerous and devastating, and closely related to the other mental distortions of ideology. But neither the good nor the bad, nor their permutations, are to be understood except in the whole historical context.

2.

Nations as we now know them only started to come into existence some five or six centuries ago. In the Middle Ages allegiance was local, to the village, the town, the feudal lord, the King—the latter not necessarily of an ethnic realm; and beyond that to a larger, supposedly universal, entity—the Empire, Christendom, Islam. In Europe the official language of the entity was not the vernacular but Latin—as was Arabic in Islam.

The emergence of nationhood took several different forms. In England, and certain other countries, the interplay of social and other strata gradually developed in a series of ad hoc adjustments to the community-as-a-whole. The nation, conscious of its existence, evolved before the idea of a nation did. The state did not create the nation, but merely came to represent it.

In most of Europe, on the other hand, the national idea preceded its realization in a national state, which only came into being as the result of revolutions or wars.

In France an older—though still immature—national consciousness was given full form by the Revolution. The successes of England in science and commerce and even war, in contrast to the French failures, were part of the mix. That something went wrong among the French intellectuals is clear enough, and can be summarized as their having misunderstood and absolutized the scientific and political practices of the more advanced country—just as the Russian intelligentsia was to do a hundred years later. They thus felt empowered to create a utopia in the name of the People and the Nation, as well as to demonize all opposition in the name of Reason.

Before the Revolution French peasants would not ordinarily think of themselves primarily as "French." It was the Revolution, the Republic One and Indivisible, that consciously created or aroused the Nation. Nationality, not only in France, was henceforward for a long time almost always associated with progressive or revolutionary-democratic views and politics. But it was, as it was not in England or Scotland or Switzerland, the state that in effect brought it into being, and that formed it, administered it and represented it from above.

In Germany, too, the idea of the nation preceded the nation. From early in the nineteenth century, intellectual activists pursued the nationalist aim far more narrowly and obsessively than had been the case in French Revolutionary thought. Though this movement sometimes had Jacobin-style manifestations, it was not the left but an evolving political-military-philosophical establishment that created Germany. German nationality after the debacle of a liberal and revolutionary effort in 1848 was taken over and realized by the Prussian monarchy nearly twenty years later. Once again this was "from above." The new Second Reich was an extraordinary chimera. On the one hand, it had what has been called a pseudoconstitutionalism with a party system and parliament, within which the various political tendencies were given freeish run and at the same time assimilated to the imperial order. On the other hand, real power remained with the Kaiser and his militaristic and irresponsible coteries, who channeled the national feeling into war. (The long-held ideas that World War I came about through accidental concatenations, or that it was due to commercial rivalries, has been abandoned by most historians, and it is now clear enough that the Kaiser's regime was inherently headed for war).

After defeat in 1918, the German constitutional parties emerged as, for a time, in possession of much of the real power. And with luck a democratic evolution might have taken place. But clearly its basis was shaky and shallow.

Above all, as George Lichtheim notes, the new style of nationalism that opposed it "had its strongholds in the schools and universities," unlike in the French situation, where the teachers were predominately of the left. Hitler's first cadres, as he himself said, were officers and—students.

It is only fairly recently that a Western country like Germany can be said to have qualified as a mature nation-state. So it may be thought that we can hardly expect early evolutions in less "civilized" areas. This may not be the way to look at it; for there are regions where the negative type of national evolution which took place in Germany does not appear to be the natural direction—that, as it were, they are farther back, but on a better road.

3.

Other European nations are also of comparatively recent origin in their present forms.

In Hungary, for example, the official language was Latin. The Hungarian Kingdom was not Magyar: and the ethnic identification of Hungary with Magyardom only emerged in the second quarter of the nineteenth century.

In the Balkans, Western maps of that time show "various Slavonic tribes." Only towards the middle of the century do we find—for example—a real Bulgarian national consciousness. More broadly, Anne Applebaum notes of the whole of Eastern Europe:

> There were, until recently, no nations in the borderlands—or at least no nation-states in the sense that we know them now. There were the nobility and the invaders—the Poles and Russians and Germans and Tartars and Turks—who sometimes changed roles, defeating one another, only to be defeated in turn. There were the peasants: the Estonians and the Livonians who spoke Baltic tongues, the many descendants of the Slavic tribes—Volhinians, Podolians, Polesians, Galicians, Braclavians, now known as

Ukrainians or Belarusians. Jews, more Jews than were found anywhere else in the world. Scattered among all of these peoples there were others: colonies of Armenians, Greeks, and Hungarians, Tartars and Karaims, the descendants of war prisoners or merchants or heretics or criminals.

In the eighteenth century, if a borderland peasant were asked about his nationality, he would probably have replied "Catholic" or "Orthodox" or perhaps simply used the Polish word *tutejszy*—which means "one of the people from here." It was, she adds, in the nineteenth century that the children of the *tutejszy* began to assimilate national ideas from the cities and the intellectuals.

Russian "nationalism," too, in the usual sense of the word, was also a fairly recent development. The old Russian Empire was not seen as an ethnic, or even cultural, entity, but merely as—an empire: *Rossiiskii*, the word we translate as "Russian" in speaking of the Russian Empire, does not have the ethnic connotation of *Russkii*. It stands for the imperium itself, Russian and Orthodox in content, no doubt, but only partly so identified.

It is true that the earlier (and gradual) Russian annexation of Ukraine had led to the suppression of Ukrainian cultural institutions, but this was at least in part because Ukrainian was regarded—as indeed it was by Lenin—as merely a peasant dialect of Russia; and even here full Russification only came later.

The Russian state was of course, more than almost any other, founded on a principle opposed to citizenship in the normal sense. A British journalist (in the *New Statesman*) quoted a Soviet official as remarking to him in 1971:

> Our country has no civil tradition. The taste for association, for organising communal life together, for getting to know each other and taking decisions together, never really existed in Russia. Between the czar and the moujik there was nothing; equally between one moujik and another there was nothing except for essential personal relationships. We were and we remain a huge body, colossal even, but shapeless and deprived of articulation, of that political fabric on which the modern states of Europe were built.

The feeling of nationality that arose in Russia was thus distorted, like much else in that unfortunate country, by its particular state form.

4.

In general, ethnicity, in the sense of language-cum-tradition, has in recent generations been the accepted basis for nationality, the national state. This has settled down in Western Europe but is still giving trouble in Eastern Europe, and has great potential for harm in areas where ethnicity has not yet emerged as a decisive form of self-identification, on this or any other basis. Its peaceful development remains the central feature of all aspiration to tolerable nationhood in our time.

On the other hand, "self-determination" has to face the difficulty that however the borders are drawn, scores of millions of people are, and will be, in states of which they are not the central nationality. Any solution implies, again, a great deal of mutual tolerance and cooperation not now often available; and international enforcement where not. As Elie Kedourie has written, self-determination, like other simple ideas, was accepted as a doctrine.

We should not, indeed, take it for granted that cultural self-consciousness, even linguistically supported, necessarily produces "nationalism." I remember an interview in *London Magazine* with Dylan Thomas, Welshness incarnate. This was at a time more verbally puritanical than ours, and the interviewer reported that he had asked Thomas his views on Welsh nationalism and that "his answer consisted of three words, two of which were 'Welsh nationalism.'"

Still, in many areas archaic tribal loyalties and hatreds persisted in only inadequately eroded form into the present day. But even then they did not, on the whole, acquire anything like their present virulence until the first half of this century. As Senator Daniel Patrick Moynihan has pointed out in his book *Pandemonium*, there was interethnic hostility all over Eastern Europe, with occasional massacres and pogroms; but nevertheless different "racial" groups coexisted until a couple of generations ago. "Ethnic cleansing," even though certain types of nationalists intermittently indulged in it, was never the policy of a state, nor the whole practice of populations.

Poles, Jews, Germans, Ukrainians, Russians lived by the millions in a vague general hostility. But only with the "scientific" anti-Semitism of the last years of the nineteenth century, did anti-Semitism become a program, an Idea; and even then it was sporadic. The Russian Civil War saw pogroms on a large scale, still mainly in the tradition of ancient tribal or religious or class hatreds. But until the 1930s there were still many Jewish towns and villages all over Eastern Europe; and it is said that one could drive in a cart from Vienna to the Sea of Azov and stay in a German village every night.

The Nazis, when they invaded the Soviet Union, did not at first find it difficult sometimes to incite the local peasantry in razzias against Jewish settlements. But they complained that apathy would then ensue, and that true genocidal operations did not gain support.

5.

In spite of the differences of approach, we should note that nationalist and Marxist extremes of thought were similar in origin. As Leszek Kolakowski puts it (*Commentary*, May 1983), "In many respects the socialist critique [of nineteenth-century societies] clearly converged with attacks coming from reactionary romanticism and from emerging nationalist ideologies."

Again, both elements looked back as well as forward, claiming the past as well as the future. Pursuing this tradition, the National Socialists' historical myths sometimes directly overlapped those of the Communists: both saw the peasant rebellions in sixteenth-century Germany as predecessors of their own revolutions. One of the leading heroes of Engels's *The Peasant War in Germany*, Florian Geyer, had an SS division named for him.

Totalitarian absolutisms in fact developed from revolutionary populisms. Unlike the older despotisms, the new movements required this identification with "the people," "the masses." The overwhelming claim of the collective to the individual's allegiance thus emerged as the basis not only of Communism but also of Fascism and National Socialism. Like Communism, once in power these subordinated the individual to the State, as representing the Community. Community was of course differently defined under the two ideologies, in spite of resemblances in the actual practice of the regimes; and it is in some such context as this that we can seek part of the difference between the variants of political mania.

It was only with the coming of World War I that Mussolini, hitherto a leading figure in Italian left-wing socialism, transferred the notion of mass identification with a class to mass identification with a nation. The submergence of the individual and of relations between individuals, and the destruction of noncentralized civic phenomena, remained the program (both Lenin and Trotsky said that only Mussolini could have led an Italian revolution). It was argued by such sophisticated exponents of Fascism as Giovanni Gentile that the individual best expresses himself as part of mass experience.

But for Mussolini the nation was not defined by ethnic dogma (Italian Fascism only becoming anti-Semitic under German influence in the 1930s). For the Nazis, *Blutgefühl*, the instinctual and archaic motivations, were pushed to the fore, so that the sane feeling of patriotism was distorted into a raging racialism transcending civilized morality. For the Communists, it was extreme "rationalism," reliance on supposedly perfect theory, that transcended, in principle at least, the natural affections for country or family. But reliance on reason alone is itself irrational. It neglects the instinctual or deep-set elements of the real human being. Thus the distinction between the National Socialists and the Communists in terms of one overstating the instinctual and the other the rational is over sharp. As Chesterton remarked, a lunatic is one who has lost everything except his reason. The result is paranoia. It is notorious how rational paranoiacs sometimes appear to be.

National Socialist ideologizing was more than its crude and simple racialism. The central message, inculcated on a massive scale in the press, in Party gatherings, in universities and in schools, was the new identification of the German individual with the nation and the state, in a higher mode than that of the older society, transcendental, mystical, scientific and philosophical. If we fail to take this into account, we miss the central drive of National Socialism. And this was what constituted its mass appeal to Germans, including much of the intelligentsia.

For, as we know, Fascism and National Socialism did not lack intellectual supporters. Not only was Gentile a serious philosopher, but he was also a devoted Fascist until killed in 1944 by adherents of a different interpretation of Hegel. Heidegger, whatever one may think of his work, fully supported the National Socialists.

Fascism and National Socialism relied, as we have said, on the social pseudoscience of the late nineteenth century—not in quite as sophisticated a form as that of the Marxists, but still enough to gain the militant allegiance of, for example, two German Nobel Prize winners in physics. (These ideas had also overlapped with trends in "progressive" thought, as with the progressive H. G. Wells's well-known comment that the "backward" races would disappear as humanity went forward.)

6.

Above all, as Leszek Kolakowski puts it, there was the fact that "no modern society can dispense with a principle of legitimacy, and in a totalitarian society, this legitimacy can only be ideological. Total power and total ideology embrace each other."

Without this transcendent justification, such natural human characteristics as pity, laziness and compromise might have intervened. As Hitler said, without ideology violence could not be relied on. On the moral and human side, a basic dogma shared with Marx's is that unappeasable strife is the driving force of our society, and of all others yet found.

As the late Hugh Seton-Watson, dean of British Sovietology, noted, Hitler's Nazis were "fanatics with an ersatz religion" who rejected not only Christianity but also traditional morality as such. He adds, "Moral nihilism is not only the central feature of National Socialism, but also the common factor between it and Bolshevism."

But identification with the masses was in all these cases more than a mental generalization. It also, obviously, involved a psychological mechanism—of the sort Kierkegaard refers to when he writes that

> people flock together, in order to feel themselves stimulated, enflamed and *ausser sich*. The scenes on the Blocksberg are the exact counterparts of this demoniacal pleasure, where the pleasure consists in losing oneself in order to be volatilised into a higher potency, where being outside oneself one hardly knows what one is doing or saying, or who or what is speaking through one, while the blood courses faster, the eyes turn bright and staring, the passions and lusts seething.

Everywhere we come across the ease with which people passed from Communism to what were in theory its most virulent enemies— Fascism and National Socialism. Several Italian Fascist leaders, like Bombacci, had held positions in the Comintern—as had Jacques Doriot in France, who even led a French pro-Nazi military formation on the Eastern Front in World War II.

Hitler himself said that Communists far more easily became Nazis than Social Democrats did. On another occasion he remarked, "the Reds we had beaten up became our best supporters," a point also noted by others. A remarkable firsthand example is given by Patrick Leigh

Fermor in *A Time of Gifts,* his famous account of his walk across Europe as a penniless eighteen-year-old in 1934. In a German workmen's bar late one night he made friends with a group of young factory hands just off a late shift. One of them offered to put him up in a family attic. There he found what seemed to be "a shrine of Hitlerism"—flags, photographs, posters, slogans, emblems. His new friend laughingly said he should have seen it last year—all "Lenin and Stalin and Workers of the World Unite." He and his friends were Communists and used to beat up Nazis in street fights. Then, "suddenly," he had realized that Hitler was right, and he and his friends were now SA men. "I tell you, I was astonished how easily they all changed sides," he said.

The more recent extreme left, of course, incorporated the irrational element of Nazism. It was the Red Brigade's Ulrike Meinhof who said at her trial, "Auschwitz meant that six million Jews were killed, and thrown onto the waste-heap of Europe for what they were: money-Jews [*Geldjuden*]" (*Frankfurter Allgemeine Zeitung,* 15 December 1972). We may note, too, that in the Khmer revolution the Communist leaders declared that "in Kampuchea there is one nation and one language, the Khmer language. From now on the various nationalities do not exist in Kampuchea." The victims, such minorities as the Chams, were subject to decrees like "The Cham mentality is abolished."

These may be taken to mark a final convergence of the Communist and Nationalist Ideas.

As to the detritus of the old-style ideologies, we have seen how they were for a long time prevalent among the political intelligentsia in the underdeveloped countries, taking on a "nationalist" hue. It was some years ago that George Lichtheim, himself a committed socialist, rather tartly concluded (in his *A Short History of Socialism*):

> In the populist ideology (which is eternally the same under every sky and in every clime) "the people" is seen as a body of virtuous toilers confronted by a handful of native and foreign exploiters whom it is the Party's (or the Leader's) duty to expel or repulse, so that the nation may accomplish its destiny. Thus nationalism is equated with socialism, the community is seen as essentially classless, and the ruling elite appears as the historical incorporation of the General Will, even though it may never go to the trouble of actually consulting the people under its control as to their real desires. Maoism, Castroism and "African Socialism" constitute

different variants of this peculiar ideology. The differences are important, but the intellectual content is in every case pretty much the same. As for the effectiveness of this creed, an ideology that promises people both the defence of their (tribal or national) traditions and painless economic growth under conditions of social equality and justice for all will never lack an audience.

This is not so true today, but it retains too much of its validity.

7.

It follows from all this that the evolution of viable nations or other such cultures adequate to participate in a true international community is not to be achieved without time and trouble. There remain ethnic and other groups with "memberships" of millions who may become focuses of nationalist movements, whether balanced or extreme or both. The future of much of the world has not yet declared itself.

Our, and every sane person's, overriding priority is a peaceful world, or at a minimum a world in which major wars are prevented and weapons of mass destruction are not used. To call the problem "international" is apt not only in its obvious connotation but also in the sense that the real world today consists of an array of independent, if sometimes partially interdependent, states, most of which we usually call nations.

Internationalism suggests an attitude to the world based on mutual accord *between* nations. It is or has been faced with two main problems: there are nationalisms that have been wholly, or largely, incapable of accepting such cooperation; and *also* there are supposed internationalisms that are in principle against nationality as such. The supranational world-state idea, urged by many rational liberals for a century or so, is not plausible in any but a very long run, and certainly any excessive haste, or attempt to impose it by fiat, would produce strong and violent resistance. It could only emerge over a very long period of concord among its components. Its meretricious immediate attraction is as a quick-fix "Idea."

National feeling is natural. It is hardly a matter of choice. Everyone is born into a culture or ethnicity (and those who repudiate it usually become, with equally strong feelings, no more than the quislings of some other grouping). Orwell calls all such allegiances, including that of allegiance to a culture hostile to one's own nation, "nationalisms" in that they contain irrational devotion to a group idea.

The malign nationalisms seen today are only in part a reversion to primitive gang loyalties, but in part a distortion of reasonable national feeling into the ideological absolute of identification we have spoken of earlier.

This is not to say that national sentiment can ever be entirely without some hostility to, or at least solidarity against, other nations. It sees itself, at least to some extent, in terms of "we" as against the "they" who are not among its membership. This can be, and often is, restrained in a reasonably mild and unhostile form. Attempts to eliminate it entirely by decree or by spurious or premature internationalism can hardly succeed. As with all our problems, it is a matter of adjustment, not perfection.

The world can be seen as containing evolved nation-states and states which, even if in some cases ethnically or territorially based, are not yet mature components of an international order. Obviously, the national "sovereign" state has not proved a marked success in a number of areas—Somalia, for example, where there was not even any ethnic problem (as against class and gangs). Then there are what amount to pirate states, in effect not recognizing (though sometimes constrained to observe) any rules of international behavior: Iraq, Iran, North Korea, Libya and so on. With, in some cases, the prospect of or the actuality of making or obtaining nuclear weapons.

These have to be coped with urgently over the interim, but in the long or medium run a really stable international order is possible only on a basis of adequate nations and national states.

8.

It is not so much that "democracy" as such is incapable of aggression, as that only states which represent rather than repress internal variety, which are themselves based on consensuality, which tolerate divergent cultures and ideas, which are not themselves enslaved to unquestioned dogma, are likely to have a reasonably cooperative attitude on the international scene. In the West the old "irredenta" wars seem to be over. This is not the case elsewhere, and the last thing the world needs is a repetition of the alternate excesses of annexation that beset Europe over nearly two centuries. This again implies insistence on the acceptance of borders not wholly satisfactory to any. And this can only be done by encouragement of the moderate and enforcement on the immoderate.

Nations must subsist within an international community, just as individuals must live within a particular society. This sort of general remark has often been made, and what it amounts to is that in spite of a reasonable autonomy in each case, there are actions between nations, as between individuals, which cannot be tolerated. We have not yet reached the stage where an effective "International law" operates. But we are now, in principle, in a position to reach it.

The inescapable conclusion seems to be that the more mature nations, which are also in general the most powerful, have an interest in promoting proper nationhood everywhere, while also in preventing threats to peace that arise in the meantime. Peace, in this context, is not a vague general aspiration. There are states that cannot possibly be seen as members of a peaceful world community, and that, as we have said, in some cases have, or soon will have, nuclear arms. And there are minor aggressions of little apparent importance, but which it is in our interest to prevent or defeat, if only to discourage others.

All this presupposes a reasonably united will among the evolved nations. This is not unachievable. But it hardly now exists.

Even as to that united will, we should not imagine that the developed democracies themselves are identical in every respect. It is not a matter of cooperation between a set of discrete but undifferentiated entities. In his *England, Your England,* George Orwell comments: "One must admit that the divisions between nation and nation are founded on real differences of outlook. Till recently it was thought proper to pretend that all human beings are very much alike, but in fact anyone able to use his eyes knows that the average of human behaviour differs enormously from country to country. Things that could happen in one country could not happen in another."

This is true, as Orwell implies, even among countries at about the same level of political development.

When one argues against excess devotion to "the nation," one is not thereby opposed to allegiance to such polities; when one argues against excessive identification with a particular ethnic or other group within a society, one is not denying all allegiance to such groups.

The basic problem is not so much the *sentiment* of nationality but the *Idea* of the nation.

9.

A fearful example is Yugoslavia. Recent events there are clearly based on older enmities. Nevertheless, here, too, the nations or groups concerned had lived in no more than a smoldering and occasional hostility for centuries. The savage Serbian policy of ethnic cleansing is a recent development (though prefigured by the Nazi-style wartime Pavelic government in Croatia). The Serbian leaders, and Milosevic himself, are mostly ex-Communists who thus transformed their earlier totalist ideology into "nationalism" in the worst sense.

Meanwhile, it is important to note that the outburst of nationalist extremism in Serbia was not spontaneous but, on the contrary, incited in the most calculating and cynical fashion by the Milosevic regime. The use of racial persecution had indeed been seen in the Balkans in the early 1980s, when the Bulgarian Communist chief Todor Zhivkov launched a massive Bulgarization campaign against the Turkish minority. Previously there had been virtually no trouble between them and the Bulgarian majority. It was created solely from above, and the damage is only now being repaired. And this is a positive sign and an indication of hope.

The ideologizing of nationality attitudes elsewhere is, as ever, proving destructive both physically and psychologically. It goes, moreover, with a tendency to ethnic "Balkanization" *within* countries until lately more or less assimilative or unitive. (As I write, we see another willful creation of ethnic confrontation in the Algerian schism with the Berbers.) Nor should we forget that different perspectives are to be found in different countries, some favorable, others not.

10.

That traditional national cultures are very different one from another has often only been accepted in a superficial way, both in theory and in practice. It was, for example, held—and still often is—that the institution of a free market would everywhere automatically produce a Western-style "Economic Man"—an illusion perhaps now dispelled by the past few years of Russia's experience. As David S. Landes has shown in his recent *The Wealth and Poverty of Nations,* "If we learn anything from the history of economic development, it is that culture makes all the difference."

Another commonly held tenet, as we have said, is that the creation of the right institutions is in itself the key to political and politico-economic development. In the long run, this certainly has a positive effect. But in his deeply researched *Making Democracy Work*, Robert D. Putnam has unarguably shown (in the case of the continuing differences in civic attitudes in the provinces of Italy) that it can be a remarkably slow process.

In the case of Latin America, the Alliance for Progress, launched under the Kennedy administration, was based on a supposedly scientific view of the nature of the original economic "takeoff" into sustained growth in countries like Britain. It was to "transform the American Continent." That not much of it is left is due to its simplistic assumptions and its failure to take into account the full cultural milieu, as a number of Latin American scholars warned at the time, and has lately been examined clearly by Claudio Veliz (in his *The New World of the Gothic Fox*). He quotes, on the whole Latin American problem, Mario Vargas Llosa's comment that such approaches are doomed

> to be ephemeral unless they are preceded or accompanied by a reform of our customs and ideas, of the whole complex system of habits, knowledge, images and forms that we understand by "culture." The culture within which we live and act in Latin America is neither liberal nor is it altogether democratic. We have democratic governments, but our institutions, our reflexes and our *mentalidades* are very far from being democratic. They remain populist and oligarchic, or absolutist, collectivistic or dogmatic, flawed by social and racial prejudices, immensely intolerant with respect to political adversaries, and devoted to the worst monopoly of all, that of the truth.

In fact, the hundreds of years of the closed (and bureaucratic) culture of the Spanish Empire, and the nineteenth-century impact on it, and on its elite, of post-Napoleonic European radical (but equally *étatiste*) notions, are not easily shed.

None of this suggests that these countries and cultures cannot adapt to the rule of law and economic liberties. No one who has been in contact with the Latino work ethic in California (where the flake population is largely Anglo) could doubt that. And in Spain itself, always less cut off from Europe than its overseas empire was, a long process has resulted, now, in a modern state—though it was only sixty years ago that it was shaken by what the historian Hugh Thomas has called a civil war between two counterrevolutions.

II.

With Africa we find, from the nationality point of view, a more complex set of problems. And we should first note that ethnic strife may take place even within single territories—in Rwanda as in Bosnia.

"Tribal" societies with a genuine consensual tradition existed over much of the sub-Saharan area almost up to the present day. "Tribal" is nowadays usually used as a hostile adjective, but it should not be. It is, of course, true that (as in Western Europe) there were polities of a despotic character in Africa—in the south, for instance, where at various times war and the mass movement of peoples left groups of broken men to be incorporated into new nations tribal in form but for a time despotic in character; and in the Niger Basin in the eighteenth century, where social collapse and distortion were produced by the Arab and Western slave trade. But it may be doubted whether these centralized dynastic states lasted long enough, for the most part, to truly eradicate the *traditions* of consensus. On the other hand, the present states of Black Africa, with very few exceptions, have no *ethnic* unity (the major exception, Botswana, appears as a model of nonviolent and consensual development).

Hence it is widely held that in Africa the old frontiers, inherited from last century's colonial divide-up, need reconsidering. On the other hand, it seems that in some cases a transethnic political class, or general elite, using English (or perhaps French or Amharic) has established a national unity, but that in others this has failed.

We might note in this context, though, that the attempt in India to impose Hindi, while understandable enough, has already had fissiparous results. And while the fact that many states of Africa use the English or French language by no means implies any automatic reliance on Britain or France, nevertheless, combined with the traditional links, the languages certainly constitute a closer tie than otherwise subsists between Africa and the West or any other part of the world and hence link the continent with examples of "advanced" economy and polity.

The earlier basic African communities and similar "primitive" social arrangements may be regarded as societies that were in a sense civic, though they were not "open." This may, after all, have some implications when it comes to the type of state likely to be most promising there. And if this virtue resides in tribalism, it might seem that African states should indeed not be conglomerate, as they mostly are now, but should be based on a group of communities. Otherwise (or so it could be argued) the political processes within today's states are not seeking new versions of the traditional forms of balancing interests, but are tending rather to a struggle, or at best bargaining, between political intellectuals projected from different communities. However, this is not to say that the sound tribal traditions might not be transmitted through an acceptable federalism of the component nations.

For, admitting that the present boundaries are often "artificial," one cannot say that groupings of diverse, and to some degree hostile, ethnic elements automatically exclude favorable development. Britain itself has emerged from a long interaction between different racial groups. Indeed, to narrow it further, Scotland arose (not without conflict) out of the merging of four different stocks (five if one counts the Norse element). It would be worth examining some of the perspectives for the development of consensuality from a "tribal" vitality—as, for example, in Papua New Guinea.

There is now discussion of the idea of large, loose commonwealths of different ethnic groups, something like a greater version of Switzerland. There seems to be no reason why such a state should not be a very positive member of a world community. The problems are huge, but present arrangements have hardly solved them. It need hardly be said that on grounds of both humanity and interest, the West needs to help the emerging nations and discourage the emerging killer nationalisms. The policies it has pursued so far have had very limited success.

12.

All this is no more than to sketch some of the realities and possibilities of an immensely complex phenomenon. Nationality has done, is still doing, much harm. That is no reason to think it can be abolished or even seriously eroded over anything but a very distant future indeed. It is a powerful force, and while its negative manifestations need to be checked, its positive side is unavoidably the material from which any true international order has to be constructed.

◆

CHAPTER V

Totalitarian Party— Totalitarian State

I.

In the twentieth century, infallible political ideologies have been historically manifest in militarized totalitarian movements. The word "totalitarianism" is regarded by some, mainly academics, as an improper usage. This is usually argued by those concerned to avoid parallels between the Communist and the National Socialist orders, to deny its applicability to the USSR, and to suggest that there were no major or substantial differences between Communist regimes and various milder types of authoritarianism.

Since both Gorbachev and Yeltsin used it of the Soviet regime, and since such eminent political philosophers as Leszek Kolakowski and Giovanni Sartori find the concept helpful, no serious argument might seem to remain. Sartori's presentation of the matter, in particular, appears definitive. In *The Theory of Democracy Revisited,* he points out that objections to the term run largely along the lines that no state, not even the Soviet Union, actually controlled every aspect of its subjects' lives. But, he adds, no political concept is ever a complete description of a real state, and the same objection would apply to a word like "democracy." It is enough if

(a) the Idea behind a regime can legitimately be considered as totalitarian in its claims;

(b) the regime itself is in actual practice closer to the "ideal type" the word implies than to any other description.

Kolakowski sees the "total lie" as one of the characteristics of totalitarianism—that under late Stalinism not only was virtually everything falsified, but that "the borderline between what is 'correct' and what is 'true' seems really to have become blurred; by repeating the same absurdities they began to believe or half-believe in them themselves." But it is enough to say that in principle the state recognized no limits to its authority in any sphere, and in practice extended that authority wherever remotely feasible.

Nevertheless, "totalitarian" as a descriptive adjective is preferable to totalitarian*ism* as a "model"; just as, in general, isms tend to become more abstract and unreal than is helpful to our understanding.

2.

The Idea does not subsist on its own. It is not just a system of thought bombinating in a vacuum, or entering the intellectual atmosphere and being accepted as general guidance after reasonable discussion—though its proponents have sometimes presented it as such with a view to winning, or confusing, those concerned.

On the contrary, it requires interpreters. Every social and every human phenomenon has to be given correct evaluation. But this can only be done by a recognized authority.

In the sense we are speaking of, a doctrine or dogma becomes incarnate in a "party of a new type," as Lenin calls the Bolsheviks—a party based (as were the National Socialists after them) on an organizational and doctrinal command system.

Its leadership, an authoritative center with power to interpret the Marxist runes, was essential to unity and purity of thought, and to correctness of tactics. (Thus, in the biological disputes of the mid-1940s, the Communist Central Committee was the final arbiter—and was recognized as such by Communist biologists when it ruled against them.)

Not that this phenomenon is "new" except compared to the looser party system then prevalent in Western Europe. It resembles those "sworn brotherhoods" or millenarian sects of an era that had long passed (in any serious way) in the advanced countries. Its immediate roots were in the conspiratorial groups of the nineteenth century. Western social democrats, and Westernizing progressives in general in Russia itself, regarded the conspiratorial organization of the Bolsheviks as an unfortunate but understandable product of the illegal and semilegal struggle against Tsarism, which would surely be given up when political liberty prevailed. Many Bolsheviks thought the same.

The writings and actions of the revolutionary-messianic type in fact resemble each other down the centuries. And, of course, revolutionaries have admitted, or rather exalted, the resemblance. Norman Cohn remarks (in later editions of *The Pursuit of the Millennium*) that Communism and Nazism are inclined to be "baffling for the rest of us" because of the very features they have inherited from an earlier phase in our culture, now forgotten, but still appealing to more backward areas of the world. In such countries as Russia and China, the apocalyptic view was "appropriated and transformed by an intelligentsia which, alike in its social situation and in the crudity and narrowness of its thinking, strikingly recalls the *prophetae* of medieval Europe."

Both Nazis and Marxists themselves often proclaimed their affinity with the millenarian demagogues of the period of the German Peasant War, claiming that these were men born centuries before their time, but as Cohen says, "it is perfectly possible to draw the opposite moral—that, for all their exploitation of the most modern technology, Communism and Nazism have been inspired by phantasies which are downright archaic."

As with the chiliastic movements of centuries long past, modern rev-olutionaries have, as Cohn points out, claimed to be charged with the unique mission of bringing history to its preordained consummation. He notes of the earlier versions:

> And what followed then was the formation of a group of a peculiar kind, a true prototype of a modern totalitarian party: a restlessly dynamic and utter-ly ruthless group which, obsessed by the apocalyptic phantasy and filled with the conviction of its own infallibility, set itself infinitely above the rest of humanity and recognised no claims save that of its own supposed mission.

The staff, and leading figures, of such movements were and are from a more or less educated stratum. When they gain the support of "the masses" or "the nation," it is through such a network, expanded to bring in representatives of the larger and less educated sections.

As to the leaders of those earlier movements, they were mainly mem-bers of the lower clergy (Spengler interestingly compares the revolution-aries of the twentieth century with the mendicant friars), plus a few eccentric scions of the lower nobility, together with obscure laymen who had somehow acquired a clerical education: as Cohn puts it, "a recognisable social stratum—a frustrated and rather low-grade intelligentsia." (And for their cannon fodder they did not recruit the poor as such, but those of the poor "who could find no assured and recognised place in society at all.") And Cohn, noting all these resemblances to the modern revolutionaries, adds that even in the medieval context, not remarkable for tolerance or objectivity, the millenarians were "abnormal in their destructiveness and irrationality"—psychological points.

3.

In any country there are doubtless elements psychologically available for the right moment and the right regime. The Eichmann mentality existed in suspension, as it were, in Germany until it was given its head by Hitler. The particular canting scum who rose in the 1940s in Hungary were already there, even though they received their final impress and style from the Rákosis and Farkases. A morally and intellectually half-educated stratum exists, in varying form, everywhere in the world.

The true novelty of Lenin's concept was that he insisted on a party consisting entirely of "professional revolutionaries." It is often said that the Mensheviks were opposed to the whole idea of professional revolutionaries. No: they merely believed that a socialist party should include not only these but also a broader stratum. The Mensheviks, it is sometimes forgotten, were themselves (by any usual standard) on the extreme, and doctrine-dazzled, left. But Lenin saw that to allow into the party membership people with outside interests would dilute its ideological committment. He also saw that a professional revolutionary group needs money from outside, and the Bolshevik record for its whole pre-revolutionary history was—had to be—one of bank robberies, the diversion of dowries, rich donors, the embezzlement of state insurance and trade-union funds.

During the underground period, and even during and after the October Revolution, the Bolsheviks went through such doctrinal disputes as affect any such sects, as well as divergence on questions of political tactics; and many Bolsheviks believed that their party was in some sense internally democratic.

It was above all the Civil War from 1918 to 1920 which first of all made total discipline appear the central necessity, and at the same time marked the Bolsheviks off as empowered to enforce their ideas and policies in their capacity as an elite, against massive unpopularity. It was in this period that true fetishism of the Party as such became complete.

What Orwell had called a type of "nationalism," directed to a consciously assembled body rather than to a naturally evolving one, had emerged. The Party in itself became an icon, a transcendental Idea. In fact, Trotsky evoked the parallel:

> None of us desires or is able to dispute the will of the Party. Clearly, the Party is always right. . . . We can only be right with and by the Party, for history has provided no other way of being in the right. The English have a saying, "My country, right or wrong," whether it is in the right or in the wrong, it is my country. We have much better historical justification in saying, whether it is right or wrong in certain individual cases, it is my party. . . . [A]nd if the Party adopts a decision which one or other of us thinks unjust, he will say, just or unjust, it is my party, and I shall support the consequences of the decision to the end.

One of Trotsky's allies at the time was Yuri Pyatakov, whom Lenin had listed among the six most prominent or promising Communists. Pyatakov was generally regarded as a particularly intelligent and capable figure. In 1928 he chanced to meet a former Menshevik friend, N. V. Volsky, in Paris. Pyatakov, who had just disavowed his Trotskyite views, provoked Volsky by suggesting that he lacked courage. Volsky replied warmly that Pyatakov's capitulation a couple of months after his expulsion from the Party in 1927, and his repudiation of the views that he had held right up till then, showed a real lack of moral courage. Pyatakov, in an excited and emotional manner, replied with a long harangue:

> According to Lenin, the Communist Party is based on the principle of coercion which doesn't recognise any limitations or inhibitions. And the central idea of this principle of boundless coercion is not coercion by itself but the absence of any limitation whatsoever—moral, political and even physical, as far as that goes. Such a Party is capable of achieving miracles and doing things which no other collective of men could achieve. . . . A real Communist . . . that is, a man who was raised in the Party and had absorbed its spirit deeply enough to become himself in a way a miracle man.

From his attitude significant conclusions followed:

> For such a Party a true Bolshevik will readily cast out from his mind ideas in which he had believed for years. A true Bolshevik has submerged

his personality in the collectivity, "the Party," to such an extent that he can make the necessary effort to break away from his own opinions and convictions, and can honestly agree with the Party—that is the test of a true Bolshevik.

There could be no life for him (Pyatakov continued) outside the ranks of the Party, and he would be ready to believe that black was white, and white was black, if the Party required it. In order to become one with this great Party, he would fuse himself with it, abandon his own personality, so that there was no particle left inside him which was not at one with the Party, did not belong to it.

Pyatakov, to whose ability what successes were achieved in the industrial program of the early 1930s were due, in August 1936 wrote to the Party secretariat that he deserved censure for not having revealed his wife's connection with Trotskyism. To regain the Party's trust, he offered to appear for the prosecution if she were tried, and even personally to shoot the accused, including her. This was rejected. (But Pyatakov himself was of course the leading figure in the second of the great Moscow show trials, in 1937, and was duly shot.)

Pyatakov's was an extreme case, but well within the limits of the general Communist attitude. Even the less excitable Nikolai Bukharin was telling confidants in 1936 that it was necessary to accept Stalin, as the incarnation of the Party.

Or again, a worker Old Bolshevik, when in a labor camp in Stalin's time, told a fellow inmate, the former head of the Palestinian CP, how he and others like him had felt, even in the early twenties, that "the Party was no longer the Party we had known. We no longer had its confidence. But the last thing we could do was to stop trusting it. It was our whole life. It was still the Party."

The terror period in which Pyatakov and Bukharin and much of the Party membership perished may be seen in its personnel aspect as the "negative selection" of which post-Soviet Russian writers speak. Those who rose to prominence instead had been, as a physicist put it, "morally and intellectually crippled." By the late 1930s the Party had indeed become thoroughly totalitarianized, with the result that, as the German revolutionary Rosa Luxemburg had foreseen, life had "died out" and stultification set in. The already intellectually unimpressive Bolsheviks had sunk to a lower mediocrity.

And this was, of course, imposed on the Soviet-orientated Communist movement throughout the world. The great American black writer Richard Wright, for a time a member of the CPUSA, tells in his *American Hunger:*

> An hour's listening disclosed the fanatical intolerance of minds sealed against new ideas, new facts, new feelings, new attitudes, new hints at ways to live. They denounced books they had never read, people they had never known, ideas they could never understand, and doctrines they could not pronounce. Communism, instead of making them leap forward with fire in their hearts . . . had frozen them at an even lower level of ignorance than had been theirs before they met Communism.

In fact, but for the Leninizing of the Communists outside the Soviet Union, the Western extreme left would probably not have suffered such moral and mental degradation.

For the Communist Parties were everywhere possessed by the Leninist view of ethics and tactics. That is to say, they succumbed to untrammeled fanaticism, the use of vicious methods of struggle, and the sacrifice of everything to immediate questions of power, in any institution to which they had access. One consequence was that (as Seymour Martin Lipset points out) they gave people like Ernest Bevin and Ronald Reagan experience of Communist attitudes which prepared them for coping with the USSR.

Perhaps even more destructive was that Communists everywhere accepted subservience to the Soviets, support for any line the Soviets were taking, and belief in any dubious assertion the Soviets made: a process that left a stultified membership.

To take another example of all this, but in a rather different context, in 1956 the Polish Communist poet Adam Wazyk was called before the Politburo member Jakub Berman and lectured about his astonishing *Poem for Adults.* As he later told a Westerner, he "saw that we were governed by imbeciles." He saw that a thousand individual imbeciles, a thousand bureaucrats and propagandists and sophists, do not become possessed of some mystic collective wisdom simply by being formed into a political organization. And so it was with other East European intellectuals: they began to openly set against the alleged infallibility of "the Party"—i.e., Berman and his like—the evidence of their own eyes, and of their own minds and hearts.

The paradox is, of course, that—as earlier in Germany—the more modernized a country gets (and the more complex the terms in which political and social theory are elaborated), the more possible it is to build political machines capable of projecting the single will of an individual *propheta*. In the Soviet case, it was possible to deploy such a machine on an international scale.

4.

The primitive overidentification with a group is thus greatly exacerbated by acceptance of supposedly infallible theory. It is not even so much the unitary ideology that is the practical problem as this group-mind, with equivalent hostility to other groups.

The phenomenon of group, or gang, loyalty has been much studied in its sociopsychological context. Here it only needs to be noted that in saying "group" or "gang" we are already implying different types of it—one benign, or at least neutral, the other malign. The same is obviously true, as we have seen, of its "national" forms.

While most people are born into a nation or culture, gang loyalty proper is often a matter of accident; as with the British football hooligans. Though we need not forget that the two rival groups of chariot-race fans in Byzantium, the Blues and the Greens, in a truce in their violent struggle, united in the Niké Insurrection in A.D. 532 which nearly overthrew Justinian's Empire.

All groups are in some sense special-interest groups. Those which seek economic advantages are usually so called. But it obviously applies, too, to groups devoted to securing or preserving power or position. It is also not inappropriate for groups in which the investment is emotional, and the reward is feeling good. This is not to deny altruism, but to place it—noting, too, that it is liable to distortion when acting in the political arena; and that neither fanaticism nor failure of the critical faculty is unknown in such circumstances.

And the Leninist (and later the Fascist) conception of "the Party" produced an irrational fetishism. While particular individuals may be particularly prone to accepting the despotic-revolutionary idea, it is also the case that this acceptance, and the merger of the individual into the organization devoted to imposing that idea further, changes that individual—and for the worse.

As to the Communist leadership itself, gang attitudes flourished.

Milovan Djilas, then a leader of the Yugoslav CP, remarked that his experiences in 1944 and 1948 with Stalin and his Politburo made him feel "that these men had no confidence at all in the legitimacy of their rule. . . . They acted like a group of conspirators scheming to suppress, squash, circumvent or hoodwink the inhabitants of some conquered land, not their own. . . . Power for Stalin was a plot, with himself as chief plotter as well as the one cast to be plotted against. It was an expression of the civil war which Communists in power have always waged, and will always wage, against society."

He adds that "of course, Russia under Stalin had 'laws' and 'institutions' on the statute books, and often these were even respected in matters such as driving on the correct side of the road, regulating the electricity supply of Tomsk, or the alcoholic content of vodka. But in all things pertaining to man's spiritual and intellectual freedom, Russia under Stalin was a lawless land."

5.

This century has in fact been the first in which the groups taking over countries had the power to use the state machinery to impose doctrinally produced errors on the whole of the society.

It has always, even in ancient times, been difficult to remove the leadership of a state. But, at least until recently, it was uncommon for a state to be able to ignore, or run wholly contrary to, all economic, social and intellectual trends. The modern totalitarian state suffered few of these limitations.

It can be argued that Marx, and earlier theorists of revolution like Rousseau, did not envision mass terror, let alone the totalitarian state. It was perhaps more a matter of such ideologues propounding unattainable utopias; and of any attempt to put them into practice only being possible by such means.

Totalitarianism is, as Leonard Schapiro notes, "a post-democratic phenomenon," arising in the age of nations and nation-states, the emergence of mass society, "the age of the legitimation of power by a democratic formula," as with other aspects of the modern age, until it finally became technically possible to control an entire society and eventually to pervade it fully with the regime's propagandas and its terrors.

In the mid-nineteenth century the Russian writer Alexander Herzen said that what he feared was "Genghiz Khan with the telegraph." And in

1917 the two main points in the capital first seized by the Bolsheviks were the Winter Palace—and the Telegraph Office. This was, of course, only the first step.

It took another fifteen years before full control of society was substantially achieved. (In Germany the already existing state machine proved adequate, though soon thoroughly purged.)

Aristotle lists various methods used by tyrants, such as "the removal of men of spirit," but also additional measures like the "forbidding of common meals, clubs, education and anything of a like character . . . likely to produce the two qualities of mutual confidence and high spirits," as well as "the adoption of every means for making every subject as much a stranger as possible to every other." There follow prescriptions for secret police, spying, informers, the sowing of mutual distrust and so on—though, as Schapiro says, Aristotle's notion of tyranny nevertheless "lacks the mobilisation element, as well as the mass democratic facade."

Of course the despotisms of the past were able to enforce their orders. But they were not normally engaged in enforcing huge social, economic or conceptual changes. They underwent various erosions and breakdowns over long periods, but though military conquests and dynastic upsets occurred, these polities were static in principle, and in the socioeconomic sphere so in practice as well.

The revolutionary despotisms, coming when their predecessors had finally antagonized vast sections of the population, could present themselves as the new, the only, alternative (just as in *Animal Farm* all repugnance towards the new regime is blocked by the cry "You don't want Jones back"). They could rely, at least for the short intervening period while they consolidated, on generous impulses. And they could nourish, at least among a section of their followers, the mystique of a new—party—solidarity.

The revolutionary despotism, persisting, also incorporates the habits of the older despotism it has succeeded. Indeed, if we compare the Russia and Britain of the 1980s with the Russia and Britain of the 1830s, we will note that in Russia the previous institutions had been destroyed and new ones created, to the accompaniment of the physical destruction of the earlier classes and elites, mass "social engineering," slaughter generally and so on; while in England the institutions and the elites evolved in what is, on the face of it, a far milder and less complete fashion. Yet the Russia of 1990 was far more like the Russia of 1830 than the England of 1990 was like the England of 1830.

It is, indeed, a characteristic of radical totalitarian movements—at any rate of successful ones—that this incorporation of "reactionary" methods of nation-binding has given them extra power and appeal. As George Orwell pointed out, "The idea of National Socialism which Hitler brought to fruition was one of the most appealing demagogic inventions of the twentieth century," while the true German "Nationalist" movement under Alfred Hugenberg achieved little and the various "internationalist" Socialist bodies were ineffective.

In World War II the Communists, too, turned to the resources of a national socialism for survival. Not only were all the old paraphernalia of Tsarist officerdom and history brought into play, but anti-Semitism, usually noted for the first time in Soviet official circles in 1943–44, was also resurrected from the Tsarist past, or copied from the Nazi present.

6.

A revolutionary despotism is, for several reasons, almost bound to institute, sooner or later, a terror on a scale not to be found elsewhere. First, of course, it is obvious enough that any radical dictatorship with a program involving the destruction of whole classes or races is bound to rely on a larger degree of terror than a "reactionary" regime needs. But beyond that we should consider an even more profound point: a radical revolutionary regime usually comes to power after its predecessor has lost the minds of the thinking classes in campaigns of "critical" argument. On the other hand, the whole intent of the revolution is to institute the rule of infallible theory which alone has the right and power to bring history to its single, foreordained end. And this implies a complete reversion to precritical society, in which it is impossible to exercise the judgment on the form of state. Plainly, this is conceptually a very difficult task and must involve the destruction of the whole attitude that the revolution once deployed against the former rulers. It can only be done effectively by a most thorough use of terror against the revolutionary class itself.

7.

"Scientific" totalitarianism, which appears to be the rational, ordered form, contains greater elements of irrationality than does the civic culture. Ours, it is true, usually involves an attachment to ancient rights on a piecemeal, and even sentimental, basis not easily amenable to rationalization. But it also contains the element of debate and argument, as well as a feeling of deeper and less conscious needs, even if these have not been susceptible to adequate verbal elaboration. The totalitarian state contains within itself all the elements of a more extreme irrationality: the elimination of real debate and criticism and the idolization of pre-mature political perfectionism. In fact, the backwardness of revolution-ary despotisms resided not merely in the parallels which may be seen between them and the bureaucratic empires of the past, but also in the factors thought to constitute their modernity.

It was of course not only in totalitarian circles that the idea of a state with strong or strongish, even if less absolute, control of society became widely accepted, or that activism, often hyperactivism, to a large degree replaced the idea of good government. Totalitarianism can be seen as an extreme of ideological subjectivism, in which the machinery of state is primarily a means of enforcing the Ideas of the ruler or ruling group on a recalcitrant or refractory society.

The full pathology of an Idea is to be seen in pure form in, for example, the whole lethal activity of the Khmer Rouge. To say that no other regimes achieved quite such totality is not to say that they, too, were not possessed by an Idea, but that even in less absolute practice the phenomenon is deadly enough. Albert Camus wrote of the type, "The will to power came to take the place of the will to justice, pretending at first to be identified with it and then relegating it to a place somewhere at the end of history."

We shall consider the content, and the history, of these ideocratic movements and states in later chapters.

◆

CHAPTER VI

Into the Soviet Morass

I.

We should now consider the prime, the longest-lasting, the most globally influential example in modern times of an Idea taking over and bureaucratically enforcing itself in a major country. Above all, it was the most complete and (one would hope) the most instructive example of the confrontation between ideology and reality—a long, bitter and murderous clash. Moreover, this massive misdirection spilled over into too many minds outside the Soviet Union itself, in the West and elsewhere.

It is not my purpose here to prove that the Soviet Union was a ghastly historical aberration—but to show how and why this came about, and what its major characteristics were. We consider first its roots, the incubation of the Idea. And then, after it comes to power, its attempts to transform the social and moral order—examined under various heads: the Collectivization Campaign; the Plan; the Terror (seen as an attempt to suppress reality); the "New Soviet Man" so created; and so on.

In this chapter, we thus do not set forth the whole history of Russian and Soviet experience. We seek to present it only in its perspective as the classical example of the conditions of the emergence of totalist ideology, and its manifestations when in power.

2.

The Russia that was to provide the world with its first example of modern totalitarianism had elements that made it vulnerable (though it is fair to say that Lenin only got his chance through a series of historical accidents, and thereafter barely held on). The Russian past can be seen in this context in terms of an extreme despotism in its habits, and of a special and equally extreme reaction against that particular despotism which created an ideology-prone intelligentsia.

"Intelligentsia" is, of course, a Russian word. The condition of being an *intelligent* was defined not by intelligence but by the acceptance of the Idea—so given, with the capital letter, and defined as the total destruction of the existing order and its replacement by a perfect society run by none other than the intelligentsia. As used in the West of more or less equivalent Westerners, the term was, my dictionary says, "often derisive." But not only the epithet but even the thing was to appear in the West, an import that it would be great to see reexported. This caste became especially noticeable in the past thirty-odd years, and we shall examine it in a later chapter. But already in the early 1930s Dimitri Mirsky was able to publish in London a book, *The Intelligentsia of Great Britain.* (Mirsky, a Prince and former White Army officer, had become converted to Communism in British exile. He was shortly to return to Moscow, and a miserable death in the Gulag.)

3.

It can be hardly be maintained that Communism was no more than a continuation of Russian history. Tsarism may have been the most repressive regime in Europe, but if we take the total executions from 1860 to 1914 (mostly of genuine terrorists in 1905–10) and add in all the other victims of civil repression such as the pogroms, we can hardly reach a figure of twenty thousand odd. The current estimate for executions alone in the two-year period 1937–38 is just under 2 million. In terms of the dialectic, this is surely an overwhelming case of the quantitative becoming the qualitative. And indeed, Lenin's regime was already far more violently repressive than anything seen for centuries.

Still, the first determinant of the country's future was the fact that it had been, over the centuries, an extreme despotism. Chekhov speaks of Russia's "heavy, chilling history, savagery, bureaucracy, poverty and ignorance. . . . Russian life weighs upon a Russian like a thousand-ton rock."

The Crimean War proved a crux. In Britain it is usually looked back on as a scene of incompetence, vile hospitals, gallant disasters like the Charge of the Light Brigade. From the Russian point of view, it appears as quite the opposite—Russia, by a thoroughly sound allied strategic decision, was compelled to fight in a far-off border territory where its enemies had the better communications by sea. In the end, a defeated Russia had no further resources and had to sue for peace.

This proved, or appeared to prove, that the Russian system was a failure. The immediate result was the Emancipation of the Serfs in 1861, and the introduction of a fairly independent judicial and jury system. But apart from the establishment of minimally elected local authorities, there was no real political change in the autocracy. At the same time, as Pasternak put it (*Paris Review*, no. 24, 1960), in the 1840s, though serfdom was obviously obsolete, no tangible hope was to be seen; in the 1860s "liberal landowners have appeared, and the best among the Russian aristocrats begin to be deeply influenced by Western ideas"; and in the 1880s came "the birth of an enlightened and affluent middle class, open to Occidental influences, progressive, intelligent, artistic." The Russian Enlightenment, not yet sufficiently translated into political action, had emerged.

None of the great writers, or other effective figures in Russia, qualified as "intelligentsia." The bulk of the educated classes were not revolutionaries. They tended to hopes, and attempts, to liberalize the country. Their efforts have been neglected in much of the literature: in one sense understandably so, since they failed, and were extinguished.

4.

For there also arose, in the mid-nineteenth century, that important element outside the established order, and under the influence of Western revolutionary thought, who were completely alienated: in fact, the intelligentsia. This more traditional, or negative, reaction was to be decisive. It emerged first as "nihilism," the idea that all beliefs apart from the new notions of science had no validity and that skepticism about all values was science's main aim. This became fairly common among the "educated," but inadequately educated, young: "Students pedantic in specs, Nihilists smug in their smocks," as Pasternak was to put it.

The impact of science and technology in the early part of the nineteenth century is hard to envisage today. The physical and mental effects of the railway or of Darwin were everywhere profound. In a Russia that had no real previous experience of assimilating novelty, acute mental indigestion ensued, as with a starving man suddenly given too much food. All this shook the instinctive confidence even of the older generation, and they found it hard to answer the young nihilists and revolutionaries.

Their elders either gave way, as Ronald Hingley says in his *The Russian Mind*, to "gratifying and undignified displays of indignation," thus encouraging the young to intensify their provocations, or "pandered to the young through feebleness of spirit or a desire to court popularity"—as with the Dostoevsky character in *The Possesed*.

Nihilism proper was hardly more than a pose, giving little emotional satisfaction beyond that of the knowledge of one's superior modernity, and the ability to annoy parents, priests and others. Though on the face of it the attitude was purely egoistic and did not logically lead to the idea of revolution, in practice its adepts were recognized as fertile soil by the small and slightly older stratum that had already taken up revolutionary views. And logically or not, the two attitudes faded into one another: to reject and to destroy.

This adolescent absolutism provided an arena in which the various credos of revolution were debated, categorized and, as it were, theologized by the more sophisticated mystagogues. In the 1890s one of the most active revolutionaries, Mikhail Frolenko, felt that "we already knew so much that if the people were taught one tenth of it, Russia would become the first country in the world." As Adam Ulam points out, this "knowledge" was entirely theoretical, and if endorsed Russia would indeed become first in the world by revolutionary standards— i.e., "she would be plunged into complete anarchy!"

This intelligentsia was marked by extreme intolerance. Of the 1860s, for example, Mackenzie Wallace noted that "the press was able for some time to exercise a 'liberal' tyranny scarcely less severe than the 'conservative' tyranny of the censors in the preceding reign." It was the same phenomenon which caused Nikitenko to report, in his diary for October 1857, that "in their intolerance they [the new opposition] are becoming representatives of a new and almost greater despotism than the previous one." The liberal Herzen went further still. He claimed that "an opposition which leads a frontal attack on a government always has itself, in an inverted sense, something of the character of the government attacked. I believe that there is some justification for the fear of Communism which the Russian government begins to feel: Communism is the Russian autocracy turned upside down."

Indeed, as Hingley puts it, "the former tyranny may have been the easier to bear. . . . Even a noncomformist may bow with dignity to superior power; there is of course something far more slavish in the conformism of one who can be made to toe the line by fear of not being considered a liberal." Nearly forty years later Chekhov claimed that the political despotism of the imperial Ministry of Internal Affairs was at least equaled by that of the editorial office of *Russkaya Mysl*, the progressive oppositionist journal. He prophesied that

> under the banner of learning, art and persecuted freedom of thought Russia will one day be ruled by such toads and crocodiles as were unknown even in Spain under the Inquisition. Yes, you just wait. Narrow-mindedness, enormous pretensions, excessive self-importance, a total absence of any literary or social conscience: these things will do their work . . . will generate an atmosphere so stifling that every healthy person will be nauseated.

In the same spirit are the denunciations of the intelligentsia's "credulity without faith, struggle without creativity, fanaticism without enthusiasm," of the "dogmatism, censoriousness, woolly-mindedness, ignorance and general dottiness" so eloquently expressed in the truly liberal *Landmarks* (Vekhi) some years later. As the Russian philosopher Nikolai Berdayev put it, "Scientific positivism, and everything else Western, was accepted in its most extreme form and converted not only into a primitive metaphysic, but even into a special religion supplanting all previous religions." The revolutionary, the scientific, the utilitarian, hit, and in their crudest form. It was said of Alexander Mikhailov, the effective leader of one terrorist movement, that "an idea would get hold of him without his grasping what it was all about."

The revolutionaries were unanimous in opposing any liberalization of the regime, and any development of civil society. They stood for the seizure of power by an elite. They commonly called their principles "socialist," in the sense that their rule would suppress the market activities emanating from the West, and would introduce equality under the state for such as obeyed its orders.

These revolutionaries probably numbered no more than a few score in the 1860s, and a few hundred in the 1870s: their conspiracies, including the assassination of Tsar Alexander II, gave them fame.

5.

Lenin became a revolutionary in 1877–78, at the age of seventeen or eighteen. Revolution thus preceded Marxism as his motivation: he says that his outlook was "completely transformed" by reading N. G. Chernyshevsky's *What Is to Be Done?* Chernyshevsky, embodying the whole primitive ethic of the intelligentsia, stood for a conscious devoted elite; and above all hated liberalism and liberals. Lenin said later that it was Chernyshevsky who showed that every right-thinking man must be a revolutionary. One thing Chernyshevsky had written was that "a man with an ardent love of goodness cannot but be a sombre monster."

Thus Lenin and others like him, revolutionaries first, Marxists later, already thought in terms of a "scientific" positivism of the type to be found in France and elsewhere (and hardly distinguishable from that of some of the revolutionaries of a century earlier). Marxism gave the mental aspirations of Lenin and his colleagues something more modern and far more completely ideological. It dealt with the new phenomenon of heavy industry and the "proletarian" working class. It presented a whole theory of human history, and of the universe in general. It provided proofs of its analysis of society and the economy. It divided humanity into irreconcilable sections engaged in a struggle to the death. It guaranteed revolutionary victory, and at the same time insisted on the need to fight for it. And it was deeply opposed to liberalism and all its products.

6.

In 1902, in his *What Is to Be Done?*, Lenin, while keeping the ideological pieties of Marxism, gave them a different interpretation. In the Jacobin tradition the task of revolution was now to be entrusted not to a nebulous "class" but to a professional revolutionary elite party acting in that class's name. Lenin, like Marx before him, had become an advocate of the proletarian cause before he had seen an actual proletarian. His underground Bolsheviks henceforth, as far as possible, transformed their worker recruits into professional—i.e., paid, full-time—revolutionaries. The workers who gave some support to the October 1917 coup were those recently recruited from the peasantry; the established working class—railwaymen, printers—backed the Mensheviks. And by mid-1918 the city workers were everywhere in opposition. As to the Bolshevik top leadership, only one (Tomsky) had been a worker. None of this affected what was regarded as more real and essential than fact, more *pravda* than *istina*—the claim that a Bolshevik ideology and program were in the interests of a notional proletariat, and would thus lead to a classless society.

Throughout Soviet history a "proletarian" background remained desirable, where possible. Men who had been apparatchiks for years still ranked as proletarians. And derivation from nonproletarian strata was even branded hereditarily. The sons and daughters of priests, kulaks and merchants were long treated as second-class citizens. Solzhenitsyn notes this attitude in *Cancer Ward:*

"All right, maybe I am the son of a merchant, third class, but I've sweated blood all my life. Here, look at the calluses on my hands! So what am I! Am I bourgeois? Did my father give me a different sort of red or white corpuscle in my blood? That's why I tell you yours isn't a class attitude but a racial attitude. You're a racist. . . ."

"It makes no difference if you had ten proletarian grandfathers, if you're not a worker you're no proletarian," boomed Kostoglotov. "He's not a proletarian, he's a son of a bitch. The only thing he's after is a special pension, I heard him say so himself."

Nevertheless, the "proletarian" aspect was always stressed. When Khrushchev, soon after World War II, suggested to Stalin that taxes on the Soviet peasantry were excessive, Stalin (himself never a "proletarian") said that Khrushchev had lost his proletarian class sense. Dozens of examples could be given, from the earliest days of the regime.

In fact, we saw the effective substitution of the Party for the working class. So that even half-crazed Ethiopian army officers or spoiled rich youths in Cuba or Nicaragua could ideologically represent the world proletariat, as much as did the pampered bureaucrats in Moscow. Nor could a hint that proletarian rule was merely a code word for party dictatorship emerge.

7.

Lenin's revolution, based on this deception, or self-deception, was a triumph for the party mind. Victory in the Civil War was a near thing, and more than once the Leninists felt that all was lost. But after three years of war, plague, famine and terror the Communists succeeded in holding power over an exhausted country. Their own ideas had produced much of the disaster. First, they had, in May 1918, decided that socialism, in their sense, was now on the immediate agenda. They had abolished the market in food products, and relied on forced requisition from the peasantry. And they were proceeding to the abolition of money, free transport services and so on. But in 1921, amid peasant risings, a crumbled economy, intense worker unrest, the Kronstadt Rebellion of that Bolshevik bastion the Baltic Fleet, it became clear that the choice was between losing power and making concessions—as Trotsky put it, "The middle peasant spoke to the Soviet government with naval guns."

Lenin, facing ruin, changed tack and kept power. Over the next four years this New Economic Policy saw the revival of the economy, and some relaxation of the terror. At the same time, the remnants of the socialist opposition were suppressed and opposition groups within the Communist Party forbidden. The breathing space, in fact, amounted to an opportunity for the Communists to get their second wind, to prepare for a further ideology-based offensive.

Over the 1920s the Communists consolidated themselves in two ways: by solidifying their machinery of power and by an intensive and monopolistic propaganda barrage onto the population. At the same time, the politico-economic apparatus solidified into a new caste. The veteran Communist Khristian Rakovski spoke of the "car-and-harem syndrome" that permeated the inner party, which he saw as in effect having "private ownership of the state."

Another aspect was the Marxist (though not only Marxist) idea of heavy industry: a kind of fetishism of the machine, of technology. Lenin defined socialism as "Soviets plus electrification." Posters, from the early twenties, concentrated strongly on bright workers, men and women, standing in front of towering machinery. Indeed the "modernity" of the regime was expressed in the (then) high-tech telegraphese used for its manifestations: Sovnarkom for Soviet of People's Commissars (Sovet Narodnykh Kommissarov); Gosplan for the State Planning Commission; Gulag for the Chief Administration of Labor Camps; and so on.

When it came to agriculture, the means of higher development under socialism was to be the tractor—also a great poster theme. This would not merely give vastly higher production, but would also be the means of urbanizing the countryside in accordance with the promise in the *Communist Manifesto.*

The autocratic traditions and habits, and the utopian tradition that had arisen in reaction to it in the absence of any but the beginnings of civic experience, were the conditions of the Leninist revolution. And the new regime even, in a different sense, inherited the old imperialist expansionism which Engels had remarked on as something that would only end when Russia had "a constitutional forum under which party struggles may be fought without violent convulsions"—not applicable to Lenin's regime, in which the tradition of Moscow as the Third Rome was replaced by the Third International.

8.

The central, classical demonstration of what might be called ideological insanity in practice came with the campaign in 1929–33 to collectivize the peasantry. The history of this inhuman aberration has been told. Millions of human beings perished, and at the same time the agricultural economy was ruined.

The countrywide terror against the peasantry was based on the claims of ideology and of power. Ideology demanded that the independent peasantry be destroyed as an economic class; power demanded that the products of the countryside be taken into the hands of the state. Molotov later commented, "They say that Lenin would have carried out collectivisation without so many victims. But how could it have been carried out otherwise?" He added that Lenin would probably have done it even earlier, and that he was "sterner" than Stalin and had often decided on "extreme measures" while "rebuking Stalin for softness and liberalism."

Then, Marxism is inherently urbicentric. The peasantry represents a class naturally tending, even if not at first, to reactionary—and above all commodity-centered—motivations. For the Leninist, the peasant is an incarnation of backwardness and in the long run an enemy to be brought under control. At the same time, this urbicentrism leads to illusions about the possibility of controlling and planning agriculture on more or less industrial lines. On the record this has always been a failure. Yet it persisted, not only in fully fledged Leninist states like Vietnam but even in Tanzania, for instance.

The land of the landlords had been spontaneously seized by the peasantry in 1917–18. A small class of richer peasants with around fifty to eighty acres had then been expropriated by the Bolsheviks. Thereafter a Marxist conception of class struggle led to an almost totally imaginary class categorization being inflicted in the villages, where peasants with a couple of cows or five or six acres more than their neighbors were now labeled "kulaks," and a class war against them declared.

The necessary hatreds were inflamed; the activists who helped the GPU in the arrests and deportations, Vasily Grossman tells us,

> were all people who knew one another well, and knew their victims, but in carrying out this task they became dazed, stupefied. . . .
>
> They would threaten people with guns, as if they were under a spell, calling small children "kulak bastards," screaming "bloodsuckers!" . . . They had sold themselves on the idea that the so-called "kulaks" were pariahs, untouchables, vermin. They would not sit down at a "parasite's" table; the "kulak" child was loathsome, the young "kulak" girl was lower than a louse. They looked on the so-called "kulaks" as cattle, swine, loathsome, repulsive: they had no souls; they stank; they all had venereal diseases; they were enemies of the people and exploited the labor of others. . . . And there was no pity for them. They were not human beings; one had a hard time making out what they were—vermin, evidently.

Grossman, himself Jewish and the Soviet Union's leading writer on Hitler's Holocaust, draws the analogy with the Nazis and the Jews. A woman Communist activist explains, "What I said to myself at the time was 'they are not human beings, they are kulaks.' . . . Who thought up this word 'kulak' anyway? Was it really a term? What torture was meted out to them! In order to massacre them it was necessary to proclaim that kulaks are not human beings. Just as the Germans proclaimed that Jews are not human beings. Thus did Lenin and Stalin proclaim: kulaks are not human beings."

The Party's reply, and its rationale for everything done to the kulaks, is summarized with exceptional frankness in a novel by Ilya Ehrenburg published in Moscow in 1934: "Not one of them was guilty of anything; but they belonged to a class that was guilty of everything."

In another such novel, also published in Stalin's time, a Party man says he can no longer go on persecuting women and children. But the chief activist, Nagulnov, will not have it:

> "Snake!" he gasped in a penetrating whisper, clenching his fists. "How are you serving the revolution? Having pity on them? Yes . . . You could line up thousands of old men, women, and children and tell me they'd got to

be crushed into the dust for the sake of the revolution, and I'd shoot them all down with a machine-gun."

Or, as another activist puts it, "He thinks he is killing a bullock, but in reality he is stabbing the world revolution in the back." And Nagulnov's example was on the whole followed. It is to an activist of this period that the well-known saying is attributed: "Moscow does not believe in tears."

Former activists have written of how they kept their ideological faith right through the performance of actions against the starving villagers of which the great Lev Kopelev, later one of Russia's leading "dissidents," wrote:

> It was excruciating to see and hear all this. And even worse to take part in it. . . . And I persuaded myself, explained to myself. I mustn't give in to debilitating pity. We were realising historical necessity. We were performing our revolutionary duty. We were obtaining grain for the socialist fatherland. For the Five Year Plan. . . . Our great goal was the universal triumph of Communism, and for the sake of that goal everything was permissible—to lie, to steal, to destroy hundreds of thousands and even millions of people, all those who were hindering our work or could hinder it, everyone who stood in the way. And to hesitate or doubt about all this was to give in to "intellectual squeamishness" and "stupid liberalism," the attribute of people who "could not see the forest for the trees."

9.

The immediate result of these measures was a catastrophic decline in agricultural output across the USSR as a whole over the 1930s. The government's reaction was to base its requirements for delivery of grain from the collective farms not on actual production but rather on what became the basis of Soviet agricultural statistics until 1953—the "biological yield." This was based on the estimated size of the crop in the fields before harvesting; it was more than 40 percent higher than the reality. And in 1932 even this tenuous link to the facts failed; the figure was distorted by merely multiplying acreage by optimum yield. The grain requisitions made on this basis were ruthlessly enforced by activist squads (and, in Bukharin's view, this experience contributed greatly to the brutalization of the Party).

Such action left the peasant with a notional but nonexistent surplus on which to live. As a result, over the winter of 1932–33 major famine swept the grain-growing areas. Some 4 to 5 million died in Ukraine, and another 2 to 3 million in the North Caucasus and the Lower Volga area. During this period about 1.7 million tons (1.5 million metric tons) of grain was exported, enough to have provided about a kilogram a head a day to 15 million people over three months; and this apart from millions of tons held in state reserves supposedly in case of war. We now have full documentation that the Stalin leadership knew exactly what was happening and used famine as a means of terror, and of revenge, against the peasantry.

A census taken in January 1937 was suppressed, and the Census Board was arrested. Its figures, finally revealed in 1990, showed a population of circa 162 million. The Soviet demographers had counted on about 177 million. The population deficit, including a decline in births, was thus some 15 million, of which premature deaths due to deportation and famine are believed to amount to at least 10 million.

It was already an offense carrying five years in labor camp to refer to the famine in any way, even in the villages affected; while to blame it on the authorities led to a death sentence. An American congressman's queries, passed to the Soviet Foreign Commissariat, were answered by the claim that talk of famine was "lies circulated by counterrevolutionary organisations"; while Soviet President Mikhail Kalinin responded to offers of food from the West by saying that "only the most decadent classes are capable of producing such cynical elements."

10.

After the economic disaster of collectivization there were two possibilities: to admit failure and change policy, even to relinquish total power; or to pretend that success had been achieved. The latter course was chosen. In fact, the Idea, contradicted by reality, coped with reality by denying it.

As a result, for the whole of the rest of the Soviet epoch the country lived a double existence—an official world of fantasy, of happiness, grand achievements, wonderful statistics, liberty and democracy, and a reality of gloom, suffering, terror, denunciation and apparatchik degeneration. Arthur Koestler, who was in Kharkov in 1933, describes the disorientating effect of reading the papers, full of young men and women smiling under banners, gleaming factories, awards to shock workers, while the city's electricity only worked a few days of the week, and people were dying of hunger a few miles away.

Collectivization was, as Boris Pasternak pointed out, "a failure as well as a mistake," and the countryside never recovered. It was a failure because all its presuppositions, or Ideas, were invalid. It was not only based on the notion that a "class struggle" existed in the villages between an invented stratum of kulaks and the rest of the peasantry. It pretended that the forced entry into collective farms of the peasants remaining after the deportation of the kulaks was voluntary. And more profoundly, it believed, or at any rate claimed, that collectivization would produce an enormous increase in agricultural productivity; for, after all, the peasants were now in effect socialized and thus at a higher quasi-urban stage of development.

Meanwhile, the offensive was pursued on two other fronts. The attack on religion was resumed, with the arrest of priests, demolition of churches and a vast propaganda campaign—a purely ideological drive, of course. And a "cultural revolution" removed the bulk of the bourgeois specialists not only in academic areas but also in such practical spheres as engineering—with the result that soon most of the country's practicing engineers lacked proper training.

II.

The two different Soviet Unions now in being were manifest in a set of phantom institutions and arrangements which put a humane face on the hideous realities: a model constitution, adopted at the worst period of the terror and guaranteeing human rights; elections in which there was only one candidate, and in which 99 percent voted; a parliament at which no hand was ever raised in opposition or abstention. The Idea, the unanimous society, had, officially, triumphed—not quite unanimous yet, however, since enemies of the people remained to be rooted out.

The earlier falsifications had been shameless enough, as with the passage in a poem of Mayakovsky's in the 1920s with Soviet children asking "What is a policeman?"—the *word* "police" had been abolished. By the 1930s the country had become, even more than in Mayakovsky's time, a police state.

Terror, accompanied by a massive indoctrination effort, was obviously intended to destroy all possible resistance—to kill or imprison millions and to subdue the rest of the population. But this only takes us so far. More radically, its aim and effect was to impose the regime's fantasy of a flourishing and happy country—beset, however, by dangerous subversives—to destroy the truth as far as possible, and to uproot or prevent independent thought.

The general story of the mass terror under Stalin is well known. The original Red Terror under Lenin, less widely known, had set the scene. Lenin actually believed in terror as a good thing in itself. He had given a theoretical justification of terror as early as 1905, when he envisaged the use of it in the style of 1792 "to settle accounts with Tsarism" after the Revolution. In 1908 he had written of "real, nation-wide terror, which reinvigorates the country and through which the Great French Revolution achieved glory." Many similar pronouncements could be cited.

From 1929 full terror arrived—first against the peasantry, then against the party, the soldiery and the population as a whole. It is the classic case—to be followed by similar actions in China and elsewhere—of an ideological government inflicting enormous demographic losses on its own population.

We do not have exact figures on the population losses—as, indeed, is true even of the Jewish Holocaust. The fact that we are not certain of the human cost within a few million is itself remarkable testimony to the extent of the terror.

At any rate, we are in the realm of what Russians call the Twenty Million—that is, who died, and not covering those who survived the forced labor camps, where, as *Izvestia* put it towards the end of the Soviet period, they suffered "unbearable toil, cold and starvation, unheard of degradation and humiliation, a life which could not have been endured by any other mammal." In June 1937 Stalin complained that prisoners were being "coddled." Shortly afterwards, for inadequately fed victims in extreme Arctic conditions, fur clothing and felt boots were banned, being replaced by wadding jackets and trousers, and canvas shoes.

Modern, "Socialist" conceptions thus led to inhuman acts against populations and individuals. The sheer moral and mental corruption of the terror could be illustrated by hundreds of examples. Bukharin's widow Anna Larina tells us how in the dreadful labor camp to which she had been consigned, an NKVD officer found on her a photo of her and Bukharin's baby (who had long since been taken from her), which she had managed to hide. He yelled at her, "You bitch, still dragging a Bukharinite pup around with you," spat on the photo and ground it under his boot.

Or what would any even semicivilized person make of the fate of 170 blind, legless or otherwise incapacitated men in prison in Moscow in early 1938. Sentenced to short terms the previous year for minor offenses such as vagrancy, they were now resentenced—on the same charges—and shot, because the labor camps would not accept them.

There are thousands of stories of vicious tortures and beatings. We have the file of the notorious interrogator V. M. Ushakov, who had beaten fake confessions out of Marshal Tukhachevsky and others and was himself arrested late in 1938. He complained that he, too, was now being beaten, that he had not realized how horribly painful it was, and that besides, those he had beaten were enemies of the people. And the point, the whole point, of these tortures was, in every case, to obtain confessions which were false as to fact, but in accord with the unreal world of ideology.

As to the extent of terror against the Party itself, older Communists—like all revolutionary groups—were to some extent the product of a critical attitude, if only vis-à-vis the former political and social order. Having achieved power, they were, as we have said, in the position of having to restore the precritical attitude as far as their own ideas and organization were concerned. The dust must be swept back under the carpet, the genie restored to its bottle. But this is a staggeringly difficult task: conceptually it requires extravagant doublethink, highly deleterious to the minds elaborating it; organizationally it requires an unprecedented terror, far more than was ever needed by traditional despotism. (Mao, like Stalin, undertook a massive terror against his own party in the "Cultural Revolution".)

The arrested and accused, party or nonparty, were almost without exception innocent of the charges of treason, sabotage and conspiracy raised against them. They were, almost invariably, tortured simply and solely to make false confessions and to implicate others, suffering agonies purely to validate a vast ideologically driven paranoia. Their families were often arrested, too, as in Larina's case. "Member of the family of a traitor to the motherland" was itself a criminal category. The formerly secret legal articles covering this have now been published in Moscow, full of provisions on how wives of enemies of the people are to be sentenced to five to eight years of imprisonment; how nursing babies of enemies of the people are to stay with their mothers in labor camps until the age of one and a half, when they are to be transferred to nearby orphanages, and at the age of three to more distant ones; how children fifteen and over are to have their education supervised by the NKVD and be watched for political error, and, if necessary, "repressed." The publicly announced lowering of the execution age to twelve in 1935 was applied in many cases.

It was not merely a question of those arrested, sent to camps or shot. The whole population was directly affected: for example, after the arrest of the parent of a schoolgirl or schoolboy, the whole class, or even the whole school, would be assembled by the Young Communist activists, and the pupil harangued or forced to make a public denunciation of her father or mother. We have some of the minutes of such meetings, and revolting reading they make. But above all, every schoolmate had the story rubbed in. And the same is true, in only slightly less repulsive form, of meetings of fellow workers at the victim's factory or office.

In general, the psychological effect of these mass arrests and disappearances was thus profound over the whole of the threatened population. Even far lesser terrors in other backward countries have been shown to crush or distort the public mind. The reasons for suspicion were many. The great writer Isaak Babel had met the French author André Malraux—therefore he was a French spy. Weather forecasters had made erroneous reports—to sabotage the crop. Astronomers were arrested as terrorists—but they had already given grounds for suspicion by advancing non-Marxist views on sunspots. One of the more "objective" accusations is worth quoting. We have a top secret report by a senior NKVD official to Stalin personally on the arrest of two officials of a plastic factory that had produced 120,000 buttons with swastika patterns "for purposes of Nazi propaganda." Stalin minutes, "What a nerve." This was in 1935, before the worst period. Stalin grows less tolerant. For example, on the question of what to do with the Tatar Communist Sultan Galiev and his group, he simply writes, "Shoot all the swine." And, as has been noted by many observers, it was precisely the unpredictability of the terror in individual cases that made it so devastating, so that Stalin's whims contributed to, rather than weakened, the effect.

Sometimes the victims were subjected to public confession trials. Much more often the "trials" were secret. In other cases, there was even greater misdirection. In 1940, without her husband being informed, the wife of Stalin's old colleague Marshal Kulik was secretly arrested, interrogated and shot. Allegedly, she had simply disappeared in unknown circumstances. Others were simply murdered, as with a former Soviet ambassador to China and his wife. Or, more striking, the case of the USSR's leading Jewish figure, Solomon Mikhoels, who was clubbed to death at Belorussia's MGB dacha in January 1948 under the supervision of Stalin's Deputy Minister of State Security, Sergei Ogoltsov (and this was at a time when the death penalty had been abolished!). His body and that of a similarly treated companion were then left on a Minsk street where, it was announced next day, they had been run over by a truck. Later the same month the police officials involved were, without publicity, awarded medals (similar medals and orders without publication had been given to the NKVD team that murdered Trotsky in 1940). We now learn, too, that Stalin's senior poisoner, Colonel Maironovski, accounted for some hundred and fifty victims. These are odd insights into a massive record of terror and a total disregard of any normal moral principle.

Was the terror intrinsic? Was it necessary? Perhaps only by such methods could the regime enforce its irrational policies. Certainly the terror not simply could but actually did crush the population. Even when mass terror was abandoned in favor of normal, if notably harsh, police-state methods, it took a generation to emerge before any serious idea of change could become thinkable.

All in all, unprecedented terror must seem necessary to ideologically motivated attempts to transform society massively and speedily, against its natural possibilities. The accompanying falsification took place, and on a barely credible scale, in every sphere. Real facts, real statistics, disappeared into the realm of fantasy. History, including the history of the Communist Party, or rather *especially* the history of the Communist Party, was rewritten. Unpersons disappeared from the official record. A new past, as well as a new present, was imposed on the captive minds of the Soviet population, as was, of course, admitted when truth emerged in the late 1980s.

12.

All this was done in the service of the new order, made manifest in the "planned economy." The First Five-Year Plan, launched in 1929, in its initial form prescribed goals for fifty industries and for agriculture, but over the period that followed it was treated mainly as a set of figures to be scaled upward. The industrial growth rate originally laid down was 18 to 20 percent (in fact, this had already been achieved, in the only way

it ever was to be achieved, on paper). Stalin soon insisted on nearly dou-
bling this rate. The Plan and its successors were thereafter a permanent
feature of Soviet life.

Understanding of the economic side of the industrialization drive of
the 1930s was long confused by two factors. The first was the claim by
the Communists that they were implementing a rational and fulfillable
plan. The second, which came later, was the notion that they had in fact
secured unprecedented increases in production. Extravagant claims were
made and continued to be issued until the late 1980s. It was only then
revealed by Soviet economists that the true rate of growth in production
over the 1930s had only been around 3.5 percent per annum, about the
same as that of Nazi Germany over the same span of time (though
German products were of far higher quality). A characteristic fault was
"giantism"—the Party's inclination to build on the largest and most
ostentatious scale. One result was continual organizational problems.
More crucial, as we shall see, was that production figures were always at,
or beyond, the limits of capacity, so that maintenance and infrastructure
were neglected, with deleterious long-term results.

By the end of the 1930s it was officially claimed that "Socialism"
had been achieved. So it had, in the sense that the state, in the name of
the workers, now controlled the economy. Since it was by definition a
higher form of society than its capitalist predecessor, the corollary was
that it was more prosperous, freer, more creative and so on. In fact, the
population was on the whole far worse off than in 1914, or even under
the NEP. But such a notion was inadmissible.

Though it sounds paradoxical, it is true that, as Professor Stanislaw
Swianiewicz wrote in 1965 in his *Forced Labour and Economic Development*,
the Soviet planning method "was an outcome of the irrational forces
which have been released and are not easily to be mastered." Orders were
given by planners—who were not in a position to appear timid—and
directors had to accept them. The pressures became great to fulfill each
factory's plan at all costs. This could only be done by cutting corners,
using inferior materials, going for bulk only, ignoring ecological or
health considerations, neglecting the infrastructure—and even then
more often than not having to fake the results.

Soviet economists, as soon as they got the chance, pointed out that
the problem of setting prices was insoluble. Twenty-four to twenty-five
million industrial prices alone per annum, each backed by thousands of

pages of documentation, had to be handled by the State Commission on Prices. In the end, no one knew what the true production figures were, nor what the costs were, nor the quality of the products.

Russian economists believe that even in the 1980s, up to 30 percent of material passing through Soviet production actually lost value in the process. At the time Alain Besançon noted, of steel production figures, that these included "production of steel, production of pseudo-steel, pseudo-production of steel" and various other categories of uselessness. For where did all the claimed 80 million tons go? A quarter of it would be more than enough for armaments. There was little sign of it on roads, not much in housing.

As to the neglect of the infrastructure, there was no party kudos for keeping up the roads or sewers. So that even now there are fewer miles of paved roads in the whole ex-USSR than in the state of Ohio; and in St. Petersburg the water is thick with giardia.

A Russian in that city once said to the present writer, in late Soviet times:

> "Our roads are bad."
> ". . . Yes. Why is that?"
> "It's our weather—an isotherm runs down the Finnish border."
> "And seriously?"
> "They were built by the state."
> "Yes, but we have roads in England which were built by the Roman state nearly two thousand years ago, and some of them are still sound."
> "Ah, but then the centurion would check that the six layers of stone had been laid down. Here, the inspector asks the foreman if they have been laid down and is answered with a bottle of vodka."

In a slightly different vein, the New Zealand scholar John Jensen, who even ten or fifteen years ago used to drive round the USSR in a caravan, once warned me that with such vehicles one should not be tempted to gain speed going downhill in order to go easily up the next slope—because there may be a bridge, but the bridge, owing to divergent planning, may be inches higher than the road, with bone-shaking results.

"He drank the profits, and left the embankment to his deputies, who left it to their assistants, who left it to itself." This is in fact a description, by Thomas Love Peacock, of Seithenyn ap Sethyn Saidi in ancient

Wales. But it might have been published in *Pravda* in one of its campaigns for economic improvement. These cases of total parasitism were not, indeed, the norm. But lesser embezzlement was common enough. And *even* directors who were honest enough vis-à-vis the state could seldom achieve their norms, *even* with routine manipulation of the figures, without obtaining raw materials illegally. Paul Craig Roberts argued in his *Alienation and the Soviet Economy* that the organization of supply for enterprises could not work efficiently except by informally (and often "illegally") "directing its activities towards overcoming problems created by its own existence," with the result that the regime "succeeded only in avoiding the *appearance* of commodity production," and this only by incurring enormous losses.

The extraordinary story of the automobile plant installed by Fiat in Ukraine (the Togliatti Factory) speaks for itself. This was a prestige operation, and one conducted, moreover, under the eyes of foreigners. Yet errors and delays of every possible sort supervened. It did not start production until two years after the target date. Then there were endless troubles, and the workforce remained far larger than that which the Italians used.

Administration of the plan by ambitious apparatchiks led to extraordinary disasters. As we have said, it was more or less automatic for factory directors to fake their output figures in one way or another, thus (in Stalin's time) at least postponing the moment of arrest—or (later) disgrace. And it was normal for a party secretary in a forest region to cut down all the trees within a reasonable distance, with a good chance that he would soon be transferred elsewhere so that his output would compare favorably with that of the successor who had to harvest the logs farther off—and he in turn would leave those farther off yet for his unfortunate replacement. All run-of-the-mill stuff.

At the opposite pole to examples of apathy and corruption, we find frenzied activity on the part of individual local leaders seeking prestige. A. N. Larionov, First Secretary of the Ryazan province and a full member of the Central Committee for many years, promised in Khrushchev's time to double his province's meat production in a year, an absurd impossibility. He and his associates, however, succeeded in this by slaughtering all the milk cows and breeding stock, buying (with illegally diverted funds) cattle from other provinces, and so on. Larionov, by now a Hero of Socialist Labor and holder of the Order of Lenin, had many imitators in other provinces. Exposed, he committed suicide.

Ten years later, under Brezhnevism, we find similar occurrences. One of dozens of examples was a great efficiency drive in agriculture in the Kokchetav province. This took the form of enforced specialization, by which sheep, cattle and so forth were concentrated in the areas thought best for them. Villages where sheep farming had been practiced for centuries were left with no sheep, and dairy farms were suddenly filled with hordes of them. Pigs, however, were the greatest sufferers. They were banned on all except a few specialized farms, the rest being slaughtered immediately. As a result, meat, milk and food production in the province fell drastically. The local meat factories refused to buy pigs except from the special farms, which had not got round to producing any, so the pigs left in private hands had to be marketed in provinces hundreds of miles away.

As to built-in idiocies, as against insane initiatives, as recently as the 1980s it was found that a leading factory wishing to use the chassis of buses for their lorries was unable to get them sent from their own factory of origin except in complete bus form. After years of failing to get decisions from the Ministry, they had to accept the complete buses, knock their bodies off with steel balls, and install their own lorry bodies instead.

Another notable charactristic of the Soviet system was the fact that though the state was in most ways far more powerful and intrusive than that of, for example, the United States, laws inconvenient to anyone with pull were simply not enforced. In Brezhnev's USSR, as in America, there were laws covering food purity. The former were not, and the latter were, enforced. Similarly, after the earthquakes in California and Armenia in 1991, Mikhail Gorbachev—then still President of the USSR—was asked at a seminar I attended why the casualties in Armenia were so much higher than in California. He replied with commendable frankness that while both countries had laws about antiearthquake standards of construction in buildings, in Soviet Armenia these had not been observed.

As can be seen, the reasons for failure are not to be thought of as merely economic. The habits necessary to efficiency were effectively discouraged on a systemic basis. A striking illustration of this is in the way people in Moscow speak of a block of flats as particularly desirable because built by German prisoners of war.

Meanwhile, utopian doublethink continued. The Communist Party Program, adopted at its 1961 Congress, asserted that by 1980 there would be so much food that all workers would be fed free of charge at factory canteens; schoolchildren and students would get free clothing and books; all citizens would enjoy rent-free housing; water, gas, electricity and heating would be free of charge, as would all means of transportation; all citizens would have two months' paid vacation per year. As Khrushchev put it, by 1980 the Soviet Union would "overtake America" in everything—"food, wealth, comfort, industrial strength."

13.

The effect on the ecology was, as is now recognized, devastating. Everything was neglected or ignored in the interests of production.

Not only did this cause great direct human damage—the infant mortality rate was over three times as high as in Britain—but the much propagandized medical services were extravagantly underfinanced. In 1990 Moscow's Health Minister revealed that half the hospitals had no sewerage, 80 percent had no hot water, and 17 percent no piped water at all. And so on and so on. This was concealed, especially in propaganda to the West, until the system was on the point of collapse. The bureaucratic reaction to the disaster of Chernobyl is illustrative. David Remnick notes as typical of the regime that when told that the reactor's radiation was millions of times higher than normal, the plant director, Viktor Bryukhanov, said the meter was obviously defective and must be thrown away, while Boris Shcherbina, a deputy prime minister, refused a suggestion to carry out a mass evacuation: "Panic is worse than radiation," he said.

Then the whole structure of the economy was excessively weighted in the direction of heavy industry. This was in part on Marxist grounds, the nineteenth-century notion of the centrality of heavy industry and its role as congener of the industrial proletariat. We find ranking high among ideology-driven miscalculations the concept that investment in heavy industry should be carried out at the expense of every other economic aim. This meant treating consumer goods as a second- or third-class concern. As Andrei Sakharov put it, they hoped to have a rich state based on a poor population. But this disregard for the level of human life was not immediately ruinous. For the citizens, as Remnick puts it, "The self-deception and isolation of the Soviet Union had been so complete for so long that poverty felt normal."

However, the stress on heavy industry was also a result of the concern to create as high a level of military production as possible, in order to outface the capitalist enemy—pursued to a degree that starved the rest of the economy. The comparative, though insufficient, technical success of much of the military investment has been explained on two grounds. It had the use of the most skilled and effective workers at every level, who were thus isolated from the civilian economy, with ruinous effects on the latter. And the military itself represented a real "consumer": unlike the citizen, unable to complain if his new shoes leaked, the armed forces could refuse to take a plane that was not up to scratch, or at least in a range of specification. But in the end, as Gorbachev put it, the "insane militarization" of the economy ruined the country without outfacing the West.

14.

One of the aims of the regime was to produce the "New Soviet Man" devoted to the aims of Party and State and free from the psychological distortions and alienations of bourgeois society. This was based on the Marxist theory that social-economic conditions determine consciousness. Socialism would inevitably produce another, and higher, form of humanity.

The "New Soviet Man" was much promulgated and led a phantom existence. The reality was different, as Solzhenitsyn puts it in *Cancer Ward:* "We thought it was enough to change the mode of production and people would immediately change with it. But did they? The hell they did! They didn't change a bit." Or for the worse.

Then, as the physicist Alexander Weissberg noted in the late 1930s (of Ukrainian industry, but the point applies more generally):

> A few months later their successors were arrested too. It was only the third or fourth batch who managed to keep their seats. They had not even the normal advantages of youth in their favour, for the choosing had been a very negative one. They were men who had denounced others on innumerable occasions. They had bowed the knee whenever they had come up against higher authority. They were morally and intellectually crippled.

Thus, as a natural result of the ideocratic system, a "New Class," as Milovan Djilas had christened it, subsisted like a cancer penetrating the whole of society and sucking nutrients from its tissues. Since all reasonable intelligence tends sooner or later to reject the unreal, the ruling stratum was increasingly selected from the stupefied and inhuman. And, as Orwell points out, such ruling elites "may ossify very rapidly," because unlike other ruling groups such as aristocracies, they choose as their successors their own like. Not exactly like, no doubt, but not very different. It was indeed a "negative selection" that raised up the new personnel.

A well-known British writer on the USSR, Edward Crankshaw, who had much experience of it during and after World War II, wrote in his *Putting Up with the Russians* of the moral and mental squalor of the middle ranks of Soviet officialdom,

> whether in uniform, attached like toxic parasites to the unfortunate Red Army, or in civilian clothes. This is a milieu almost impossible for the foreigner to present to his own countrymen. I have had to work with such officials in war and peace. Their sycophancy, their barefaced lying, their treachery, their cowardice, are so blatant, their ignorance so stultifying, their stupidity so absolute, that I have found it impossible to convey it with any credibility to those fortunate enough to never have encountered it.

And they settled in permanently, or what appeared to be permanently. As Andrei Sakharov wrote in the late 1970s of the whole late Soviet apparat, down to junior levels:

> A deeply cynical caste has come into being, one which I consider dangerous (to itself as well as to all mankind)—a sick society ruled by two principles: *blat* (a little slang word meaning "you scratch my back and I'll scratch yours"), and the popular saw: "No use banging your head against the wall." But beneath the petrified surface of our society exist cruelty on a mass scale, lawlessness, the absence of civil rights protecting the average man against the authorities, and the latter's total unaccountability toward their own people or the whole world, this dual irresponsibility being interrelated.

The stultifying nature of Soviet life under these operators is well illustrated, at a petty level, in the autobiography of the great soprano Galina Vishnevskaya, *Galina*. She tells of La Scala's coming to Moscow from Milan. A representative of the company went around to the

Ministry of Culture to say that La Scala would like Galina to sing *Tosca* with them. The answer was that Galina didn't sing *Tosca*. When the Italian protested that she had sung in a Milan performance of the opera the year before, the culture official replied that Galina was not in Moscow. On learning from the La Scala representative that indeed she was in Moscow and was as a matter of fact dining with him that very evening, the official dismissed him with a promise to call him in half an hour and give him a final answer. The final answer was that Galina refused to sing *Tosca*. When the La Scala man went to dinner with her and asked if she had really refused to sing it, she answered that of course this was untrue. Upon his expressing astonishment, she explained, "You're in the Soviet Union." This is but one of several similar stories she recounts.

Under the Soviets one of the perks of power, understood at all levels, was the institutionalization of the feeling that the beneficiary could act with complete arbitrariness to those dependent on him or her. This is characteristic of all such regimes—indeed to a lesser degree of all hierarchies. But in the USSR it rose to almost transcendental heights. At the top level, one minor example: in the 1970s the Panov couple, both top ballet dancers, asked to be allowed to emigrate. This was refused, and they were fired from their jobs. There was something of an uproar in Western intellectual circles, even in the pro-Soviet milieu. This had no effect. But some years later they were allowed to emigrate. I asked a Moscow friend what was going on: the regime had had a great deal of very bad publicity, but if their policy so dictated, why had they (much too late to avoid trouble) let them out at all? He answered that the whole point was to show "who was in charge."

But this was seen at every level. In his *Moscow! Moscow!*, the South African poet Christopher Hope (with no pretension to expertise), giving a very good impressionistic view of life in late Soviet times, tells of going by rail from Moscow to Orel with his guide-interpreter. It was a very hot day, and the window was locked. He suggested to his companion that they should ask the carriage concierge-type woman to open it. He looked dubious, but agreed. When she came round she seemed offended at the request, but took out her key and opened it a little. Later, as the heat got worse, Hope asked her to open it wider. With an enraged look on her face, she then locked it up completely.

Well before the fall of the Soviet Union, I remember the future democratic leader Yuri Afanasiev agreeing with me that what was necessary for the country was the elimination of feudalism—by which status and wealth were conferred simply by the state.

The Soviet elite was rooted solely and exclusively in the political sphere, and its powers were "politically granted, politically guaranteed and politically oriented." This is pointed up by the extent to which the privileged enjoyed perquisites deriving from their status. For in addition to high salaries, the Soviet elite had access to an extraordinary array of hidden secondary benefits. An extra month's salary ("the Thirteenth Month") was routinely given as a bonus to most leading Party figures and some others. Important officials in Moscow received special extra payment in gold "rubles" with which they could purchase foreign goods in the state-run foreign currency shops: several thousand are believed to have benefited from this so-called Kremlin ration. The foreign currency shops were also of particular use to Soviet elite families, about eight thousand members of whom had positions abroad and were able to exchange part of their very high salaries in a form usable in these shops by relatives at home. Then there were several thousand sinecures; for example, those of the approximately fifteen hundred deputies of the Supreme Soviet who only had a few days' ceremonial duties per annum got one hundred rubles per month and enjoyed free travel.

As was pointed out by Mervyn Matthews in his *Privilege in the Soviet Union:*

> Another touchstone is the secrecy which shrouds the doings of the most favoured Soviet citizens. It is noteworthy that (a) words like "elite," "rich" are banned as a description of any Soviet social group, (b) no information whatever on higher salaries is printed for open distribution, (c) no official figures have so far been given for the national distribution of income, probably because this would reveal an unsocialistic degree of inequality, (d) scarcely anything is printed on elite lifestyles, or the benefits which an elite might enjoy, (e) there is nothing nearly as comprehensive as a "Who's Who" in the Soviet Union. This was due to definite Soviet censorship instructions.

Omnipresent bureaucracy and a new caste of sycophants appear to be the necessary results of the destruction of civic relations and the non—command economy.

15.

With such truths repressed, falsehoods in every field were incessantly rubbed in in print, at endless meetings, in school, in mass demonstrations, on the radio. Even more striking, for a creed based on the notion that economic class determined consciousness, was the reliance on "agitprop"—agitation and propaganda—which constituted a state-sponsored monopolistic campaign to inculcate the Party line. The population was, in effect, deafened and disorientated. Joseph Brodsky quotes Anna Akhmatova saying that no one could understand the Soviet system who had not been forced all day, day after day, to hear the Soviet radio. Leszek Kolakowski writes of the totalitarian attempts "to swallow all channels of human communication." The individual could not breathe a word of the truth with impunity. As Isaak Babel said (in strict confidence to a trusted friend), "Today a man only talks freely to his wife—at night, with the blankets pulled over his head."

On a different note, the censorship body, GLAVLIT, is believed to have employed about seventy thousand full-time staff, concerned not merely to eliminate incorrect facts and promote correct falsehood but also to ensure that the correct ideological spin was put on every published item.

Sakharov (like other heroes of this transition) says that even his and their minds were under a profound "hypnotic spell"; and this psychological distortion has left its mark on many of them to this day. Still, as we know, in the end the experiment failed. The economic and ecological decay which led up to the collapse of the regime is obvious enough. But it should be added that this meant, over the decades, that the actual and the notional conditions became more and more distinct, the falsehoods more flagrant. Fifteen or twenty years ago, when one spoke with Soviet officials one began increasingly to notice a look of shame as they presented to Westerners what were not just lies, but obvious and contemptible and discreditable lies.

So, the material decay was matched by the developing moral and intellectual crises. The latter, once it broke through, had intense grievances to feed on.

16.

The main characteristics of the Communist Idea, simply put, were and remained these. First, it was a way of seeing the world which was in the very strictest sense dogmatic; that is, it accepted the idea that a final world-view, political philosophy and theory of society had been devised, and that the nature of the perfect human order which would prevail throughout the future was known and would be realized by theoretically prescribed methods. That is, it was a closed system of thought, and one which, being "true" in contrast to the falsehood of all others, implied a closed society. As a result, in Solzhenitsyn's words, "The primitive refusal to compromise is elevated into a theoretical principle and is regarded as the pinnacle of orthodoxy." Second, this way of thinking implied that the political leadership, and political considerations generally, were on a higher and more comprehensive plane than all other elements in society and were empowered to make the final decision in all fields. Third, it was based on a view of history, and of the world in general, that saw struggles and clashes as the only essential mode of political or any other action. Other political orders—even "Communist" ones that deviated in any significant way from that of the USSR (for example, Dubček's Czechoslovakia or Mao's China)—were in principle illegitimate, to be destroyed when tactically convenient, just as aberrant political or other views within the USSR were subject in principle to total suppression.

The Idea was never to be submitted to serious argument. Even before the Revolution, Lenin had written that his aim in polemics was not to refute but to destroy his opponent. Nor were his arguments rational. *State and Revolution,* for example, is concerned to prove not that his opponents are wrong, but that they are "renegades" from Marxism. He does this by interpretations of the texts of Marx and Engels. It is a completely fideistic, as opposed to rational, approach. The paranoid component is also well seen in the typical expressions of Communist argument, recognizable as symptomatic by any alienist: *ne sluchayno*—"it is not accidental"—used of any pair or set of unrelated circumstances; and *kak izvestno*—"as is known"—used of any dubious or false assertion.

The doomed writer Isaak Babel said in private conversation (later reported to the secret police) in 1938, "Soviet power is only sustained by ideology. Without that it would be over in ten years." It permeated the whole structure. As Alain Besançon remarked:

The moment the individual accepts the language of the ideology, he allows his mental world and his sense of self-respect to be hijacked along with the language. No matter how inadvertently he may have stumbled into the use of the official vocabulary, he is now part of the ideology and has, in a manner of speaking, entered into a pact with the devil. . . . Ideology collapses when Communist power collapses. Or, if you like, ideology and language collapsed together with the legitimacy of Communist rule. The language of Communism is the power of Communism.

Even when enthusiastic belief became difficult, adherence to ideology demonstrated political loyalty—a very essential pragmatic function. It is hard to know what people really believe. As Lenin said, no one has yet invented a "sincerometer." Moreover, it is very easy to believe, or assent to, something that justifies one's own power and position, as is common historical experience—and this is, of course, the essence of Marx's "false consciousness."

Djilas noted in the 1940s that the rule of the Soviet leaders continued to be "anchored in Ideology, as the divine right of kings was in Christianity; and therefore their imperialism, too, has to be ideological or else it commands no legitimacy." He added that this is the reason why Western hopes that the Kremlin might be pressed or humored into a truly comprehensive détente was based on a misunderstanding, since "no Soviet leader can do that without abdicating his title to leadership and jeopardising the justification of Soviet rule"—as indeed happened.

As to international policy, the "class principle" was only given up when Eduard Shevardnadze became Foreign Minister in 1990. This change, as he pointed out, meant the abandonment of the idea of permanent conflict with all other political orders.

The penultimate premier of the USSR, Nikolai Ryzhkov, tells us in his memoirs that all Politburo decisions, even in his time, were taken on an ideological basis. This applied to both domestic and foreign affairs. In each case, it was a matter of, in principle, weighing the interests of the international proletarian struggle. Of course, any real connection with proletarian interests had long since evaporated. The more valid point is that all public phenomena were judged in terms of benefit to one side or the other in a worldwide unappeasable conflict.

The effort failed in the end, but how was it that it lasted so long?

Above all because the Idea became institutionalized, and the institution was the totalitarian state. It controlled every aspect of power and of thought; it penetrated in detail every aspect of the society and the economy.

In fact, the Idea, if it is to enforce itself on a population, needs to extinguish, as far as possible, even the possibility of dissent. Its aim was, after all, the unanimous society. It did not achieve it, but the attempt went far enough to be ruinous to Russia and dangerous to the whole world.

◆

CHAPTER VII

The Great Error:
Soviet Myths and
Western Minds

I.

The delusive view of the Soviet phenomenon to be found in Western intellectual, or near intellectual, circles in the 1930s, and to some extent again in the first postwar decade and later, will be incredible to later students of mental aberration.

For a long time, and to some degree still, one found factual evidence and reasoned argument facing a gradient of preconceptions not only about the Soviet Union and its hatchlings but also on all sorts of related issues.

The record of British, American and other dupes of the Soviets has been dealt with elsewhere in well-researched books by Paul Hollander and others (though the material is so rich that it would take a small encyclopedia to do justice to it). The intention here is more to consider how and why this aberration took place, to differentiate its various species, and to suggest a crucial question: Is it—or anything resembling it—likely to be repeated, and thus to endanger our future?

The approaches were from minds sunk, separately or in combination, in the inappropriate romanticism and inappropriate rationalism we considered in Chapter I.

As to the latter, George Orwell noted Bernard Shaw's early attitude to the Russian Revolution. Shaw's "bloodless rationalism" could only see in Lenin and his subordinates reasonable people with a well-considered program, and he accused Churchill of falsely characterizing them as devils when they were no more than rational human beings at work. Orwell commented that whether one regards them as angels or devils, one thing certain is that they were not reasonable men.

The more romantic, but not thereby less disastrous, motives for self-deception were often a matter of good intentions—a proverbially inadequate guide. Its bearers had turned to socialism as a means of creating a better, more humane society. But of course socialism is not a synonym for humanitarianism but a specific social and political mechanism credited with the power to produce that society.

The comfortable word "socialism" was thus a major mind-trap. It signified for three or four generations a political and economic system free from guilt. Society, instead of private persons, would run (and was running) the Soviet economy. Or rather, since society could not do so, the state would do so and was doing so for it. In any case, the great result would be the end of "capitalism." "Socialism" was what Lenin, Stalin and their successors claimed to be practicing. They came, after all, from a section of the old Socialist movement. And by the mid-1930s capitalism, private ownership, had indeed been destroyed in the Soviet Union. And what could the noncapitalist order be but socialism? And this, or something like it, possessed the minds of many in the West for another thirty or forty years.

The ethical argument, if such it can be called, seems to run:

(1) there is much injustice under capitalism;
(2) socialism will end this injustice;
(3) therefore anything that furthers socialism is to be supported,
(4) including any amount of injustice.

The idea of socialism had entered many minds over the previous couple of generations. Even when not specifically Marxist, even when not based on conscious and ideological theory, in its less dogmatic form it had received a Marxist input from the general intellectual atmosphere. In particular, it promoted the view that socialism would not only be a better and juster social order, but also that it was more modern, more advanced, that it represented a higher historical level. What was to become, in effect, the Soviet constituency in the West arose primarily among those who had accepted a belief in the possibility of attaining a good society through state power, but especially those among them who blamed their own actual economic and social orders for inhumanity. These saw the Soviet system as both anticapitalist and possessed of a generally acceptable formula for social reorganization. The Soviet Union, and Communists everywhere, were accepted as part of the "left." The lines thus drawn were between supporters of the System— Conservatives, Social Democrats ("reformists") and so on, and advocates of its overthrow. (When Hitler, from another radical perspective, was struggling for power, he divided his opponents into supporters of *das System* and enemies outside the system—to wit, the Communists.) People originally concerned with humanitarianism thus at first saw "socialism" as a habitation for it, but later began to accept the structure as sufficient in itself, even when deprived of its original purpose.

H. G. Wells has a short story in which an Eastern prince is devastated by the death of his young and much loved bride. He decides to devote himself to putting up a worthy monument to her. Her tomb is to be the focal point of a splendid dome which is the center of the magnificent new temple. The prince devotes himself to the planning and building. During the construction his ideas become year by year more ambitious, and he orders a sequence of changes, making the whole result more and more aesthetically perfect. Until one day he comes in with his architects and looks around, still unsatisfied. He goes off, returns, looks around critically, and finally points to the tomb and says, "Take that thing away."

In some such way, their Idea of socialism was built round the concept of social justice, but the form retained its admirers after the removal of the content.

There was thus an unjustified mental leap between attacking the misdeeds of capitalism and accepting the Soviet Union as a model. Lincoln Steffens had been a fearless exposer of political and financial corruption in the United States. How could he go to Russia in the 1920s and say, "I have seen the future and it works," of a barely viable terror regime? One role of the democratic media is, of course, to criticize their own governments, draw attention to the faults and failings of their own country. But when this results in a transfer of loyalties to a far worse and thoroughly inimical culture, or at least to a largely uncritical favoring of such a culture, it becomes a morbid affliction—involving, often enough, the uncritical acceptance of that culture's own standards.

By the 1930s the atmosphere in such circles was one of revulsion against what appeared to be a muddled and exhausted political system in the West, and against an economic system ("capitalism") which was then slowly recovering from crisis.

It is sometimes argued that a thinking being's allegiance should not be given to his country or his culture since it is mere accident that he is born in them. He should, on the contrary, rise above such prejudice— use his power of independent thought and judgment to discover the world's most worthy cause or country and give it his devotion.

Now it is clear that this higher-level transcending of roots, this purity of abstract motive, is seldom a true description of such attitudes. As Albert Camus pointed out of French Sovietophiles, it was not so much that they liked the Russians as that they "heartily detested part of the French." In general, people do not transcend their roots, though they may think they are doing so.

Many whose allegiance went to the Soviet Union may well be seen as traitors to their countries, and to the democratic culture. But their profounder fault was more basic still. Seeing themselves as independent brains, making their choices as thinking beings, they ignored their own criteria. They did not examine the multifarious evidence, already available in the 1930s, on the realities of the Communist regimes. That is to say, they were traitors to the human mind, to thought itself.

2.

It is true that Western societies had, and have, many blemishes. One thing fetishism of the Communist order missed was, as Leszek Kolakowski has pointed out, that the Communist societies had most of the faults of our own in more acute form; and that the claims to (for example) superior medical services were fictitious. And, above all, that, at a more basic level, the blemishes on the Western body societal, however bad, in a broader comparison could be seen as unpleasant and visible afflictions of the skin, and not, as with Soviet society, cancers of the vital organs.

Further reasons, or rather excuses, were available. The Communists were, or appeared to be, the most militant opponents of Nazism, and the most effective supporters of democracy in the Spanish Civil War, which engaged the sympathies (though naturally not the full understanding) of liberals, socialists and moderates everywhere in the West. The Communists disposed of an array of international connections, including many Western journalists, while the Francoites had a very limited audience, and similarly with the Anarchists, the left-wing POUM, and that part of the Madrid government suspicious of and under pressure from the Communists (the local Communist leaders themselves being, often reluctantly, forced to carry out the orders of the Soviet "advisers"). So the suppression of the non-Communist left in Barcelona in 1937 was seen in America and Europe almost wholly from the Communist point of view. And the apparent Soviet-sponsored defense of democracy and liberty distracted attention from the total crushing of anything resembling democracy or liberty in the Soviet Union itself.

Another factor we should not neglect is fashion. Not a very rigorous conception, but conveying better than most the atmosphere later ridiculed as "radical chic." It was manifest in a belief that those accepting it were more up to date, more à la mode than the ruck; and it went with the traditional rejection of the "bourgeoisie" in its various aspects.

Sovietophilia was thus an extravagant example of the dogmas pervasive in the 1930s in countries with freedom of press and publication. It should indeed be repeated that the same period, even a rather longer one, took psychoanalysis to be uniquely and undeniably descriptive of human behavior. In fact, though the Freudian and the Marxist views are logically incompatible, many advanced circles contrived to believe both, or combinations of features of both. They shared the characteristics necessary for a system, or supposed system, of thought required to be accepted by minds thirsty for certainties—they both claimed to be scientific and exhaustive. And both doctrines provided, separately or together, that built-in proof that disagreement was due to prejudices predictably embedded in the opponent's mind by forces understood by the elect.

Of course, Freudianism cannot be blamed for Communism; and in the Soviet Union psychoanalysis was suppressed as a bourgeois aberration. It is ironic that, nevertheless, a combination of Freudian and Marxist certainties is very evident in a whole genre of pro-Communist and anti-Western literature, including even some of Auden's verses. In these the Western bourgeoisie, or the ruling classes in general, are represented as not so much reprehensible as obsolete, decadent, worn-out, doomed—and (among other things) impotent. This notion to some extent persisted even after World War II. A left-wing journalist of my acquaintance, becoming a trifle drunk at a party, picked on a Duke, one of the North Country ones, with a loud "What use are you?" and so on. When a mutual friend said, "Well, they say he's very good in bed," this clearly infuriated the journalist more than any other counter.

3.

A further reason for self-deception was mere parochialism. People could not bring themselves to believe the horrors of Stalinism. It was far easier to attribute such stories to reactionary spite—even though hundreds of witnesses had long since reached the West. As Nobel Prize poet Joseph Brodsky put it later, many here were unable to take in the mere scope of Soviet terror and oppression, preferring to save their moral indignation for the incomparably less dreadful "mustachioed colonels." Parochialism also affected the Western academic community, which continued to produce work treating the Soviet Union as at worst a reasonable sort of system not very different from our own. Such expertise in turn justified the true pro-Soviet political stratum here, which, in fact, did not want real events, real people, let alone real reforms or peaceable progress. They wanted to reduce actuality to a psychodrama. To them all the world is indeed a stage—or an amphitheater, with themselves as the emperor and his entourage, and the rest of us as gladiators, or Christians.

Speaking of which reminds one of the pro-Stalinist clergymen met with then and later—for example, Hewlett Johnson, Dean of Canterbury, who managed to reconcile his allegiances while somehow missing Lenin's view that "every religious idea, every idea of God, even flirting with the idea of God, is unutterable vileness . . . contagion of the most abominable kind. Millions of sins, filthy deeds, acts of violence, and physical contagions . . . are far less dangerous." The present writer chanced to see "the Red Dean" peddling his line in the Balkans after World War II. The impression given was one of overpowering vanity—of "Look at me, untainted by bourgeois prejudice!"

Nor was the dean an isolated case. The record vis-à-vis the Soviets of a fairly large section of Western religious representatives merits fuller study—as with the World Council of Churches voting, time and again, to condemn various offenses against humanity throughout the world *except* in the Communist countries, in spite of attempts by clear-minded delegates to the contrary. On the Soviet Union, their conferences accepted the line advanced by its regime-sponsored church representatives (almost all of whom have since been officially identified as KGB agents, with appropriate code names).

The appeal to vanity is again obvious in such cases as that of Bernard Shaw (in what has been described as "the most frivolous episode in history") when he returned to the USSR at the height of the Stalinist famine and reported an overfed population. So with the supposedly more solid figure of H. G. Wells—another Fabian, but one who had been hostile to Communism and regarded Stalin as a dictator. When Stalin gave him an audience in 1934, Wells was won over—his trust in his own powers of personality assessment enabling him to say of Stalin that he had "never met a man more candid, fair and honest," attributing these qualities to "his remarkable ascendancy over the country since no one is afraid of him and everyone trusts him." A remarkable example of faith in one's intuition—with Wells, like others, throwing some of his not negligible public weight to the Stalinist side. Flattery of major Western intellectuals played a part, together with according them the glamour of official reception and VIP treatment (described to me by a veteran Communist as "banquet politics"). Still, a con job needs a con man *and* a sucker. In their case many suckers even managed not to take in what they saw with their own eyes, or rather somehow to process unpleasantness mentally into something acceptable. Malcolm Muggeridge describes Quakers applauding task parades, feminists delighted at the sight of women bowed down under a hundredweight of coal, architects in ecstasies over ramshackle buildings just erected and already crumbling away. It has been said that many visitors to the USSR came with Potemkin villages built into their organs of perception. Mind-set seems too strong a word: these were minds like jelly, ready for the master's imprint.

As George Orwell complained, "Huge events like the Ukraine famine of 1933, involving the deaths of millions of people, have actually escaped the attention of the majority of English russophiles." As he implies, this was an intellectual and moral disgrace on a massive scale.

4.

Stalin was, in fact, a reader of Machiavelli. He operated on a principle advanced indeed by many other sophisticated observers of human behavior—one put well in English by Henry Fielding in *Jonathan Wild*, with his leading character's principle "that virtues, like precious stones, were easily counterfeited; that the counterfeits in both cases adorned the wearer equally, and that very few had knowledge or discernment sufficient to distinguish the counterfeit jewel from the real." English literature had, of course, provided an earlier warning against Stalin's personal influence on Wells and others: "One may smile, and smile, and be a villain!" None of this readily available wisdom seems to have penetrated some minds.

The components of this deep and dangerous misunderstanding of reality were deception and self-deception, and the first could not have worked without the second. Indeed, the deception was often at a very crude level. For example, the French statesman Edouard Herriot, twice Premier of his country, actually went to Ukraine in 1933 and afterwards denied that any famine had taken place. A visitor to Kiev described the preparations for Herriot. The day before his arrival the population was required to work from 2:00 A.M. cleaning the streets and decorating the houses. Food-distribution centers were closed. Queues were prohibited. Homeless children, beggars and starving people disappeared. A local inhabitant added that shopwindows were filled with food, but that the police dispersed or even arrested local citizens who pressed too close (and the purchase of the food was forbidden). The streets were washed, the hotel he was to stay in was refurbished, with new carpets and furniture and new uniforms for the staff—and similarly in Kharkov, where he was taken to a model children's settlement. He saw the Shevchenko Museum and a tractor factory, and attended meetings and banquets with the Ukrainian Party leaders. As to his (and others') experience of the countryside, this was confined to "model" collectives—for example, "Red Star" in the Kharkov province, where all the "peasants" were picked Communists and Komsomol members, well housed and well fed, the cattle in good condition and tractors always available.

Stalin, and his whole leadership, understood human weaknesses, from which major Western figures would have considered themselves exempt. "O, what a fall was there . . . !"

5.

The conflict between Soviet reality and Western perceptions had become acute in 1933. As we have seen, the Soviet official line was that no famine had taken place. Spokesmen from President Kalinin down called reports to the contrary inventions by émigré or fascist circles, or by Western bourgeois attempting to divert their workers' attention from their own miserable life. But the Soviet line was supported by a whole range of Western correspondents and other observers in the USSR. The most influential was *New York Times* correspondent Walter Duranty (who seems to have been blackmailed on sexual grounds by the secret police).

Duranty personally told Eugene Lyons and others that he estimated the famine victims at around 7 million. An even clearer proof of the discrepancy between what he knew and what he reported is to be found in the dispatch of 30 September 1933 from the British chargé d'affaires in Moscow: "According to Mr Duranty the population of the North Caucasus and the Lower Volga had decreased in the past year by three million, and the population of the Ukraine by four to five million. The Ukraine had been bled white. . . . Mr Duranty thinks it quite possible that as many as ten million people may have died directly or indirectly from lack of food in the Soviet Union during the past year."

What the American public got was not this straight stuff but the conclusion that "any report of famine" was "exaggeration or malignant propaganda." The influence of his false reporting was enormous and long-lasting.

Duranty received the Pulitzer Prize for "dispassionate, interpretive reporting of the news from Russia." The announcement of the prize added that Duranty's dispatches were "marked by scholarship, profundity, impartiality, sound judgment and exceptional clarity," being "excellent examples of the best type of foreign correspondence." *The Nation*, in citing the *New York Times* and Walter Duranty in its annual "honor roll," described his as "the most enlightening, dispassionate and readable dispatches from a great nation in the making which appeared in any newspaper in the world."

At a banquet at the Waldorf Astoria to celebrate the recognition of the USSR by the United States, a list of names was read, each politely applauded by the guests until Walter Duranty's was reached; then, Alexander Woollcott wrote in *The New Yorker*, "the one really prolonged pandemonium was evoked. . . . Indeed, one got the impression that America, in a spasm of discernment, was recognizing both Russia and Walter Duranty."

There were a number of reporters like Malcolm Muggeridge, and other Westerners who had given firsthand accounts of the realities.

Thus the Western world was faced with, in effect, two different stories about the famine (and about various other Stalinist massacres). Why did an intellectual stratum overwhelmingly choose to believe the false one? None of this can be accounted for in intellectual terms. To accept information about a matter on which totally contradictory evidence exists, and in which investigation of major disputes on the matter is prevented, is not a rational act.

For people who claimed to have used their brains, one can surely suggest that they had a duty, a *moral* duty, to look more carefully at the evidence.

6.

Academics may in the long run have been even more influential than people like Walter Duranty in peddling falsehood, if only from their particular claim to special knowledge and to the disinterested pursuit of truth. Moreover, politicians, media and public took them seriously, and right through the Soviet period each ill-informed Western politico or editor retained a supposed expert to support his own preconceived opinions.

It was in the 1930s, just when the Soviet system was in its very worst phase, that major validation of the enormous set of falsifications with which this was concealed came for the first time from Western academics of the highest standing.

The stars were, of course, Sidney and Beatrice Webb, the deans of Western social science, leaders of the Fabian Society, founders of the London School of Economics. The motivations of the Webbs are reasonably clear, and may be divided into two main attitudes, which we find in different forms throughout Western pseudological writing on the Soviets. First of all, as with others, for them "socialism" was the society of the future, in which a government representing the people would provide a planned economy, with beneficial results. They thought they saw socialism in the USSR, and, of course, so they did. This led, as is normal in academic self-deception, to their excusing some of the undemocratic reality and denying the rest. As a result, their work was of a genre common in literature, but hitherto never applied to a real country—utopian fantasy.

The Webbs' second contribution to this field was also to persist until quite recently in some academic circles: they accepted as true the facts, figures and so forth published by the Communists. They thought that the electoral system, the trade unions, the cooperatives existed in reality in the form which in fact existed on paper only.

The Webbs' book, seen as the last word in serious Western scholarship, ran to over 1,200 pages, representing a vast amount of toil and research, all totally wasted. It was originally entitled *Soviet Communism: A New Civilization?*, but the question mark was triumphantly removed in the second edition—which appeared in 1937 at precisely the time the regime was in its worst phase of gloomy, all-embracing terror.

Their view of what they reckoned as the exile of a million-odd families of "kulaks" was that "the Soviet government could hardly have acted otherwise," and indeed that "strong must have been the faith and resolute the will of the men who, in the interest of what seemed to them the public good, could take such a decision." When it comes to the famine, they say there was merely some local food shortage—due, anyhow, to "sabotage" by the peasant population. On the faked Moscow Trials, they take the view that the confessions of the accused were due to their "behaving naturally and sensibly, as Englishmen would were they not virtually compelled by their highly artificial legal system to go through a routine which is useful to the accused only when there is some doubt as to the facts," and that Western observers at the trials were convinced that the confessions proved genuine conspiracies, and that their reading of the transcript gave them the same impression. They advance "a detached and philosophical interpretation"—to the effect that conspiracies were known in England and France some centuries ago, that Russian revolutionaries were by nature plotters, and that Lenin had predicted in 1922 that for a long time to come there would be doubts, uncertainty, suspicion and treachery—a "forecast," they added, "which was borne out by the evidence in the Moscow Trials of 1937." They argue that after revolutions "little intellectual freedom on fiercely controversial subjects is apt to be allowed," citing the fact that for several generations after the English Revolution of 1688, Catholics had no electoral rights. Not quite the same thing as mass executions, one may think.

Of the hundred-odd shot in secret on the morrow of the Kirov murder, they say that they were "undoubtedly guilty of illegal entry and carrying bombs," when the only evidence was an official announcement to that effect (they have all now been rehabilitated).

The Webbs' subheadings include: "The Emergence of a Communist

Conscience," "The Vocation of Leadership," "Ethical Progress in the USSR," "The Maximising of Wealth" and "The Success of Collective Agriculture." And they speak of "the sense of freedom and equality" among the Soviet nations.

Another British academic, the highly influential Professor Harold Laski, took a similar view of the trials, with particular praise for Stalin's villainous prosecutor Andrei Vyshinsky, who was "doing what an ideal Minister of Justice would do if we had such a person in Great Britain."

It is significant that the Webbs, as well as Laski, had little knowledge of history and approached the evidence from the point of view of analytical social and political science. We shall come across later examples of this often long and laborious, but essentially worthless, type of approach.

Another leading British academic of the period did not even have their excuse of arrogant ignorance. Sir Bernard Pares, Britain's leading Russianist, had opposed the Soviets, but changed his mind on arriving in Moscow late in 1935, instantly feeling that the Bolsheviks "were Russia." He went on to believe the Soviet version of the trials, adding his own fatuous contribution—that "the bulky verbatim reports were in any case impressive." Once again, this inability to imagine that official documents could be a pack of lies—and we shall find that even in the 1990s!

The Webbs were not Marxists but were veterans of the Fabian idea of intellectuals penetrating, and transforming, opinion. Their theme was state control of the economy, and socialist-intellectual control of the state; and when Beatrice Webb's protégés won control of the London County Council, the Labour members were put under far tighter discipline than those in the House of Commons. She, like that other Fabian socialist H. G. Wells, had earlier favored eugenics, though not going to Wells's length of suggesting that the non-European races had no future. This positivist and authoritarian outlook saw much to praise in the USSR.

What can we conclude? It is clear that people like the Webbs admired the ability of the Soviets to enforce their ideas. For them, as for so many, one is reminded of Orwell's remark that they always speak of what things would be like "under" socialism—under, with them on top. And they seem less concerned with the humanitarian side of the socialism they professed (and thought they saw in the USSR) than with modernity, efficiency and other attributes of the properly organized future. As to the "modernity," Russia was indeed (through no fault of its new ruler) a backward country. But its direction, seen in its posters celebrating the tractor against the horse, its telegraph-era abbreviations—was of progress made, or about to be made, real.

There was also even a special operation to make Soviet penal life look attractive, with a model prison at Bolshevo and a model wing in the Leningrad Transit Prison. Enthusiastic comments came from Westerners—such as Lenka von Koerber with her book *Soviet Russia Fights Crime.* The Webbs, D. N. Pritt, Harold Laski and other prominent Britons saw and warmly welcomed the vision of this progressive treatment of an old social problem. The value of these operations was understood in high Kremlin circles. In newly published police documents we find under late Stalinism that the Politburo, in full session, heard a report on "The visit of the English delegation of the community of Quakers to an Industrial Corrective-Labor Colony of the Administration of the MVD for Moscow Province, on 27 July, 1951." One progressive, indeed, Jerzy Gliksman, who had reported favorably on Bolshevo, was to find himself in camps more truly indicative of Soviet practice in the field and to write a vivid book on them.

On the intellectual level it is revealing to see some of the most respected minds in philosophy, literary criticism, the sciences, falling into the fundamentally simplistic political scholasticism, and in too many cases into the mental idiocy of pure Sovietophilia. This alone is enough to discredit any idea that the notions harbored at any given time by a section of intelligentsia are to be taken seriously, except as symptoms requiring treatment.

7.

In this case many had become addicted, to a greater or lesser degree, to Marxism. (I don't think "addiction" is too strong a word: perhaps someone will consider founding a curative organization called Marxists Anonymous.) At the same time, and mainly as part of this phenomenon, many, as we have seen, became firm believers in a large array of falsehoods about the Marxist states, in particular the Soviet Union.

But let us first insist that it was possible to have radical socialist views without being deceived about the Soviet regime—or, if temporarily deceived, soon undeceived. On the far left, the Anarchists, of course, never had any use for the Marxist-Leninist dictatorships. Conversely, there were people with right-wing attitudes who were successfully taken in by flattery and falsification—the millionaire American ambassador to Moscow Joseph Davies being a prime example.

Still, the great bulk of those who forwarded the Stalinist myth in the West were, whether Communist or not, members of an amorphous progressive intelligentsia. The Communist Parties in the West were not the only carriers of radical socialist ideas. But they were the best organized, and the best funded. Best funded because of massive Soviet subvention. Best organized because they had adopted the Leninist quasi-military principle of "democratic centralism."

But the Westerners who became to one degree or another addicts of the Stalinist regime went far beyond the Communist Party membership. They were, generally speaking, from the educated classes—in itself a reflection on the insufficiency of education itself to save its products from absurd errors. As for formal academe, "political science" does not sufficiently take into account those other categories of reasons for political error: vanity, credulity, sophistry and all their combinations or variants.

Even apart from those who wholly accepted the Stalinist line and saw the Soviet Union's falsified image rather than its reality, the whole intellectual atmosphere was in fact pervaded to a greater or lesser degree by extravagant misperception.

We should note the rarity in the past of what would now be regarded in the West as normally humane behavior. Westeners often excluded the mere possibility of the mass terror of the Stalin period in Russia. Nor did they grasp that an established state could go to such lengths.

8.

Let us return to the "Moscow Trials" of 1936–38—the three public, and massively publicized, events at which a series of major Soviet figures confessed to espionage, terrorism, treason and sabotage and were then executed. Rejection of these grotesque spectacles became the great test of unacceptability by the Soviet Union and the Communist Parties everywhere. The black Trotskyite C. R. L. James said to a friend, "This will open people's eyes"; his colleague replied more realistically, "No, it will close them." And so to a large degree it turned out.

Stalin, when one of his police generals expressed doubt as to the probable Western reaction, is said to have retorted, "They'll swallow it." For some it was hard to cope with. When Stephen Spender asked a

Communist friend what he made of the trials, the answer was "What trials? I've given up thinking about such things long ago."

Others were more enthusiastic. John Strachey, influential as, among other things, a supposedly non-Communist member of the three-man committee of the supposedly independent (and mass-membered) British Left Book Club, wrote, "I believe that no one who had not unalterably fixed his mind on the contrary opinion could read the verbatim reports of the trials without being wholly convinced of the authenticity of the confessions." He added, "I can only say that no man can advance his political education more than by studying this supreme historical document of our time."

As Julian Symons (himself of the radical though non-Stalinist left) says in his *The Thirties,* the Western intelligentsia who supported the Spanish Republican cause had generous motives, "nor did most of them realise for some time that they were pawns, used deliberately not for Spanish but for Russian ends." But when it came to the Moscow Trials they had no motive but a selfish refusal to face disillusionment—the (as he puts it) "winter wind of reality." His final judgment is, "But they had not been deceived. In relation to the Soviet Union they had deceived themselves, and in the end one has to pay for such self-deceits."

Some of these preconceptions had set in at an early and impressionable stage of life, or in connection with the professional or political allegiance and antipathies formed then. The Australian poet James McAuley wrote penetratingly of the pro-Communist phenomenon: "During the thirties and forties Australian intellectual life became subjected to an alarming extent to the magnetic field of Communism. All sorts of people who would regard themselves as being non-Communist, and even opposed to Communism, in practice were dominated by the themes and modes of discussion proposed by the Communists, danced to the Communist tune, and had serious emotional resistances to being identified with any position or institution which was denounced by the Communists as 'reactionary.'" He adds that "one reason for all this was that schools of thought genuinely independent of and opposed to Communist suggestion were in this country not well organised and publicly *present.* They lacked *prestige,* that magical aura which captures the minds of the young in advance of argument and establishes compelling fashions." And let us recall that it was a much (though wrongly) admired Australian historian, Manning Clark, who wrote that Lenin was "Christ-like, at least in his compassion," and was "as excited and loveable as a little child."

At any rate, whether in Australia or the United States, Britain or France, the mood was the same. Koestler speaks in his autobiography of the time when London was full of "the thousands of painters and writers and doctors and lawyers and debutantes chanting a diluted version of the Stalinist line."

9.

These delusions trapped some Westerners into total allegiance to the Soviet Union, and this included acting as direct agents of its secret intelligence services. It is astonishing to find not just the odd example but large numbers of cases of this type of mental warp. Much of the story is only now emerging, or is only now being fully confirmed—and much remains to be discovered. This secondary product of the Stalinist penetration of Western scientific and governmental circles became evident in the 1940s and 1950s, though many, even of the moderate left, especially in America, did not accept the fact.

So we find a sort of mirror-image McCarthyism, with anyone detecting or alleging espionage or other underground activity in favor of the Soviet Union being denounced for "smearing" those concerned. This was particularly noticeable among scientists. But it expanded to all fields. Those subjected to years of slander and professional persecution and to whom apology is now due and overdue include such names as Edward Teller, treated, as Andrei Sakharov put it, in a "mean" fashion by the main body of physicists. Whittaker Chambers was represented as an "unstable, pathological liar," and so forth. He has, of course, been vindicated—not perhaps as to stability but certainly as to truth. Elizabeth Bentley was typically described in David Caute's *The Great Fear*—as late as 1978!—as a "neurotic liar." She, too, was totally vindicated by the documents published by Yale University Press a few years ago.

Though the American Communists denounced those like Chambers and Bentley who had defected from Soviet control, it was not only Communists who took up the theme. Those who had been involved but later thought better of the Stalinist enterprise, and done their best to expose the underground network devoted to the destruction of the United States in its favor, were attacked as renegades and informers. They were indeed in a sense renegades, though those who had deserted democracy for Stalinism surely were at least equally deserving of that epithet. They had "informed"—at a time when those they were exposing had been "informing" the Soviet secret agencies. But it is the childish tone of the attacks on these deserving characters that is most striking—they were treated as "snitches."

In seeing the motives of those who became Soviet spies as ideological, we must also surely look at their psychological makeup. This seems to have varied, and is in any case hard to establish. Of the British spy rings and also of the blindness of the establishment on which they battened, Anthony Powell, a novelist without any special interest in politics, makes some very shrewd observations in the second volume of his autobiography, *Messengers of Day.* He speaks of the slight connections he and friends of his had with Donald Maclean and Guy Burgess. He quotes his friend Adrian Daintrey, the painter, a man without the least interest in politics, as quite clear as early as 1935 that Maclean was a Communist, while he himself noted the drunkenness, violence and conceit that led Maclean into trouble with his superiors—who, however, positively basked in their own tolerance and magnanimity in letting him get away with it. Maclean was "the fonctionnaire who wishes to be 'different,' a not unfamiliar category, carried to its logical conclusions; the complete reversal of conventional behavior, while remaining in conventional circles." But Burgess, only a temporary government employee, was "a notorious scallywag, to whom no wholly baked person, among those set in authority, would ever have dreamt of entrusting the smallest responsibility, or access to secrets of even a low grade classification. In fact, if Maclean is the supreme exemplar of the civil servant who wants to be 'different,' Burgess is equally representative of the manner in which official bodies (noticeable, too, in the army) lack as a rule the faintest idea of what an individual is 'like.'" Powell had personally met Burgess once, and described him at the time as "nauseating"—his main point, however, being that the meeting had taken place "in the house of a distinguished member of the Treasury."

These traitors were misled, one of them, Anthony Blunt, tells us, about the USSR. But to be in error is not the same as to become a traitor. One may feel that those who undertook a life of crime, of treason and espionage, were under a particularly strong duty to examine the record of their prospective employer; and that in the case of Burgess, Maclean and their accomplices this lack of intellectual skepticism was in itself already so irresponsible as to constitute a moral offense. Blunt's excuse for his later activism was that he could not "betray his friends"—who were betraying the millions of his compatriots. The moral squalor of this principle of a Cambridge clique—to put one's friend (i.e., Burgess) before one's country (i.e., Britain)—does not even now seem to strike Blunt's not very various defenders.

So we find that Blunt's defense rests mainly on a false appeal to anti-Fascism (since he spied on through the Nazi-Soviet Pact) and a recourse to the Mafia morality of solidarity in crime. He fails, except in passing, even to rise to the level of defending his right and duty to follow his Stalinist convictions.

But what should be our answer to such a defense, whether from the Blunts or the Joyces, the Berias or the Eichmanns? I have yet to see a better answer than John Sparrow's thesis that their guilt "is not mitigated by the fact that they believed their aim to be a good one; they must be judged ultimately by reference to the cause to which they dedicated themselves. . . . If it seems hard to condemn a man on moral grounds for an intellectual error in the choice of ends . . . the answer is surely that the lie that betrays him is a lie in the soul; that the causes men dedicate themselves to . . . reveal the kind of person that they really are." Blunt and Burgess and the others brought to a rotten cause a rottenness that was already in them.

The detection of such horrors is the job of the security services. But there is a political element, in that—in Blunt's case at least—there was some feeling expressed that he should not be further victimized, though the victims of this gang included a Soviet secret police defector sent back to torture and death, and scores of Albanian democrats sent to their deaths in a betrayed incursion.

At any rate, a problem remains, in that a number of minds are still tolerant, or at least forgiving, of offenses committed on "ideological" grounds with which they feel some sort of vague sympathy. This recalls what Peter Viereck once described as the "awful cocktail party chic of tolerance" towards totalitarianism—the sort of thing that led to the denunciation as fanatics of academics who objected to too hospitable a reception in the United States of literary KGB veterans at a time when Joseph Brodsky and the like were sweating it out in the Arctic.

As to scientists, it might have been thought that the number of those who were admittedly guilty of espionage—Fuchs, Nunn May, Pontecorvo, etc.—had been enough to destroy the image of scientists as being immune to the Stalinist virus. But there seems to be no connection between scientific prowess and any immunity to totalitarian ideas (as we have seen with the Nazis). What was odder was the argument to the contrary from a wide range of scientific minds themselves not Communist. An absurd example was the rallying of his fellow anthropologists in defense of the Soviet agent Mark Zborowski. But the sciences gave many examples of what was no better than at best a professional loyalty or a personal tie taking precedence over objective fact. As late as the 1990s there were many who were almost ostentatiously "in denial."

10.

Another area of misunderstanding was to be seen in business circles. Ronald Hingley, a frequent visitor to the old USSR, once wrote that the biggest Western dupes he came across there were scientists and businessmen. In both cases there were many exceptions. But misunderstanding of the whole nature of the order had some odd results in the economic field.

Extravagant misconceptions about the Soviet and East European economies had been endemic in all sorts of circles. Representatives of high capitalism had, off and on since Lenin's time, seen it as in a mirage, as a universally promising venue for trade and investment.

Astonishing bouts of optimism about the possibilities of American-Soviet trade recurred. Sometimes this went with the idea that the more the trade the better the political relationship (though Russian-German trade had reached its highest points in 1913 and 1940).

The Soviet Union had, in fact, become largely autarkic. When the United States recognized the USSR in 1933, trade between the two countries declined throughout the following decade to a level of less than one sixth of what it had been before.

During World War II various economic experts in America predicted (in the words of Eric Johnston, then President of the Chamber of Commerce) that "Russia will be, if not our biggest, at least our most eager customer when the war ends" (*Nation's Business*, October 1944). He was supported by a poll carried out by *Fortune* magazine in 1945, which showed that business executives had more faith in Soviet postwar intentions than any other group in the American population. The same magazine estimated that U.S. exports to the USSR would range between one and two billion dollars, while the U.S. Bureau of Foreign and Domestic Commerce had suggested (in October 1943) that not less than a third of American exports would go to Russia after the war. In fact, U.S. exports to Russia during the postwar period were much less than 1 percent of the total.

Such misreading of the Communist system continued. A more materially damaging example came in the 1980s, when (encouraged by governments) Western banks gave vast credits to Poland, which merely prolonged the misery, lined pockets and led to the writing off of the debts, so that, except for crooks, *no one at all benefited!* (It was particularly irritating that Chase Manhattan, with whom I once banked, gave the Polish government better terms than what we ordinary depositors were allowed.)

A more general misunderstanding of the Soviet economy remained widespread in the West. Alain Besançon noted in 1980:

> The Soviet economy is the subject of a considerable volume of scholarly work, which occupies numerous study centres in Europe and the United States and which provides material for a vast literature and various academic journals. But those born in the Soviet Union, or those who approach Soviet society through history, literature, travel or through listening to what the émigrés have to say, find that they cannot recognise what the economists describe. There seems to be an unbridgeable gap between this system, conceived through measurement and figures, and the other system, without measurement and figures, which they have come to know through intuition and their own actual experience. It is an astonishing feature of the world of Soviet affairs that a certain kind of economic approach to Soviet reality, no matter how well-informed, honest and sophisticated, is met with such absolute scepticism and total disbelief by those who have a different approach that they do not even want to offer any criticism—it being impossible to know where to begin.

The fullest study, sponsored by the CIA, was highly misleading. They did not, it is true, actually accept official Soviet figures. But they took them, since they were the only figures available, as the basis of their analysis, assuming that they were distorted or exaggerated in certain respects, but still useful. In fact, they were not distorted, they were *invented.* Once again, there was a defect in the imagination of the Western researchers. In *1984*, Orwell has Winston Smith sitting in front of the telescreen watching a minister announcing to triumphal trumpets that 50 million pairs of boots had been produced last year.

Winston Smith, quite apathetically, and with no special political thought, says to himself that for all he knows, no boots at all were produced. Orwell understood Soviet statistics; academic economists didn't.

And all this is to say nothing of such comments as that of John Kenneth Galbraith in 1984, in the true Webb tradition, that the "Soviet system has made great economic progress in recent years. . . . One can see it in the appearance of solid well being of the people in the streets," adding that, in particular, unlike Western economies, the Soviet "makes full use of its man-power"—a staggering misstatement.

II.

The original euphoric approach appeared to die of shock following the signature of the Nazi-Soviet Pact, the invasion of Poland, the war against Finland and seizure of the Baltic states. Western true believers, including most of those in Soviet spy rings, indeed held that the Soviet Union was the unique hope of future progress, and that its actions must still be supported, whatever the twists and turns, in what it saw as the necessities of foreign policy. But most earlier Sovietophiles went into a sort of mental hibernation, from which they emerged when Hitler attacked the USSR in 1941. Odder still, earlier non-Communist liberal delusions also reemerged: in particular that Stalin could be trusted to cooperate in a wartime and postwar alliance for peace and progress.

To different degrees, this much affected governmental circles in the West, in spite of a long accumulation of evidence against it, until well into the postwar years. By the late 1940s two matters seemed clear. First, that the Stalin regime was pursuing a foreign policy of hostility to the West, and an internal policy of suppressing all Western ideas. At the same time, a vast body of evidence had been available about the terror, the Gulag, the whole truth. Moreover, what remained of the imaginary high ground had been destroyed by Orwell, Koestler, Serge and the other strong minds now emerging. (The British Communist leadership had a special meeting on how to combat Orwell, Koestler and the brief but very effective quarterly *Polemic,* edited by the highest-ranked British officer in the Spanish War, Humphrey Slater—which may for comparative purposes remind us that all three of the successive commanders of the British Battalion in the International Brigade in Spain, with many others, had now left the Communist Party, realizing that they had been made use of.)

12.

However, the Stalinists rallied. As before, opposition to Communism was almost never countered by rational argument. As George Orwell wrote, critics of the Soviet system were called "rabidly anti-Communist." He adds:

> The upshot is that if from time to time you express a mild distaste for slave-labour camps or one-candidate elections, you are either insane or actuated by the worst motives. In the same way, when Henry Wallace is asked by a newspaper interviewer why he issues falsified versions of his speeches to the press, he replies: "So you are one of these people who are clamouring for war with Russia." There is the milder kind of ridicule that consists in pretending that a reasoned opinion is indistinguishable from an absurd out-of-date prejudice. If you do not like Communism you are a Red-baiter.

The United States, though not Western Europe, had the McCarthy experience. (Russians have seriously suggested to me that he was a Soviet agent—he *had* had Communist help in his own election in Wisconsin!) At any rate, he disgraced anti-Communism in the eyes of many, by wild or false accusations.

McCarthyism was a temporary aberration. Its longer-term effects were that in some intellectual circles, by a sort of mind-clenching, the term was used not only of false accusations of collaboration with the Soviets but also of true ones. His naming of Professor Owen Lattimore as the leading Soviet agent in the United States was absurd (a false accusation, rejection of which, to this day, leads to denial of the plain fact that Lattimore was an active and devoted adherent of the Soviet cause).

"McCarthyism" remained a potent myth in intellectual circles. In fact, it figures in many historical tests in universities as a major matter in American history—with accounts of the realities of Soviet penetration of U.S. agencies omitted. Indeed, the myth remained so strong that when Angela Davis—not only an admitted Communist but actually the CPUSA's vice presidential candidate—came to speak at Stanford University, the student paper referred to her simply as an "activist." When queried on why they didn't, truly and legitimately, call her a Communist, the editor said that this would be McCarthyism!

More broadly, the epithet has almost achieved the comprehensive applicability Orwell noted of the word "fascism." In the late 1990s I note it used by the Russian ambassador to Bulgaria of that country's government, when it complained of espionage; and by the Italian press (*"macartismo"*) when the *Los Angeles Times* printed an article pointing out that the film *Il Postino* was about a Stalinist writer indoctrinating a young man to go to his death in the Stalinist interest, thus supposedly causing it to lose an Oscar.

In the 1950s the lines thus drawn had led many on the left, at least in the United States, to refuse, as we have said, to credit any accusations of treason in favor of the Soviet Union. It is hard to see how anyone who had read Nathan Glazer's excerpts from and analysis of the court trial of the Rosenbergs could have had any doubt that the Rosenbergs served as Soviet agents. Something similar could be said of the Hiss case.

At the time, American politics were also very heavily traumatized by the Communist takeover, in 1949, of mainland China. Blame for this disaster ran largely along partisan lines. The Republicans, or their Senate leadership, had moreover for some time supported McCarthy. When McCarthyism collapsed, the Democrats, or a large section of them, attacked genuine investigations of real Communist penetration as part of the McCarthyite "witch-hunt." Richard Nixon and other members of the House Un-American Activities Committee (and their counterparts at Sacramento) were held to have been mean, partisan, unjudicial, tricky, driven by ambition. No doubt such points are legitimate; but they should hardly be allowed to obscure the main issue. Was Nixon right? He was.

13.

In other Western countries experiences differed. Nevertheless, in France, in particular, non-Communist, or anti-Communist, attitudes were subjected in academe to all the persecution available to those without control of the machinery of state. The evidence of Soviet reality, such things as the Gulag, was met by the dominantly influential Jean-Paul Sartre with two arguments. First, that the evidence was unofficial (though he accepted precisely similar testimony about French misconduct in Algeria); second, that such evidence would throw the French proletariat into despair. He added, "As we were neither members of the party nor avowed sympathisers it was not our duty to write about Soviet labour camps; we were free to remain aloof from the quarrel over the nature of this system, provided no events of sociological significance had occurred."

French intellectual servility to Stalinism reached its zenith when, in

January 1953, the announcement was made in Moscow of the discovery of the "Doctors' Plot," in which leading Soviet physicians, mostly Jews, were accused of plotting to kill Soviet leaders on the instructions of Zionist, American and British intelligence. A group of leading French doctors at once—not even waiting for the supposed evidence—publicly denounced their unfortunate Soviet colleagues, who were, however, declared innocent by Moscow a couple of months after Stalin's death.

Meanwhile, Stalin's death had evoked a funerary ode by Pablo Neruda (omitted from the current English edition of his works). Neruda, calling Stalin "the moon" and "the maturity of man and the peoples," writes that we must learn his "sincere intensity" and "concrete clarity" and take pride in the title "Stalinist." However, "the light has not vanished" since (Neruda rather lamely concludes) "Malenkov will continue his work."

The German record is even more unbelievable. Many West German academics, journalists and others were successfully deceived, not about distant Russia but about their own countrymen's existence in next-door Communist East Germany. Delegations were successfully potemkined. And in particular, the economic state of the "German Democratic Republic" was grotesquely misunderstood—as became obvious after the Wall fell. Moreover, this was largely a debacle of German academe. As Timothy Garton Ash has said, "Whole West German institutes were devoted to failing to understand the East German economy."

The prominent intellectuals and others thus deceived were at best naïve; but they were neither morally nor intellectually entitled to such naïveté. At worst, they were conscious agents of what they knew, at some level, to be a terrorist dictatorship.

I register such things not so much for their intrinsic importance as in the context of what can only be called a form of mental incapacitation.

14.

As the Soviet Union became less dreadful under Stalin's successors, it became less popular in the West. This was partly because knowledge about its horrible past was now widely available, partly because the regime's ability to prevent access to its actual condition was now less effective.

In 1956 Khrushchev's Secret Speech, detailing some of the frame-ups and tortures carried out by his predecessor, alienated many.

At the time of the execution of Imre Nagy in 1958, the leader of the

British Communist Party, Harry Pollitt, privately told the *Pravda* correspondent in London that "the basic reason for the weakness of the English Communist Party is the policies of the CPSU. All our crises come to us from abroad." Pollitt, the *Pravda* man added, had said that the sentence on Nagy was "a failure from the point of view of the situation in the Western countries." Of course, this was, in one sense, because no effort was made to produce a faked public trial. Once again we see the USSR as more unpopular in the comparatively moderate post-Stalin period than at the height of Stalinist terror—*because* of the completeness of falsification in the earlier phase!

Difficulties had already arisen over the original intervention against the Hungarian Revolution in 1956. Ilya Ehrenburg, then a member of the Communist Front World Peace Council, reported in December of that year that many of its branches were against "our action," with only "the Brazilian, Austrian and Finnish movements" remaining supportive. But what is surprising and symptomatic is that there was a persistent drift back from this shock therapy into a renewal of pro-Soviet delusions. The invasion of Czechoslovakia in 1968 was even more a rubbing of sensitive noses in reality. Again, while many were permanently cured, the 1970s saw (for example) Britain's Labour National Executive Committee holding "party to party" talks with the Communist Party of the Soviet Union, represented by Stalin's veteran Comintern thug Boris Ponomarev—and this at just the time when Moscow was rearresting the octogenarian leaders of Baltic Social Democracy, who had already served long sentences for, in effect, Labour views. But the then NEC, or its advisers, contrived not to know these things.

The matter of the Soviet past and present was thus grasped only temporarily and inadequately. Still, each new outbreak of disillusionment brought its contribution of understanding. Professor Mark Almond at Oxford has argued that the debacle of the Sandinistas had an even greater effect on the older revolution-groupies than did events in the Soviet Union itself.

On the other side of the account, one of the most extraordinary changes in the European consciousness was what took place in France after the publication there of Aleksandr Solzhenitsyn's *The Gulag Archipelago.* Over quite a short period, and no doubt it would be simplistic to credit it merely to that one cause, not only did the Soviet Union lose its appeal, but Marxism itself became (as is now said) only viable among an older stratum of village schoolteachers. French intellectual circles had experienced something like a Marxist monopoly. Now this was suddenly and catastrophically ended—so much so that French intellectuals now complain about the primitive Marxism found in other Western countries.

15.

As with the Webbs in the 1930s, we still find in the 1960s examples of admiration for the USSR precisely because it was bureaucratic. C. P. Snow, in his relations with the Soviets, favored fearful cultural apparatchiks like Alexei Surkov and Yuri Zhdanov out of what I called "Burintern solidarity." I added that

> one is reminded of the controversy between Lord Acton and Bishop Creighton, when the Anglican was inclined to excuse Innocent III's persecutions on administrative grounds, while the Catholic condemned them absolutely for reasons of inhumanity. Each of these solidarities—the bureaucratic and the humanist—in fact transcend mere political and religious allegiance. On any barricade I can think of, there is many a communist I should prefer to have on my side than Snow.

In the West full understanding and direct pro-Soviet views were indeed now incompatible. Various "social" falsehoods still circulated— for example, that the Soviet health service was in an admirable condition. In fact, the main distortions were now that the USSR was not an ideal but still an economic and social success; that it was at least better than, or no worse than, America; that it was a normal political entity in international affairs; and (for anti-Americans, but here not untruly) that it was anti-American.

And even to this day one reads such comments in Western academe as that anti-Communism strongly resembled Communism, the two being merely opposite and contrasting ideologies. Like antifascism and fascism? But the point here is not the obvious one (that to be against Communism meant for most people opposition to terrorist dictatorship) but that Western academics can still speak in this way— even perhaps think in this way.

Understanding that Stalin (and his regime) was monstrous and murderous is a minimum requirement for acceptance into civilized discourse. It should also have been clear that the post-Stalin Soviet Union, though no longer employing mass physical terror, continued to enforce a set of erroneous and virulent ideas on the minds of the citizens, and to punish dissent.

All the same, many only partly taken in by the Soviet line remained unconvinced that the issue was important. They realized that lies were being told and terror inflicted, even that the USSR did not look all that good. But they did not care; they still felt a measure of attraction to it, and an ability to forget the negative side. Some still saw the USSR as a respectable Socialist state; others as, if perhaps sometimes insufficiently active, a revolutionary standard-bearer for the world leading the Guevaras and such to victory.

It is true that, unlike the Cubans themselves, many revolutionary groups were now anti-Soviet on sectarian grounds, being (for example) pro-Beijing instead—the facts of Maoism having not yet emerged so starkly as those of Stalinism. Still, on Central American matters in particular, the old revolutionary romanticism fitted into Soviet policy. This adolescent revolutionism has proved hard for reality to reach. A friend of mine was in the main hotel in Managua when the results of the election in which the Sandinistas were defeated came through on television. He tells me that several West European leftists present broke into tears.

The Sandinista story may remind us of the projection onto very different countries of a variety of concepts long unfamiliar in the West, but having something of a romantic or emotional appeal. We still see the idealization of supposed "peasant revolutions" of one sort or another, which will distribute the land to the "peasantry." We heard a lot about Mao Tse-tung's movement as a peasant uprising with agrarian reform as its central aim, and similarly with the Vietcong. This long-standing attitude, transferred from country to country as its expectations are, over the years, seen to fail by all but the most verbal-visioned, seems based on a whole set of muddles. It is usually found in countries like England and America, where peasants have long ceased to exist— and where most of the proponents of "land distribution" elsewhere would not urge anything similar at home. The peasants of many Third World countries are indeed to one degree or another "oppressed," though not as much as under collectivization in Russia or the equivalent despotic disaster in Ethiopia. And, as Orwell says, it is common for revolutionaries to hate the system much more than they pity its victims. This would mean that, at least in many cases, ideology becomes a sort of mental trap. And when its bearers come to power they are, or are often, stuck with a program that produces far worse suffering among the peasantry than what was theirs under the original oppressors.

The secondary infection, by which revolutionary myths fill the minds of some members of the intellegentsia in our own countries, is something we cannot afford. How easily it can happen is revealed in almost incredible fashion by the student demonstrations in South Korea calling for unity with North Korea on North Korean terms. It has been explained that these students were very ill informed about real conditions in the North; but the probability seems to be that they were well enough "informed" but rejected the information as coming from their own establishment.

The advantages of the "left" regimes and movements in the eyes of the world media have thus not disappeared. They do not have to pursue "left" policies so much as to adopt "left" stances. Anthony Howard, then editor of the left-wing New Statesman, once pointed out that if Huey Long had only used left-wing phraseology he would have enjoyed wide support from the New York and London intelligentsia.

Much of the world thus emerged in many minds as a simple pattern of progressive states—good and never called dictatorships, and right-wing states—bad, and often oppressive (similarly, "death squads" were always right-wing). All determined by preconception—sometimes roughly applicable, sometimes absurd. We may note, though, that this was, and still often is, very largely directed at areas of the world of which the enthusiast has no direct knowledge, and that once imprinted he or she becomes immune to genuine information—as with the Soviet prototype.

Above all (as we shall develop in a later chapter), many agreed with the charge that Western intentions and armaments were to blame for the Cold War. It was largely on this basis that Soviet influence was—again!—brought to bear, with joint action by committed Western Communists and an array of progressives, as with the CND (Campaign for Nuclear Disarmament) in the United Kingdom. This mass organization publicly encouraged, and used the organizational skills of, the British Communist Party—that is, of a keen supporter of Soviet nuclear armaments. A friend of mine was at a public meeting when an open Communist, one of the speakers' platform, said that American policy would result in atom bombs on London. "Who'll drop those bombs?" my friend asked. And answer came there none.

16.

Meanwhile, both politicians and media now—still—sought the expressed opinions of "experts" on the Soviet phenomenon—some of whom were indeed under the influence of the remnants of Stalinism in the academy, but others of whom were well-meaning crackpots, or concerned to give the USSR, past and present, a fair deal. The whole question of "good motives" thus arises. But if you are in any sort of public position, or one in which you can in any way influence the public and the political leadership, and your judgment is, or could be, disastrous, the excuse seems inadequate.

Incredibly enough, as with the de-demonization of Hitler by the "institutionalist" academics in Germany, a new wave of Webb-style attitudes to the Stalinist phenomenon splashed over academe in the late 1980s—just at the time when the Soviet authorities themselves were massively validating the appalling realities.

A certain proportion of academics seem—and not only in this context—notably prejudiced against realities and persuaded by smoke and mirrors. We shall consider this phenomenon in its broader aspects, that is, in connection with the whole question of negative forces in education, in a later chapter. But meanwhile, we should note that knowledge and understanding of the Soviet phenomenon in particular was—and still is—deficient in the very professional circles supposedly devoted to its study.

As a broad generalization, we may say that in the postwar period, and into the sixties and seventies, the study of Russia was largely carried out by professors whose various expertise had taken them into active participation in matters of military and foreign-political importance. They were veterans of reality as well as of study. The deskbound professor of the prewar period, who was to emerge again in the next academic generation, was much less in evidence.

One of those then writing was Merle Fainsod, who in 1953 produced his excellent study *How Russia Is Ruled,* which he revised well in 1963. And here, alas, we are led into the first signs of trouble. After Fainsod's death, by a mischance too complicated to go into here, the task of producing a new edition fell to a young scholar, Jerry Hough.

Hough changed the title to the more polite *How the Soviet Union Is Governed,* and used the prestige of the original, adding, "By Jerry F. Hough and Merle Fainsod. Revised and enlarged by Jerry F. Hough." But the "revising" consisted of reversing and distorting the whole work.

To take a particularly revealing example: Fainsod's index gives over sixty references to forced labor camps; Hough's revision gives none. Again, while Fainsod spoke of millions of victims of Stalinism, Hough had a totally contrary view, speaking in terms of ten thousand or so shot. In his pseudo-Fainsod he takes the same view, though there and later admitting a possibility of "a figure in the low hundreds of thousands." Of course, even then the question was how many millions, or tens of millions, as is now fully confirmed in Russia. A single one of the mass graves lately dug up there holds more than Hough's original estimate. We should note that Hough's version of Fainsod was—and still is—a textbook.

Hough (who, it may be noted, was trained in institutional and socio-logical formulations rather than in history) also described Brezhnev's Soviet Union in strange terms. "The Soviet system [is] a very participa-tory one"; "the regime has become more tolerant of individual icono-clasm, including political dissent, than it was . . . in the Khrushchev era"; "Brezhnev came to power promising normalcy, and it was a pledge that he kept"; the Soviet Union is "a parliamentary system of a special type." "Pluralist" was a term also much used, not only by Hough (who also saw the Soviet and British constitutions as similar).

Hough is to be taken into account if only because he still figures (or did until very recently) as a guru on television and in the other media. And he was an influential precursor of (though not as negative as) the "revisionists" who came to notice in the late 1980s.

These formed a group which claimed to present a truer picture of the Stalin period than that prevailing among what they called "Cold War" Sovietologists. Their general theme was that the terror had been fairly minor—one American proponent wrote (like Hough) of "thou-sands" executed and "many thousands" imprisoned—the dead later raised to over 30,000, later still to over 600,000. This last figure relies on two KGB documents from the 1950s and 1960s. Both can be shown to be invalid. The first was repudiated by the Security Ministry General who made it public. The second produced figures for 1939–40 much lower than the proven executions of March–April 1940. Moreover, con-siderably higher figures have been given by the government, party and security officials concerned. The establishment of such figures is always one of the most refractory of historical tasks; and earlier historians had given estimates based on the evidence then available which were in certain respects too high, though long since suitably amended. But for the new sect, playing down the extent of the terror was not the only point: they also held that terror is not in any case of major importance, since institutional and social changes were the true essence of the period—though terror affecting millions directly and the whole population indirectly might also be thought of as a social phenomenon. They were also interested in the rise of new cadres, but not in the criteria for their promotion—servility, brutality, and coarseness of mind, constituting what, as we have said, is now called in Russia a "negative selection" of the new ruling class. Nor were they interested in the methods of personnel change—the denunciation and execution of predecessors. Others of this school wrote of the collectivization in a similar vein, as a social change, and they praised the party emissaries from the cities who effected it—i.e., bullied the peasants into submission.

Part of the trouble seems to be that they were (like Hough) sociologists by training, rather than historians, and sought (in rather the same context as that which produced Marxism) the structural rather than the essential, the form rather than the content. This also led them, like the Webbs before them, to accept official documents as better evidence than what they referred to as "anecdotal" accounts—that is, the firsthand testimony of actual witnesses which contradicted the official picture. As we now know, this unofficial evidence was vastly superior to the official, and even when not conclusive was not simply one vast fake, like the Communist product.

Once when I referred to the 1939 Soviet census as a "fake," one expert replied that no census was perfect, but that I was not thereby entitled to pick and choose which census I accepted. My objections to the 1939 census were: that the census taken in 1937 had been suppressed and the Census Board shot for "diminishing the population of the Soviet Union" so that the new Census Board had some incentive to exaggerate the numbers; that these new figures were announced in 1939 before the new Census Board had delivered its figures; and so on. All obvious enough, and Soviet publications soon confirmed the obvious—that millions reported in the 1939 document "existed only on paper." Yes, official, "documented" evidence was totally worthless—and a tiny modicum of common sense should have made this plain even to an academic.

Of course, Soviet materials published in the late 1980s and the 1990s have destroyed these and similar delusions. Or so you might think; but you would be underestimating the skill of the academic mind in devising evasive stratagems. Even in the true sciences, deep intellectual investment in what turns out to be fallacy is not easily given up.

Some of these scholars manqués were praised in predemocratic days in articles in Moscow by reactionary Soviet writers, who described them as "objective"—a traditional Soviet expression meaning reasonably uncritical of the old official line. In *Pravda* of 2 October 1990, the establishmenteer Professor Viktor Danilenko observed that there was a "new look" in foreign Sovietology. This was, he said, "welcome," for (in his view) it had "sharply raised the prestige of the professors of Sovietology. . . . Anti-Sovietism has begun to disappear from the works of contemporary Sovietologists." Just as it had in the time of the Webbs!

As one who was himself categorized a few weeks later at a plenum of the Central Committee, by the Stalinist writer Alexander Chakovski, as "anti-Sovietchik number one," I am well qualified to define this anti-Sovietism Danilenko complained about: determination to deploy the realities of Soviet history and the nature of the Stalinist mind-set. The revival of Stalinist attitudes in some circles in Russia in the mid-nineties has similarly led to a search by Moscow hard-liners for arguments from Westerners supporting the pro-Soviet stance.

The proponents of perverse reinterpretations were not in themselves very impressive, but they seemed novel and so "exciting" to uninformed editors, obtained academic posts and thus indoctrinated students. For even apart from revisionists proper, as the postwar years rolled on, the veterans had been increasingly replaced by a more mediocre (and less experienced) generation. Students were instructed that true scholarship must not be "judgmental." In lay terms this meant not only that verdicts, however soundly and factually based, must be avoided, but also that lines of research likely to lead to verdicts were discouraged. The safe subjects were those like "Cotton Prices in Uzbekistan"—thus peripheral research began to be the road to tenure.

Truly deleterious approaches, though sometimes published by university presses, are probably of little effect in improving the Stalinist image in the public mind, or even in the mind of what may be called the general intelligentsia as apart from a narrow academic substratum. A less indefensible, or less obviously indefensible, rehabilitation of the October Revolution is still occasionally, though not often, to be met in rather more impressive circles. At any rate, one historian, though Marxist historian, of repute and influence, Eric Hobsbawm, has lately argued:

- that Lenin in 1917 won the rural masses by his support, "contrary to the socialist programme," of the division of the land among the peasantry. Yes, he tried this maneuver, but they voted overwhelmingly against him in the elections he then held;
- that the proletariat were pro-Bolshevik, then and later, and indeed pushed Lenin forward. But the experienced proletariat—the railwaymen and the printers—opposed the Bolshevik takeover. And even within the new proletariat at the big factories such as the Putilov Works, where the Bolsheviks had gained organizational control (though not on a program of one-party dictatorship), workers were criticized by Lenin within weeks of the seizure of power for lack of "zeal and discipline" and the "stubborn tradition" of asking the Soviet government for less work and ("even worse") more pay. In 1918, of course, the factories voted in Mensheviks and other non-Bolsheviks and came out in massive strikes that Lenin put down (in his own words) "mercilessly," with major workers' risings in several industrial towns; while in 1921 the workers in Petrograd were closely linked with the Kronstadt Rebellion;
- that Lenin did not enforce socialist measures (this based on a remark of his in January 1918). But from May of that year he did enforce extreme "socialist" measures—as he several times admitted (and admitted as failures) after they were abandoned, under huge popular pressure, in 1921. In one of several similar comments he said: "We made the mistake of deciding to change over directly to Communist production and distribution";
- that "the Russian Revolution was made by the masses." Odd, then, that the Bolsheviks only got a quarter of the vote at the height of their popularity in the elections that followed—a good deal fewer than the British Conservatives in their 1997 debacle—and a minority even in Petrograd;
- that "one of the few achievements of the Russian Revolution which not even its enemies deny is that, unlike the other defeated multinational empires of the First World War, the Hapsburgs and the Ottomans, Russia was not broken into pieces." Well, yes.

Yet Hobsbawm, writing on our era, has been warmly welcomed in British liberal establishment circles.

17.

The phrase "Cold War attitudes" is still applied by certain academics to those of us who played a part in, or took an anti-Soviet view of, the long confrontation. These attitudes supposedly lead to our inevitably distorting the facts of history and being inappropriately judgmental.

They do not seem to grasp the idea that we might have become judgmental, and anti-Communist, after, and because of, learning the facts.

The author did indeed take part in the Cold War, first at the Foreign Office in what amounted to the period's equivalent of the Political Warfare Executive of 1939–45. Then he takes some pride in having briefed Senator Henry Jackson, who acknowledged this debt in several speeches (e.g., in the Senate, 27 September 1972 and 11 February 1977). Then he advised Margaret Thatcher over the whole of her period as leader of the opposition and Prime Minister, even drafting her first Iron Lady speech.

Far lesser offenses than these are held by the new anti-anti-Communists as disqualifying their perpetrators from the right to study, analyze and comment on Communist phenomena. My own legitimate scope is even more constricted by the fact that I also took part in the Hot War against Nazi Germany, and am thus also disqualified from studying National Socialism. (And, similarly, all Jewish scholars are obviously too prejudiced to embark on any such project.)

A last-ditch defense by the misinterpreters of the USSR is that while those who took a soft view of the regime were mistaken, those who took a hard view believed the regime could not be changed. This is untrue. I and as far as I know almost all those who took the "hard view" had continually expressed agreement with Orwell's remark that it would "either democratise or perish."

In general, radical misapprehension was more common among academics than among the Western public. Such academics were all too often not only inexperienced but also, as we have said, for the most part ignorant of the possibilities of history. They had no background of knowledge, let alone "feel" for the great slave empires of antiquity, the millenarian sects of the sixteenth century, the conquerors of medieval Asia. When Stalin procured the death of 6 or 7 million peasants in the terror-famine of 1933, he was doing no more than what Tamerlane had done—"laying waste" a rebellious territory with hunger rather than fire and sword. Any socioeconomist could tell us that this was rationally speaking impossible and therefore didn't happen—just as Tamerlane could not have erected that "pyramid" of seventy thousand skulls at Ispahan, for it would obviously have been "economically counterproductive."

One reason, in this sphere as in all the others, is clear. Some academics had not the imagination necessary to comprehend the alien phenomenon of the Soviet state, an aberrant entity not to be understood by accepted methods. All this by no means destroyed serious understanding of the Soviet past and present, but it did serve to confuse the issues.

This is demonstrated past argument by the record of the Wests' supposedly thinking classes on the Stalin regime. At this point I cannot resist quoting the dictum of a well-known American critic, Fredric Jameson, which puts in more dramatic form a view still, or again, to be found elsewhere. He says that Stalinism was a "success," having "fulfilled its historical mission to force the rapid industrialisation of an undeveloped country." This is, of course, fallacious on several grounds. Russia had already been fourth or fifth among industrial economies before World War I; Stalin's industrial advances could (as Russian scholars like Nikolai Shmelev and American scholars like Holland Hunter have long since demonstrated) have been achieved on the foundation of the 1929 economy, without collectivization, famine or terror; the advances were far and away smaller than claimed; the gigantism of enterprises was a grave distortion, as was pointed out to the Stalinists by (for example) Western automobile manufacturers; and Soviet-style industrialization was by world standards an anti-innovative dead end. In the circumstances, it is unclear how, or by whom, Professor Jameson felt empowered to speak for History.

One might suggest that a course on the credulity of supposed intellectual elites should be one of those given, indeed made compulsory, at universities—even, come to that, at theological colleges.

More generally, and not only in academe, this misunderstanding of a major force on the world scene could have proved disastrous in the period between the end of World War II and the collapse of the Soviet Union. As it was, its influence made the pursuit of a rational foreign policy difficult. It hardly needs saying that we must do our best to avoid, or prevent, anything resembling a repetition—in fact that the lesson should be learned.

CHAPTER VIII

◆

Launching the Cold War

1.

We do not propose to give a full history, or present a complete analysis, of the Cold War—that permanent crisis in international relations which held the world in its grip over the decades. We will, rather, examine certain basic elements, consider certain cruxes, and in particular present the Soviet ideological concepts that were its driving force, and the various methods of political or mental struggle that marked or defined it.

2.

Even during World War II Stalin's cooperation with the Western Allies was entirely a matter of realpolitik. And that cooperation was almost entirely one-way. The United States and the United Kingdom were at a disadvantage. Not indeed in practical terms. On the contrary, Stalin was desperately dependent on Western aid. The West, and especially the United States, provided huge supplies of essential equipment. It was of course in the interests of the Allies, and of the world in general, that the Soviet armies should defeat Hitler. But in return for the aid the West received little but further (and often impossible) demands, abuse and promises. What Stalin was able to get away with in connection with the Allies was quite remarkable.

Americans and Britons who served with their countries' military or political missions in the USSR tell the same story. At one point Churchill had to threaten to stop the convoys to Murmansk if Royal Navy representatives were not treated tolerably. One of dozens of examples of bad faith was Moscow's refusal, while the war was still being waged on land and sea, to allow American naval experts to see the captured German experimental U-boat center at Gdynia and thus help in the protection of our convoys.

On the Western side, over the years of the war, but dating back to the earlier self-deceptions of progressive opinion, we come across sheer ignorance, plus inept egoism. Harry Hopkins, to take one example, seems just to have accepted an absurdly fallacious stereotype of Soviet motivation, without making any attempt whatever to think, or to study the readily available evidence, or to seek the judgment of the knowledgeable. He conducted policy vis-à-vis Stalin with mere dogmatic confidence in his own (and his circle's) unshakable sentiments.

Some level of misreading of Soviet attitudes had indeed penetrated not only influential areas of the American establishment but also government circles, including the State Department itself. In his *Memoirs,* George Kennan says:

> The penetration of the American governmental services by members or agents (conscious or otherwise) of the American Communist Party in the late 1930s was not a figment of the imagination of the hysterical right-wingers of a later decade. Stimulated and facilitated by the events of the Depression, particularly on the younger intelligentsia, it really existed, and it assumed proportions which, while never overwhelming, were also not trivial. . . . [b]y the end of the war, so far as I can judge from the evidence I have seen, the penetration was quite extensive.

Kennan tells us that pro-Communist moods in the State Department had already resulted in the dissolution of the serious and professional Russian Department. Similar actions followed: some on a lesser scale, such as the Pentagon's mislaying of a senior American POW report on the Katyn Massacre.

Even during the war period Stalin committed acts almost ostentatiously offensive to civilized opinion. For example, the arrest and execution of Henrik Ehrlich and Viktor Alter, the leading figures in the Jewish Social Democratic Bund, on charges publicly given by the Soviet embassy in Washington as having tried to stop resistance to the Nazis. In 1945 we see the disappearance of Raoul Wallenberg.

It seems harder still to believe that any faith in Stalin might have survived one of his most open and treacherous acts early in 1945. The leaders of the underground Polish State and Army were induced, under Soviet safe conduct, to come out of the underground and negotiate with the Stalinist authorities. These were the men who had succeeded in Poland, unlike in any other Nazi-occupied country, in keeping the national organizations in being. They were headed by official representatives of the legal Polish government, allies of the West since 1939. When they emerged in March 1945, under the Soviet guarantee, to negotiate, they were arrested (and, after nine months in the hands of NKVD interrogators, "tried" and sentenced to long terms of imprisonment).

This extravagant proof of duplicity and repression against legitimate representatives of an ally did lead to Western protests; but these were not followed up. Instead, the United Kingdom and the United States brought pressure on the legitimate Polish government in London to come to some accommodation with the Communist puppet Committee then installed in Warsaw. If this was done (they said) Stalin would allow a multiparty coalition to rule democratically, so long as Soviet interests were not harmed. What actually happened, of course, was that Premier Stanislaw Mikolajczyk and others went to Warsaw and joined the Communists as a minor partner in the coalition, which was then recognized in the West as the legitimate government of Poland. Within a couple of years Mikolajczyk and the other democrats were in exile or jail, and the Communists had total power. Thus, by means of a brief charade, Stalin had obtained both complete Soviet control and recognition of it by the West, and all this *before* what we regard as the beginning of the Cold War!

3.

The Soviet assumption that all other political life-forms and beliefs were inherently and immutably hostile was the simple and central cause of that Cold War. Not merely were "capitalism" and "imperialism" sworn enemies of Moscow; this also applied to all non-Communist Socialists and all non-Stalinist Communists. This ideological compulsion saw the "world-historical process" as an unappeasable struggle between the Stalinist social order and the rest.

From the Communist viewpoint, there was never any question of a permanent accommodation between the USSR and the "capitalist" world. The choice before Stalin and his regime in 1945 was thus not whether to seek permanent and stable cooperation with the non-Communist sphere. It was to decide whether in the new period there should be a temporary relaxation, a reining back, of the ideology's inherent expansionism. From 1923 to 1939 the USSR had not pressed forward, but played a defensive game.

It has been argued that even in 1945 Stalin had not decided on his tactics for the postwar period, and that he for a time heeded the advice of such figures as Maxim Litvinov and Ivan Maisky, who, while suggesting hard bargaining with the West, nevertheless urged a strategy of accommodation for ten years or so (and as to taking "socialism" to Western Europe, another twenty).

Stalin himself, in no way abandoning confrontation in the long term, seems to have seen that the Soviet Union was exhausted by the war and would need a period of recovery and reconstruction. In 1945 he told the Yugoslav Communists, "The war will soon be over. We shall recover in fifteen or twenty years, and then we'll have another go at it." Thus, even from the point of view of a Soviet Union committed in principle to a global struggle, there was a case for a pause, and Stalin, himself physically exhausted in the latter half of 1945, may have considered it.

But the objective rationale did not match the subjective factor. It soon became clear that Stalin and his entourage regarded any relaxation as, apart from anything else, a seedbed for incorrect ideas and autonomous stirrings in the USSR itself: for something like political and ideological disintegration.

That is to say that the Cold War, as it actually turned out, was not inevitable. But over a longer period some similar confrontation must have developed, unless and until the whole mind-set of the Communist Party and its leadership eroded.

4.

At a 1990 conference on the Cold War in Moscow in what was still the Soviet Foreign Ministry, I got the warmest applause from both Soviets and Westerners when I said that Stalin and the Stalinists had waged it "not only against the West and the peoples of Eastern Europe but also against the peoples of the Soviet Union."

In 1945–46 Stalin was faced in his own empire with two problems—both, from his point of view, intractable except by political and mental repression.

First, in the East European countries he had overrun, and whose acceptance of overriding Soviet interests he felt he needed on both ideological and military grounds, it seemed impossible to secure reliable pro-Soviet regimes except by Communist-controlled dictatorships. This could not be effected except by the progressive repression of all democratic and pro-Western parties and ideas in the countries concerned; and thus must inevitably lead to Western reaction, particularly as it was flatly contrary to a whole series of agreements.

Second and even more crucial, in the USSR itself the war, and the alliance with Western powers, had caused a dangerous—to Stalinism—mood of hope for national and international normalization and relaxation.

The USSR was now exhausted, and the United States was strong. Against this, Stalin, as in the past, felt able to squeeze proportionately far more military investment out of his battered economy than would have been possible in the West. And American strength, with the major exception of the nuclear weapon, was not deployable; while Western Europe remained weak and powerless—and in France and Italy large and powerful Communist Parties and Communist-dominated trade unions were deployed on the Soviet side.

In November 1945 Maxim Litvinov, at that time Deputy Foreign Minister of the USSR (who, as his wife told me, had become not merely tactically but even ideologically disenchanted), was asked by the American envoy Averell Harriman what the West could do to satisfy Stalin. He answered: "Nothing." In June 1946, still in that post, he warned a Western journalist that the "root cause" of the confrontation was "the ideological conception prevailing here that conflict between the Communist and capitalist worlds is inevitable"—that is, no more than the doctrine long since announced by Lenin that "a series of frightful clashes" were bound to occur between the two systems, leading finally to the world victory of Communism. When the correspondent asked Litvinov, "Suppose the West would suddenly give in and grant all Moscow's demands? . . . Would that lead to goodwill and the easing of the present tensions?" Litvinov answered, "It would lead to the West being faced, after a more or less short time, with the next series of demands."

The view, the ideological concept, that the world was an arena in which the socialist or proletarian forces were locked in a lethal struggle with the imperialist or bourgeois forces, a struggle in which no lasting accommodation was possible and which would eventually end in worldwide Communist victory, lasted until 1990, when, as we saw, Shevardnadze denounced both in doctrine and in practice the conception of an international "class struggle," to be concluded only with the victory of "world socialism."

This was the essential dynamic of the Cold War, confirmed as to its later development by a number of Soviet high officials. For the crux of the international scene was (and is) the relationship between different political cultures with alien histories, attitudes and beliefs. As early as 1946 T. S. Eliot wrote in an extraordinarily perceptive essay introducing *The Dark Side of the Moon:*

> We are, in fact, in a period of conflict between cultures—a conflict which finds the older cultures in a position of disadvantage: from lack of confidence in themselves, from divisions both internal and between each other, from the inheritance of old abuses from the past aggravated by abuses due to the hasty introduction of novelties. The liberal . . . assumes . . . that the cultural conflict is one which can, like political conflict, be adjusted by compromise, or, like the religious conflict, be resolved by tolerance. . . . The frantic attempt, either through assembling representatives of more and more nations in public, or through discussions between representatives of fewer and fewer nations in private, to find a political solution to what is not merely a political problem, can . . . only lead to temporary and illusory benefits, unless the deeper problem is faced and pondered.

5.

In Stalin's time, but also in the pre-Stalin and post-Stalin Soviet Union, the dominant attitude to the outside world can best be described as a siege mentality. The obverse of this is, indeed, a sortie mentality. It has sometimes been suggested that the Cold War was a conflict between two "ideologies," equally (or so it appears) closed. But the Western approach was not an "ideological" one at all. It is important that this confusion of the issue be ended—if only because it features in low-level comment even now. The Western culture had, in a general way, a view of politics which included political liberty and the rule of law. It did not have a universal and exclusively defined mind-set.

Western resistance to Communism included proponents of an eventual Socialist society—for example, Ernst Reuter, who was the brave mayor of Berlin during the blockade in 1949, and the Social Democratic leader Vaino Tanner, militant in the Finnish resistance to Stalinist aggression.

It was in the London left-wing weekly *Tribune* (and at the same time in the *New York Times* of 10 March 1946) that Arthur Koestler published a remarkable article. He said, in part:

> No political treaties and trade agreements can guarantee peace as long as this world remains psychologically divided into two worlds, with persecution-mania on one side, growing alarm on the other. . . . Psychological armaments should be made an object of international negotiations and of political bargaining just as armaments in the air and on the sea. . . . The measure of "psychological armament" is the extent to which a government obstructs the free exchange of information and ideas with the outside world. A country which builds a Maginot line of censorship from behind which it fires its propaganda salvoes is committing psychological aggression. . . .
>
> Psychological disarmament should be made a bargaining object in all future negotiations, and given high priority on the political agenda. It should be made the pre-condition of concessions in the geographical, economic and scientific field. To get it accepted, the use of all levers of pressure, political and economical, would for once be morally justified.

6.

If Stalin had imposed his regimes in Eastern Europe rather more slowly and carefully, American demobilization and withdrawal from Europe might have taken place as at first planned, after which he could have moved gradually to the offensive.

This fails to take into account the pressures which, as we noted, had built up in the Soviet Union itself. One finds a consensus among those who speak of the country at the end of the war. It was strongly felt that the efforts and sacrifices must result in better things. Boris Pasternak tells us how a "presage of freedom was in the air." Andrei Sakharov recalls that "we all believed—or at least hoped—that the post-war world would be decent and humane." Vasily Grossman shows us a war hero fighting not only against the Nazis but also against the Soviet labor camps where his relatives had perished. Konstantin Simonov, a more orthodox writer, describes how the individual qualities developed in a soldier, "his mother wit, his intelligence, his courage," presented a danger to the Soviet regime.

Moreover, "Ivan had seen Europe," finding even Poland and the Balkans far more prosperous than the USSR, while the wartime alliance had to some extent encouraged thinking about Western ideas among the intellectuals. All in all, a dangerous mix from the Leninist-Stalinist point of view, and one which, if it had not been ruthlessly countered, might indeed have led to a disintegration of the system and saved the world from fifty years of danger and suffering. The following years saw a bitter struggle waged against the West and against Westernizing, or democratizing, tendencies in the Soviet empire.

There is no need to retrace the whole process by which the Soviets interpreted the Yalta and Potsdam agreements guaranteeing free elections in Eastern Europe into ruthless Stalinist takeovers. The peace treaties with Hungary, Romania and Bulgaria guaranteed free democratic rights to all antifascist parties. Any disputes were to be settled by the ambassadors in these countries of the three powers (the USSR, the United States and the United Kingdom). When the democratic parties were in fact persecuted and destroyed, the American and British ambassadors demanded the consultation provided for by the treaties. They were told that no "dispute" existed, so no meeting need take place.

It was not until 1946 that hopes of a Soviet return to "normality" were seen by the practical leadership of the West to be misconceived. Over 1945 and 1946, and even more in 1947 and 1948, Soviet actions first shook, then destroyed, such illusions. The democratic parties of the United States, Britain, France, Italy and Germany and the other West European states saw the realities and, however reluctantly, took up the challenge. They were faced, over the whole period, not only by the armed ideology of the Soviet Union but also in their own countries by ignorance and confusion over the mere facts—sometimes from converts to the hostile cause, sometimes from well-meaning innocents unaware of the real issues.

Attempts were later made by some Westerners to deflect the blame, or much of it, onto the West. For example, Isaac Deutscher, the influential anti-Western historian, stated that "it was only after the Communists had been ejected from the French and Italian governments that Stalin began to eject the anti-Communists from the Eastern European governments." In fact, it was in January 1945 that Vyshinsky's ultimatum secured the expulsion of Julius Maniu and the democratic parties from the Romanian government. Nikola Petkov and the Bulgarian equivalents were out by that summer. In East Germany the Social Democrats were destroyed in April 1946. Mikolajczyk and his Peasant Party had been excluded from the Polish government by

February 1947; and in the same month the Smallholder leadership in Hungary had been accused of conspiracy, and their Secretary-General was under arrest. It was in May 1947 that the Communist ministers left the governments of Italy and France.

Nevertheless, this canard was repeated by Eric Hobsbawm, as late as the 1990s, in his *The Age of Extremes*—arguing that in 1947–48 the Communists were eliminated from Western governments and that in Eastern Europe the Soviets "followed suit" by eliminating non-Communists from their governments. It is too much to ask of such analysis, erroneous as to fact, that it go on to concern itself with the even more striking point that in the West the Communists were not "eliminated" from legal opposition, while in Eastern Europe the non-Communist opposition was crushed and its democratic leaders executed or jailed. (At a Moscow seminar in late Soviet times, I found that their establishment historians were saying that both the USSR and the West were to blame for the Cold War in Eastern Europe, with the Soviets backing the "extreme left" and us backing the "extreme right." In fact, all of the parties supported by the West were well left of center, with the possible exception of the Romanian Liberals, who might be called moderate rightist. The younger scholars at this seminar without exception put the entire blame on the USSR.)

The Stalinist momentum, following these earlier successes, led to the coup in Prague, the Berlin blockade, and the full Communist confrontation with the governments of the West.

7.

A recent Moscow article suggests that if Stalin had not believed (quite rightly) that the Soviet Union would soon make its own nuclear weaponry, he might have adopted a less aggressive strategy, even perhaps accepting the Marshall Plan. Whatever may be thought of that, it is certainly true that the emergence of the American nuclear weapon in 1945 profoundly affected the thinking of everyone concerned with international affairs.

American possession, and for a time monopoly, of the bomb indeed marked a crucial change in Stalinism's operational context. From 1945 there could no longer be much hope in Moscow that the United States would be unable to project its military power. Over the decades the bomb led to restraint: neither the West nor the Communists could really face a nuclear war; and though things were sometimes unpleasantly dangerous, we can agree with Thomas Powers when he says that in a sense the winner of the Cold War was the atom bomb.

The American bomb meant that the West had at its disposal, for the time being, a weapon giving it an advantage more than compensatory for any inferiority in other military and political fields. The United States, also relevantly, had a bomber force the Soviet Union could not match. This was largely true, and of high deterrent value, even after the first Soviet bomb was tested in 1949.

As is now generally admitted, a Soviet bomb would not have been achieved for several years more but for the success of Soviet espionage in obtaining secret information from Western scientists associated with the Manhattan Project. That is to say, political ideas in the minds of certain capable physicists and others took the form of believing that to provide Stalin with the bomb was a contribution to world progress. They were wrong. And their decisions show, once again, that minds of high quality in other respects are not immune to political or ideological delirium. (As we have noted, the German Nobel Prize physicists Johannes Stark and Philipp Lenard were extreme Nazis.) In the Soviet case, those involved thought they knew better than mere politicians like Churchill. They didn't.

Knowledge of the horrifying power of the new bomb had a profound psychological impact on the Western public. Those who became involved in the various "Peace Campaigns" usually thought that concessions by the West, rather than deterrence, would or might save the world. That the Soviets had no real concern for internationalizing in the nuclear sphere was made clear when the UN Scientific and Technical Committee, which included Russian and Polish scientists and the Communist Professor Frédéric Joliot-Curie, reported unanimously that inspection and control over the whole process of production was desirable and technically possible. Vyshinsky, as the Soviet representative, rejected this view as "an assault on State sovereignty" (on 9 November 1948). In the UN Political Committee, he put it bluntly: "We are not obliged to subordinate ourselves or to render an account in this matter to any international organs."

The Soviet leadership both under Stalin and later wished to avoid nuclear war. But it never abandoned, until 1991, the basic policy of irreconcilability with all other political systems and ideas, nor the ultimate aim of Communist victory on a world scale. Nor did its military doctrine ever abandon the nuclear option, especially on the tactical battlefield.

Fortunately, Moscow retained enough prudence, or sanity, to understand first the power of the Western deterrent and, second, its own failure to disintegrate the Western will by psychological or political warfare.

It seems even more fortunate, given the Maoist attitude to nuclear war, that Communist China played no decisive role. The Soviet leader Mikhail Suslov reported to the Central Committee in 1962 that "when a Czechoslovak journalist, in a conversation with Tao Chu, a member of the Central Committee of the CCP, pointed out that in Czechoslovakia, where 14,000,000 people live, the whole nation might perish in the event of thermo-nuclear war, he was given the reply, 'In the event of a destructive war the small countries of the Socialist camp will have to subordinate their interests to the general interests of the entire camp as a whole.' Another responsible official of the Chinese People's Republic, in a conversation with Soviet representatives, asserted that Comrade Togliatti, Secretary-General of the Italian Communist Party, was wrong when he expressed concern for the fate of his people and said that in the event of thermo-nuclear war all Italy would be destroyed. 'But other peoples will remain,' said this official, 'and imperialism will be annihilated.'"

This comes, indeed, from a partisan source—from the Soviets. But it is in accord with Nehru's conversation with Mao Tse-tung when the latter said that in a world war, even if half the population were destroyed, socialism would be victorious and soon make up the deficit. This takes the totalitarian view to its logical extreme, and not many Communist leaders would have subscribed to it, openly at least. Still, it well illustrates the possible dangers of their attitude that all other political life-forms are to be regarded as hostile—as fundamentally, irretrievably hostile, and destined in one way or another for destruction as soon as this might be feasible.

8.

Stalin knew that the United States was, as he put it, the most powerful state in the world. This was especially true from a Marxist point of view, that is, economically. And taking the West as a whole, vis-à-vis the "Socialist camp," it was even more apparent. How could the Communists hope to prevail against these "objective factors"? Lacking the economic and technological power to outmatch the West, the Soviets could only hope to achieve their ends by massive deception of the Western publics and governments.

So when the leaders of the West learned their lesson, they had to cope not only with their opponents *à l'outrance* in Moscow, but also with the sections of their own publics who, to greater or lesser extents, accepted Moscow's disinformation.

Politically, the West went through a very vulnerable period. Even so, American—and potentially West European—power was such that it could not be faced directly. This was especially so after the formation of the North Atlantic Treaty Organization and the blocking of Communist power in France and Italy. So, as was to be the case throughout the Cold War, this Western defensive strength was attacked as being inherently aggressive. The central theme of the Soviet operation against the Western public mind was "peace." Every mobilization of Western power, every Western failure to accept Soviet proposals in negotiation, every speech, book, broadcast or article by a Westerner conveying the facts about Stalinism, were branded as offenses against peace. Vast "Peace Campaigns" were launched in the West, with agitation, mass meetings, polemics in the press and on the radio. All this at the cost of millions of dollars.

The West's response was on a much more limited scale, and, at that, most of it was from individual sources. George Orwell's and Arthur Koestler's dramatizations of the madness of Stalinism were probably more effective than a vast pro-Soviet demonstration in Trafalgar Square. But this was because the nature of Soviet reality was itself showing through the fog of official misrepresentation. Its own actions increasingly shook would-be sympathizers. A number of reputable firsthand accounts of life and politics in Stalin's empire were appearing, and sound analyses of its nature were being written.

Western governmental counteraction in itself was, by Moscow's standards, small-scale and low-funded. Its one highly effective counterstroke was to subsidize radio's Russian and East European services—in particular the politically informed broadcasts of Radio Liberty and Radio Free Europe. The Soviet response was a huge and incomparably more expensive jamming operation, which was only partially successful. Of course, anyone caught listening to it was subject to immediate arrest. Apart from that, Soviet citizens had nothing to go by except the vast and penetrating voice of Soviet propaganda, which portrayed the West as fascist cannibals (a quite normal image) and induced a measure of mass psychosis in much of the population. The way in which ignorance prevailed as late as 1987 was strikingly illustrated by the Moscow correspondent Xan Smiley (*Daily Telegraph*, 14 December 1987), who said that "I often mention that compulsory national service in Britain and America was abandoned about a generation ago—and they always look at me in disbelief. Everything here is mentally geared up for war. Readiness for war against capitalism is part of education. We in the West, it is assumed, are psychologically even readier."

Western government leaders engaged in the struggle for the support of their own citizens mainly with general pronouncements, though there were very occasional direct polemics at the international level, as when the UK delegation to the United Nations officially presented it with the secret Soviet Forced Labour Codex.

Two initiatives in the intellectual arena were, however, of great value. Under a presidential instruction, American secret funds were provided to the Congress for Cultural Freedom, almost all of whose members were from the moderate but anti-Communist left. They produced an array of literary-political journals in the West—*Encounter, Preuves, Quadrant* and so on—which successfully ended the fairly easy ride pro-Soviet intellectual circles had enjoyed in the 1940s. When, many years later, it was revealed that *Encounter* was financed by "CIA money," there was a minor row about various editors not having been told what was, after all, a secret. It was never alleged that the CIA, or the American government, had intervened in any way in the editing, and many contributors, including a Marxist professor and a leading counterculture spokesman, sprang to *Encounter*'s defense, with the Labour, later Social Democratic, leader Roy Jenkins commenting aptly that if the CIA had supported the periodical, this was to its credit.

The other effective governmental action of which I am aware was the founding by Labour Foreign Secretary Ernest Bevin of the Foreign Office's Information Research Department, in which I myself served for a number of years until 1956. Repeating, on a far smaller scale, the Political Warfare Executive of the Hitler war period, its role was to discover, analyze and make available to journalists and others the real facts—and real views—of the Soviet milieu. The full history of these attempts to present, and success in purveying, the Western investment in the political struggle is yet to be written. Apart from these instances, it will reveal an extraordinary combination of shortsightedness and credulity.

At any rate, to counter the huge Soviet investment in ideological and political warfare, there was always reluctance in Western political circles to funding countermoves—even though these were based largely on making the realities of the Communist order and Communist actions clear to the citizens of both "camps." Nor was this shortsightedness merely a result of a pro-Communist, or détente-deluded, left.

9.

The Soviet ideological offensive was, of course, differently conceived. It was naturally concerned to represent Soviet actions and ideas in the best possible light. As to actions, this took the form of denial in some cases and verbalism in others—the phrase "People's Democracy" was a special part of the panoply.

This had effects with some minds: on the forced labor issue, to which we have referred, a French intellectual, Jean Lafitte, when a witness at the Rousset libel trial in 1950, was asked, "If labor camps like those which have been described to us do exist at Kolyma, would you agree to condemn them?" He answered, "If I am asked, 'If your mother is a murderer, would you condemn her?' I would reply: 'Sir, my mother is my mother and will not be a murderer!'"

An extreme case, no doubt, but there were plenty of extreme cases, and many more who were prepared to regard such matters as either unproven (despite hundreds of witnesses to the facts) or as immaterial. Immaterial, that is, in the context of taking a comfortable view of the USSR. But, of course, to have such misconceptions of a world power was to build one's world view on sand.

In addition to the eclipse of critical standards of judgment which marked those whose allegiance was to the Soviet Union and the Communist Party, we find an accompanying penumbra of less committed misunderstanding which obscured the realities over a far wider section of Western society. Or, to use a different metaphor, to those symbolic birds the hawk and the dove should be added not only the cuckoo but also the ostrich.

The fear of war, and now, more lethally than ever, of nuclear war, led many to believe, or fear, that their own governments could avoid it by pursuing policies acceptable to the Soviet government—even, in many cases, to the belief that surrender might be a better option than deterrence. But of course even a world effectively conquered by the USSR would have been beset by an endless cycle of schisms and rebellions, fought with the utmost ruthlessness and with every available modern weapon. As early as 1944 Milovan Djilas, who was then a leading Yugoslav Communist, was told by a Soviet general that "when Communism has triumphed throughout the entire world, then warfare will take on an ultimate bitterness." We know that Stalin and the Communist chieftains of Eastern Europe planned an assault on Communist Yugoslavia itself, which was abandoned in part because of their then overriding fear of the West. In Hungary in 1956, the first open clash came between two Communist-headed governments (together with a barely averted war between the USSR and Poland). In 1968 the Communist USSR invaded Communist Czechoslovakia; and in the following year full-scale battles between the Communist USSR and Communist China were in progress on the Ussuri River, with all-out nuclear war a near thing. In 1978 the war between Communist Vietnam and Communist Cambodia occurred; and later the fighting between Vietnam and China. As the Soviet general told Djilas, eventually the proliferating sects and factions of Communism "will undertake the reckless destruction of the human race in the name of the human race's greater 'happiness.'" You might be Red *and* dead.

Public debate on the ethics of defense produced a variety of arguments and raised a variety of problems. On the issue of deterrence, it may seem that the prospect of nuclear warfare was so humanly intolerable that whatever deterred it was morally justifiable. But the counterargument also derived from the intolerableness of nuclear war—that if deterrence failed, the moral burden of using the nuclear weapon could or should not be faced.

These dilemmas are familiar enough. Various moral pronouncements attempted to reconcile them, at least in part. But when the hierarchies of the Roman Catholic Church in America and France issued contradicting statements, less professional moralists may have felt that these were all too often attempts to square the circle and provide a balm to the consciences concerned. At any rate, it seems obvious that if we accepted deterrence in any sense at all, the deterrent must be adequate, and unquestionably adequate, to deter. To seek to solve the moral problem by paring down the deterrent to a point at which its deterrence value no longer carried full conviction would have been to have the worst of both worlds. Yet this is where we seemed to be pointed by those who wanted to be able to say abashedly, like the girl with the baby, that we had a deterrent, but only a little one.

Needless to say, other views also had their contradictions—in particular unilateral nuclear disarmament, which carries the corollary that it would encourage conventional war, which would swiftly become nuclear.

10.

So far, we have examined the main and major causes of the extremely dangerous period that followed the end of World War II.

All this is sometimes disputed on the grounds that Western policy over the years can be faulted for mistakes; and not only mistakes but destructive and self-defeating reactions.

It was urged against Western policies that some of those states we had as allies in the Cold War were otherwise deplorable—authoritarian or dictatorships. Yes, and in the war against Nazism it was similarly argued that Britain at first was allied only with an undemocratic Poland and a corrupt France; that the Gaullist Free French who then supported us ruled only colonial territories; that later our most effective ally was the Greek military dictatorship of General Ioannis Metaxas, who in 1941 won the first Allied victory over Fascism. Then we had the feudal Ethiopian regime, which we restored to power. Later still, Britain and America took as their principal allies Stalin and Chiang Kai-shek, neither of them stainless democrats. And similarly with the alliances of the Cold War. In fact, it is impossible to take seriously a notion of world politics that suggests a stainless record, unviable outside the sphere of those the Scots call the Unco' Guid.

Indeed, it could be argued that some more moralistically pretentious democratic governments, such as that of Sweden at its worst, were on balance an asset to the Stalinists rather than to our side.

Another phrase much sneered at by hesperophobes was "the Free World." They were able to point out all sorts of imperfections within the Western sphere. But in comparison with Stalinism, this was rather like saying the expression "pure water" is absurd—all sorts of salts being in solution even in the best. So (it might be said) there was no essential difference between it and brine.

Of course, none of this is to suggest that the West acted throughout in an impeccable manner, beyond all moral criticism. No political process—not even Gandhi's—could ever merit such an accolade.

CHAPTER IX

◆

Missiles and Mind-sets:
The Cold War Continues

I.

The period between Stalin's death in 1953 and the emergence of the Brezhnev regime in 1964 saw continued progress in Soviet armaments: the detonation of the first deliverable hydrogen bomb in 1953, the launching of the first satellite in 1957—the latter marking the achievement of an intercontinental ballistic missile.

The satellite launch, followed by other Soviet space achievements, had a major propaganda effect. There was a strong impression that the Soviet Union deployed a superior science and technology. And this was, of course mistakenly, thought to have produced a "missile gap" in which the United States was outgunned—though in fact the Soviet Union had not really caught up in terms of effective deployment.

The Cuban missile crisis in 1962 was, in this context, an attempt to outflank America's general superiority. The Soviet retreat was accompanied by much, though unpublicized, comment in Moscow military and political circles to the effect that the USSR would never again be caught in a position of weakness. The period that ensued and that only ended in the Soviet collapse at the end of the 1980s saw the continuity of the totalitarian mind-set. In one sense, the Soviet leaders, especially after Khrushchev's fall, were not red-hot ideologists. On the other hand, their minds were such that they had no other way of conceiving, or even justifying, their role. Even if doubts had entered one or another mind—as, however minimally and vaguely, they seem to have entered Khrushchev's—they could barely find expression. His successors were

men who—unlike Khrushchev and his generation—had had no experience whatever of pre-Soviet times. They were all mere products of the
apparatus. They had no other way of "thinking." Their view of the
world remained that of sectarian hostility to all other sources of political ideas and political power, and an almost ineradicable conviction that
struggle on a world scale was their historical mission.

Tactics, and the assessment of opportunity, varied with Marxist
assessments of the balance of forces. So in the mid-1960s, the time
when Stalin had, in fact, foreseen that the USSR would be in a position
to "have another go," we entered the second main phase of the Cold
War—on which we shall go into more detail. For it is at about this time
that a decision seems to have been made in the Kremlin to take on the
West in armaments and on a world scale.

The expression "offensive against the positions of imperialism"
began to appear regularly in the Soviet press in 1965. The first use of
the phrase seems to have been by Brezhnev in an address to the congress
of the Romanian Communist Party on 20 July 1965, when he noted
that "some years ago" the Communist Parties had already concluded
that the relation of forces had shifted in their favor, and that in the
meantime this had reached such a stage that "the progressive forces are
now on the offensive." The call for this "offensive" was formalized in
the manifesto of the Communist Parties in November (*Pravda*, 28
November 1965).

As to the scope of Soviet ambitions, in June 1968 Foreign Minister
Andrei Gromyko flatly asserted in his speech to the Supreme Soviet:

> The Soviet Union is a great power situated on two continents, Europe
> and Asia, but the range of our country's international interests is not
> determined by its geographical position alone. . . . [T]he Soviet people
> do not plead with anybody to be allowed to have their say in the solution
> of any question involving the maintenance of international peace, con-
> cerning the freedom and independence of the people and our country's
> extensive interests. . . . During any acute situation, however far away it
> appears from our country, the Soviet Union's reaction is to be expected in
> all capitals of the world.

Though, of course, equivalent Western reaction to events in Poland was
illegitimate.

One would have thought Gromyko's claim to a place in the sun was unequivocal. Yet some Westerners extracted a fairly harmless intent from it. They argued that all Gromyko urged, and so all the Soviet Union wanted, was the status of a global power coequal with the United States. On this argument, the Soviet Union for decades put in an enormous effort and overstrained its economy for the right to have its opinion "listened to" in discussions of world problems! And if we interpreted it as meaning that the Kremlin simply wanted a half share with the West in every sphere, it remained nonsense. Were we really to envisage a peaceable world in which every country was ruled by a stable coalition of Communists and democrats? Or alternate countries that were Communist and non-Communist, with no attempt to spread the power of the former into the latter?

The idea that Soviet expansionism was in later years simply a "great power" matter hardly holds up. We need not, indeed we cannot, sort out the components of the expansionist motivations. We certainly cannot exclude an "imperialist" element in the mix, but there are a number of arguments against overstressing it. First, the expansion, except in Afghanistan, was not in the Russian interest area. And in fact, the army leadership, naturally the keepers of strategic tradition, still thought in terms of Europe and Asia and resisted the new trend. The various Soviet adventures overseas were, of course, tied up with the enormous naval expansion of the Khrushchev and post-Khrushchev era, both effect and cause of this new transoceanic colonialism—though, as ever, rational thinking on naval deployment seems to have been lacking. A prominent official of the period once asked me exasperatedly how they could have built a big fleet in a sea it could not get out of. (It is true there are supposed to have been plans for a seizure of the Straits, by *Spetsnaz* troops, but even if that were plausible, the ships would have been sitting targets.) The navy was extremely expensive, and contributed greatly to the economic burden of military production. And that level of production was itself an argument against any but a commitment to arms at all costs.

And meanwhile, all theoretical pronouncements, both public and secret, gave the essentials of Soviet foreign policy, as enumerated by Gromyko in his book *The Foreign Policy of the Soviet Union* (Moscow, 1975):

> The Communist Party subordinates all its theoretical and practical activity in the sphere of foreign relations to the task of strengthening the posi-

tions of socialism, and the interests of further developing and deepening the world revolutionary process.

2.

But the USSR, and the whole Soviet bloc, were still economically far weaker than the USA and the West. In that context, further steps were taken to persuade the West not to match the Soviet armament drive. This was the Soviet concept of "détente."

Brezhnev stated the political results he sought from "détente" clearly enough: "In conditions of international tension, in bourgeois countries, the reactionary elements become active, the military raise their heads, anti-democratic tendencies and anti-Communism are strengthened. And conversely, the past few years have shown quite clearly that, in conditions of slackened international tension, the pointer of the political barometer moves left" (speech to the Conference of European Communist Parties at Karlovy Vary, 24 April 1967).

Translated out of Sovietese, this signified that from the Soviet viewpoint, détente was intended to weaken Western vigilance, making it easier for appeasers and pro-Soviet elements to come to power.

The ideological struggle, Soviet leaders often insisted, should be continued, and even intensified, during a period of détente. As Brezhnev put it, "Our Party has always warned that in the ideological field there can be no peaceful coexistence, just as there can be no class peace between the proletariat and the bourgeoisie." On 27 June 1972, at a dinner for Fidel Castro, he added:

> While pressing for the assertion of the principle of peaceful coexistence, we realize that successes in this important matter in no way signify the possibility of weakening our ideological struggle. On the contrary, we should be prepared for an intensification of this struggle and for its becoming an increasingly acute form of struggle between the two social systems.

Soviet insistence on the continuation of the ideological struggle was often misunderstood. As Walter Laqueur remarked, in the West "Soviet insistence on the continuation of the ideological struggle is all too often not taken seriously"—because the concept of such struggle is alien to Western thought. People were, Laqueur argued, inclined to think that Soviet pronouncements were merely a matter of lip service to doctrine.

In fact, however, "ideological struggle is not something which concerns the philosophers. It is a synonym for political struggle, and political struggle, needless to say, means power, not only the power of ideas, but also some far more tangible things." Laqueur added that the notion sometimes held by Western statesmen, that Soviet policy was difficult to understand (and he quotes Chancellor Willy Brandt directly to that effect) was only the case "if one refuses to take seriously what Soviet leaders are saying" and if one refused to compare their sayings with their actions.

Thus, this "ideological struggle" was not a matter of winning well-conducted philosophical debates at international congresses—though even as to theoretical argument, Lenin cogently said that his controversial methods were "calculated to evoke in the reader hatred, aversion and contempt . . . calculated not to convince, but to break up the ranks of the opponent, not to correct the mistake of the opponent, but to destroy him."

Through the entire "détente" period, the Soviet "ideological" offensive went ahead. At home in the USSR, there was a continuous flow of propaganda (the viciousness of whose tone is still perhaps not sufficiently appreciated abroad) against the internal evils and the international aggressiveness and militarism of the West, blanketing the country with harsh abuse and plain lies. Abroad, every possible medium was employed to blacken the Western governments and their friends, to assist their enemies, and to undermine their military defenses and their political will.

During the last years of the regime, Soviet officials, including spokesmen for the Central Committee's Foreign Department, wrote that the Brezhnevite "détente" was a deception; that the Soviet stance remained expansionist; but that the Western governments' reaction prevented any substantial gains—i.e., that in spite of all their efforts, our policies remained effective.

3.

A common misconception in the West was (and is still) that there was an "arms race" between the United States and the USSR for which Washington was at least as much to blame as Moscow. As to arms races in general, as the British historian Michael Howard has pointed out, there have been arms races that did not lead to war, and wars that were not preceded by arms races. Andrei Sakharov, from his unchallenged moral position, even suggested that an arms race might have a sobering effect by proving how fruitless, as well as how dangerous, the results must be.

It may be appropriate to give the view of another Soviet physicist (and Nobel Prize winner) who had himself barely avoided execution. Lev Landau's conversations, as reported to or bugged by the KGB, are on record. On I December 1956 he said: "If our system cannot fall apart in a peaceful way, then a third world war, with all the horrors it would create, is not avoidable. Therefore the question about the peaceful liquidation of our system is, in essence, a question of the fate of humanity." On 4 December 1956 Landau said: "I am of the following belief: if our system is liquidated without war—no matter whether it be by revolution or evolution—then a war will not occur. Without fascism there will be no war."

Generally speaking, the Soviet arms effort over the period from the mid-sixties to the mid-eighties proceeded at the maximum feasible rate, almost regardless of the occasional bursts of American rearmament. (There were, of course, particular investments in response to particular Western armaments.) And arms control treaties were as far as possible negotiated with a view to their compatibility with Soviet military planning. (Or were, on occasion, broken, as with the Krasnoyarsk radar.)

And once again we come across the widespread notion among a stratum in the West that the establishment of facts and the expression of opinions unwelcome to the Soviet regime was itself an act of "Cold War." I remember that a short biography of Lenin I did for Frank Kermode's Modern Masters series—a fairly mild one, too, by modern standards—was denounced as a "Cold War" production by the London *Times.*

This notion of Moscow taking offense and therefore hardening their policy was common in the West. There was no real warrant for it. Of course, so long as they believed that going through the motions of being offended would influence Western policy makers, they went through the motions. But, as Gromyko said, the Politburo based their policies not on whether or not they were offended, but solely on what would give them a real advantage.

But even if this is not accepted, such acts as George Bush's refusal to receive Andrei Sakharov's widow Elena Bonner (unlike Mrs. Thatcher or M. Mitterand), as with President Ford's refusal to receive Alexander Solzhenitsyn, were clearly based on the notion that advantages could be obtained by not offending Moscow.

Moscow did not reciprocate. At that very time, the Kremlin gave a lunch for Georges Marchais, the head of the French Communist Party— that is, we could not receive the wife of a man persecuted merely for the expression of his opinions, while they could receive the organizer of a political machine devoted to the overthrow of the Western order!

We need not trace the details of the Soviet campaign in the West. A few examples will suffice. Thus the Soviet investment in the anti–neutron bomb campaign in Western Europe alone is estimated at around a hundred million dollars. And this was a single operation. As to the detail, there are numbers of cases of hitherto unsuspected journalists, peace activists and others proving to be Soviet agents, sometimes caught with large sums from Moscow having been traced to them. A typical case was that of the French journalist Pierre-Charles Pathé, sentenced in 1980 as a KGB agent (whose Soviet controllers worked at UNESCO) with the role of spreading disinformation on behalf of Moscow. Literally hundreds of articles based on information falsified in the KGB "service A" were put out by him, full in particular of allegations against the CIA. The KGB's aims are obvious enough. What is extraordinary is the wide success of these operations.

The record of a great part of the West German media was a dreadful example. Strong words, no doubt, but surely not too strong when one considers that their representatives, as we have noted, saw East Germany as not only politically but even economically successful—and this in spite of GDR-sponsored trips through the actuality, in their own near neighborhood and with no language barrier.

4.

One result of the Western mood was that in negotiating for a nuclear agreement, the mere aim of getting an agreement, and thus presenting the Western publics with a success, sometimes led Western governments to accept unsatisfactory commitments.

The negotiations for various treaties were of course conducted from the American side with the Soviet government, and from the Soviet side with the American government *and* the American and Western publics. The history of these negotiations and treaties is complex. Here we are only concerned with the views taken, the mental atmosphere. The susceptibility of the West to deception was seen at two levels: that of the fairly influential Western minority who to one degree or another tended to pro-Soviet views; and those among, or with a direct influence on, the Western foreign policy establishment who to one degree or another believed that the Soviet Union was at least an unexceptional member of the international community.

To put it another way, "idealists" thought the Soviet Union to be a good society, and "pragmatists" thought it to be a normal society. Both were wrong.

As we have said, this is understandable in part because of the extreme mental pressures of the nuclear confrontation, and the apparent inability of Westerners to influence the other side as compared to that side's political input to the Western publics and governments.

Between the United States and the USSR, as the other and initially roughly equal major nuclear power, negotiations on arms control were rightly seen as essential; it is fair to say that such moves to some slight extent cooled down Kremlin paranoia. But the dangers in the international sphere were not to be mastered by détente—nor were the Soviet leaders moderate-minded men equally seeking accommodation.

We have spoken earlier of the mental quirks which led a section of those Westerners critical of their own society to temper the wind to the failings of that society's enemies. This applied, of course, not only to comparing Western social faults to the imaginary social triumphs of the Soviet Union but also to the Soviets' supposedly more acceptable foreign policies. A search on Nexus of the use in American newspapers of the word "bellicose" of various leaders in the post-1979 period gives: Reagan—211 times, Thatcher—41, Brezhnev—5; and this in a period covering the Afghan war. As to those still further out, I noted (a perfectly ordinary example) the Catholic bishop of Stockton, California, bad-mouthing his own government as totally untrustworthy, but urging as a solution to our international troubles the reposing of total trust in—the Soviet leaders!

It is extraordinary to remember the uproar from his political opponents which met Ronald Reagan's characterization of the USSR as an "evil empire." I chanced to be, with Richard Pipes, at a seminar in the State Department when the about-to-be-delivered speech was circulated to us. We both thought it unwise, and indicated as much to the rather righteous speechwriter—mainly because of the expected reaction, which in fact occurred.

It was proclaimed that Reagan had called for a "crusade"—which he hadn't. (The truth of the "evil empire" phrase was of course later publicly endorsed by post-Soviet leaders, including the then Russian Foreign Minister Andrei Kozyrev.) An interesting feature of the phrase was that it had less effect in the non-English-speaking countries of the West, in the absence of alliteration.

This is not the place to discuss the details of the negotiations, the treaties and the proposed treaties between the United States and the Soviet Union. It will, however, be appropriate to consider how they were affected by the accompanying struggle for the minds of the Western publics and governments.

There is a never-to-be-forgotten observation of de Tocqueville's:

> It is especially in the conduct of their foreign relations that democracies appear to me to be decidedly inferior to other governments. . . . A democracy can only with great difficulty regulate the details of an important undertaking, persevere in a fixed design, and work out its execution in spite of serious obstacles. It cannot . . . await their consequences with patience.

This led to several lapses—in particular SALT II. As Lord Chalfont, former Labour Minister, said at the time it came before the U.S. Senate, in words applicable to the whole dangerous mishandling of the issue over the years:

> It is argued by people both in this country and in the United States that, if the Senate were to fail to ratify this treaty or outrage the Russians by demanding any form of amendment, the prestige of President Carter and of the whole American Presidency would be undermined; and that this would have effects upon the world balance of power altogether disproportionate to the importance of the SALT agreement. I find this argument difficult to follow. If the treaty itself is bad and ineffective, then it seems to me that it would be far more dangerous to accept it uncritically than to say so now while the Senate is in the process of debating the ratification. It will be no good saying it afterwards.

Andrei Sakharov sanely advised:

> Western leaders must not create the appearance of success in disarmament negotiations without real achievements: doing so, they would

deceive their own countries and—worst of all—provoke a unilateral disarmament. The danger is real because of both the tight secrecy in socialist
countries and the short-sightedness and domestic political maneuvering
of certain Western politicians, who are prepared to jeopardise the delicate
global balance for transitory political situations at home.

Fortunately, there were thoughtful senators and others who presented that body with careful analysis. In particular, the late Senator Henry
Jackson pointed out the slapdash acceptance of negative detail. He
noted that even SALT I had allowed a Soviet superiority in crucial
fields, and that neither SALT gave even the appearance, let alone the
substance, of equality between the Soviet Union and the United States.

In 1976 a team of selected "experts" had reported to the U.S. government that Soviet intentions were peaceable. After various objections,
a "B team" headed by Richard Pipes was formed. It concluded that the
USSR, though up to a point cautious, was prepared to fight and win a
nuclear war—an assessment later confirmed by Soviet military and
other documents. Where Western advocates of détente Brezhnev-style
have commonly denied that Soviet policy envisaged winning a nuclear
war, V. V. Zagladin, First Deputy Head of the International Department
of the Central Committee, noted as early as in 1988:

> In the 1970s and the first half of the 1980s the roots of many mistakes
> were in the conceptual approach. Repudiating nuclear war and conducting
> an active struggle for peace, we nevertheless proceeded from the assump-
> tion of the possibility of victory in a possible conflict. Here is the source
> of confrontation in relationships with the West. Only when the foreign
> and military policy concepts were adjusted away from that, only then did
> the foreign policy of our country become consistent. (*Komsomolskaya
> Pravda*, 26 June 1988, p. I)

The Communist armies, as we now know, were on a very short notice
for an invasion of West Germany, with the certainty of a tactical nuclear
exchange. And military thinking in Moscow inclined to a view that
nuclear war, while to be avoided, was winnable. From our point of view,
such a peace was always shakily based. And it depended on the Soviets
being denied superiority in military technology—as to not only missiles
but, for example, tank effectiveness.

But for the moment, the problem remained. At one point—an egregious example to be sure—we saw a ploy by the Soviet leadership that if their demands were not heeded, "harder-line" figures would prevail in the Kremlin. Stalin had already used this on Edward Stettinius in 1945! In the Brezhnev era, I remember Averell Harriman, who had been to Moscow as envoy of President-elect Carter, telling a group of us at the Woodrow Wilson Center that if the United States did not accept Brezhnev's demands, his "harder-line" rivals (so Brezhnev had himself told Harriman) would take over. This argument, not unknown in other spheres, amounts to saying: "If you don't give me what I want voluntarily, my successor will take it by force."

It is sometimes asserted, even nowadays, that "cold warriors" were committed (often "ideologically") to a dangerous, provocative and aggressive policy towards the USSR. I will quote some passages from a book I published on foreign policy in 1979, *Present Danger:*

(a) A programme for peace today must have a three-fold aim: first, it must prevent the destruction of the Western culture; second, it must work continually for the maintenance of a permanent truce between the two cultures, accepting for practical purposes the present existence of a divided world; and, third, it must hope for, wait for and encourage the emergence of the principle of civic consensus in the more backward despotic sphere, leading to the eventual establishment of a stable world peace.

(b) Perhaps the most realistic attitude for the West, barring total and unforeseeable change in the Kremlin, is to understand the dangers and revert to a sensible policy of unprovocatively matching the USSR in armament, and blocking Soviet expansionism. . . . Such a "temporary" suspension of expansionism would allow the positive forces in the USSR time to develop: even perhaps produce an evolution towards sanity, a gradual crumbling of the ideological foundations in the ruling group itself. If the regime survives, hopes of peace would centre on such a limited evolution towards the progressive abandonment of its total claims in the world. This can best be attained by denying the Kremlin the possibility of achieving these aims and at the same time making clear the advantage to be gained by cooperation rather than conflict.

(c) Our foreign policy should have the short term aim of preserving world peace between antagonistic cultures, and the long term hope of securing not just a truce, but a truly peaceful world. The way to achieve this is not through aggressive crusading, but by example on the one hand

and, on the other, by encouraging the evolution of despotic cultures from the economic, intellectual and civic stagnation which is the result of their present policies.

(d) The [Soviet] weaknesses at home imply a point beyond which the USSR could not match the West in armaments, simply from over-strain of the economic base. There can be no need for panic about a limitless arms race. Once the West committed itself to reasonable strategic and conventional parity, and to firm diplomatic action, the USSR would have little choice—whatever its longer term intentions—but to accept the situation.

This became, in effect, the policy President Reagan was to pursue with such success.

5.

It was also, sometimes, argued that negotiations on arms would be jeopardized if we included the human rights issue in the discussion.

The late Charles Frankel, in his *Human Rights and Foreign Policy*, pointed out that the human rights issue in its narrower sense can never be the sole moral touchstone of foreign policy, since, as he put it, "a desire to maintain peace and prevent bloodshed is not an immoral desire." There are and were areas in which our status is merely humanitarian. If the Soviets treated their peasants as serfs, or beat up arrested criminals, we might have felt and said that this was bad behavior, perhaps even symptomatic of a bad attitude likely to have some relevance to their international stance, but not a key issue.

But, as Koestler had urged in 1946, the free movement of people and ideas was another matter, and one absolutely central to the whole confrontation: it was not only our sympathies that were engaged, but our interests too. For the way in which the Kremlin treated those advancing Western ideas when they were in its power—that is, within the Soviet Union—was a wholly clear indication of the way in which they would have treated the rest of us if they had had the opportunity. That is, the "ideological" warfare against bearers of Western ideas inside the USSR was one and the same as their campaign against the West.

Glasnost was in fact one of the conditions, the main condition, for ending the Cold War.

When in 1975 the Helsinki Agreement was drafted, "Basket Three"'s guarantee of progress in the free movement of people and ideas was inserted, at the insistence of some of the smaller European states, quite specifically as essential to any lasting and reliable peace.

The Final Act at Helsinki asserted flatly that

> the participating States recognize the universal significance of human rights and fundamental freedoms, respect for which is an essential factor for the peace, justice and well-being necessary to ensure the development of friendly relations and co-operation among themselves as among all States.

Helsinki's "Basket Three" was an attempt to get from the Soviets, in exchange for other concessions, an implementation of these general points and the beginning of a free movement of people and ideas; the West had no other political demands. It will be noted that we asked no more than what we already granted: Communist ideas circulated freely in the West and Western citizens could move freely about the world. Nor did our negotiators make any unreal demands for immediate and total fulfillment of these points: the terms of the agreement were "gradually to simplify and to administer flexibly the procedure for exit and entry," "to ease regulations," "gradually to lower," "gradually to increase" (just as the Jackson Amendment asked for a relaxation of the restrictions on emigration, not instant freedom). Indeed, Helsinki was a most modest start, merely seeking a sign of the beginnings of Soviet tolerance towards their own citizens, even those who might not share the ideas of their government or accept its claim to control their every move.

Helsinki was intended to inaugurate a new epoch of goodwill. In Russia itself we would have seen, had its provisions been carried out, "the effective exercise of civil, political, economic, social, cultural and other rights and freedoms all of which derive from the inherent dignity of the human person and are essential for his free and full development."

The Politburo was in something of a dilemma, for in the USSR, meanwhile, the dissident movement had arisen, with underground publications. In Stalin's time such efforts would have resulted in execution. Brezhnev's KGB chief told the leadership that the arrest of a few thousand people would destroy the movement. Numbers were in fact arrested and sent, often to die, to the Gulag. The survivors carried on. Heavy-handed public trials were not a success—for the first time, writers like Yuli Daniel and Andrei Sinyavsky were openly sentenced for their writings; in Stalin's time the purged were at least accused of terrorism or espionage. And above all, major figures like Solzhenitsyn, and later Sakharov, now emerged, to eliminate whom would have shaken world opinion. So the persecution remained halfhearted—Solzhenitsyn expelled from the country, Sakharov exiled to Gorky.

There were other factors, but there is now no doubt that the leadership was concerned to avoid action likely to destroy Western illusions about Soviet actuality.

In the West, however, it was actually the human rights issue that persuaded the Western political public of the basic intransigence of the Soviet regime. The repressions were not enough to destroy non-Communist ideas at home, but they were enough to disgust the Western world.

Progress was slow even on the small scale of permitting the reunification of American-Soviet families. It is hard to think of any earlier despotism that would have taken the Soviet position. The tardy, reluctant, incomplete action on this, which even if fully implemented would have affected a few hundred at most, was scarcely up to a bare-minimum requirement for membership in any remotely civilized community of nations.

The successes in matters of direct Western interest had always been such things as President Kennedy, in 1963, suspending cultural relations until Professor Barghoorn was released, President de Gaulle threatening to expel the Soviet ambassador unless Michel Tatu's Russian wife and stepchild were allowed out—both almost instantaneously successful.

Unsimilarly, when a young British lecturer, Gerald Brooke, was sent to labor camp for smuggling anti-Soviet pamphlets into the USSR, several of us made public protests, but the Foreign Office kept telling me not to rock the boat because quiet diplomacy in Moscow had already elicited hints of release. They even went to the abject length of continuing (against the wishes of its staff) the Soviet teacher exchange program with the polytechnic at which Brooke taught. After a year or two Brooke was released, and immediately told me that I had been right, and that such was the view in their own cases of all the political prisoners he met. Anatoli Scharansky, for example, said the same—that quiet diplomacy was useless unless backed by public outrage.

But, far more important, the supposed triumphs of quiet diplomacy were no more than extracting individual exceptions from a major background of repression. Scharansky nobly pointed out that his own release counted for little if it merely compounded the nonrelease of hundreds of others. While we rejoiced at the result of cases like Scharansky's, we often failed to remember that the role of such celebration was to throw the fate of many others into obscurity, and to provide a false—or at any rate cheaply bought—aura of respectability to the jailers.

I recall in the Nixon period how American envoys en route to Moscow on missions of quiet diplomacy about selected dissidents would rather anxiously ask the late Leonard Schapiro and myself whether the approach was the right one. We always answered no: a power could not base its policies on the hostage principle. As it was, the USSR, in exchange for making a few exceptions to its general line of conduct, was able to virtually silence the American government's public voice on the broader issue.

One reason was certainly a *déformation professionelle* of the diplomatic establishment. Since diplomats' forte is negotiation, they believe negotiation to be good in itself; and negotiation proper is a quiet matter. But the Soviets did what their interests required when the alternatives seemed less acceptable, and negotiation was merely a technical adjunct. To believe otherwise was to fall into the fallacy of the entrepreneur who thinks that a skeptical and experienced customer is more affected by the salesman than by the product. We need diplomats and salesmen to handle our policies and products, but there is more to international and economic affairs than that. Nor are these lessons obsolete.

In general, negotiation with the USSR was thus skewed not only by constituencies in the Western body politic but by misconceptions within the Western governmental and diplomatic apparatus. At that time, I recall speaking to a group of American senators. Another Sovietologist had told them that it was wrong to "pressure" the USSR. Several seemed to agree. But when I pointed out that "pressure" was merely a hostile term for "If you want us to do something you want, you must do something we want," and that this was the most elementary politics, put that way, they saw it at once.

The Brezhnev regime was to some extent trapped by its wish to combine excessive weapons policies and expansionism in the African and other areas with a simultaneous attempt as far as possible to project a positive image in the West. This had two major results. First, it meant that though they might suppress the voices of dissent in the USSR itself, they could not take the KGB's advice and arrest them by the thousand, nor could they employ their full measures of repression against people in the world's eye. They clearly did not feel that their image could survive a total ban on emigration. When they signed the Helsinki Agreement, with its guarantee of the free movement of people and ideas, they found it hard to handle the unofficial Helsinki Watch Committees that sprang up among their subjects. And in general, they now had, and could do no more than contain, a dissident movement—something the USSR in its prime had never faced. And the times were ripe, the exhaustion of the Soviet idea so far gone, that this small beginning was already shaking the system.

Again, cultural exchanges, things designed for—and fairly effective as—a means of giving the regime a good image, also meant more and more contact with and knowledge of the West among a growing section of the Soviet intellectual class.

And the arms negotiations, even though of limited effectiveness, gave the Soviet foreign policy experts contact with the West and some feel for the true attitudes of the Western governments. It is in this class that one finds, in the early period of *glasnost*, the most striking criticisms of Soviet foreign policy. Thus, again, unwanted truths penetrated the echelons of the apparat. Moreover, after such treaties it became increasingly difficult to represent the West as mad aggressors; or, rather, though internal propaganda on these lines persisted, it became increasingly implausible.

6.

Yet the basic problem in the West remained an often inadequate conception of the Soviet psychology.

The defect was not, strictly speaking, one of intellect or intelligence. Not even of judgment, in the abstract. It was, rather, one of the imagination. There are minds of apparently high IQ, people of apparently great experience, who are unable to conceive of minds and men markedly different from themselves. Chamberlain and Roosevelt were not "stupid." They simply lacked the scope needed to envisage alien minds as they really were. They were not, in a crucial sense, "men of the world."

For the capacity to envisage the alien is not distributed according to any of our usual intelligence tests. People can be able, clever, but not in the deepest sense wise. Examples of a run-of-the-mill academic or bureaucratic or even political "brilliance" are not seldom regarded as adequate in the responsible offices of the West, with disastrous results.

Shakespeare, in fact, was a better guide to the modern world than—in particular—certain circles with an inordinately powerful influence on the West, for he even produces characters, like Cassio, who typify the inability of inexperienced minds to understand the Iagos of the real world.

It is easy enough—for any of us—to fall into the trap of thinking that others think, within reason, like ourselves. But this trap is precisely the error that must be avoided in foreign affairs. It was probably less common till the present century. Gladstone could scarcely have felt that the Mahdi was approachable in terms of Western liberalism. But nowadays the alien political orders had a new advantage. While a Sultan or Shah with turban and scimitar, with titles like Commander of the Faithful and references like the Peacock Throne, would not have appeared to be within the usual concepts of George III, in this century the equally—indeed, far more—alien political rulers of the USSR and elsewhere dressed in a version of Western clothing and spoke a dialect, however perverse and false, of the political language of the West.

When they were with Westerners, they talked with amenity and amiability. I have myself heard from very high-level Western negotiators remarks that showed a total ignorance, or ignoring, of other firsthand evidence—such as the coarse snarling and jeering by Brezhnev and his group at the handcuffed and helpless Dubček and his colleagues when they were paraded as prisoners before the Politburo in 1968.

The notion of a "reasonable" set of Soviet leaders—that is, of men more or less assumed to have motives generally regarded as natural by well-meaning American academics and others—long bedeviled policy towards the Soviet Union.

If Churchill was not deceived as to Hitler, this was not a matter of intelligence, but rather of a knowledge of history, and of evil. Chamberlain could not conceive of anyone whose attitudes were not more or less within the limits of those prevalent in the Midlands. What was and is essential is a grasp, if not of the particulars of a non-Western history, and political psychology, at least the notion that such may be totally different, totally aberrant, from our point of view. Some camouflage (as in the Soviet case) works better than others. All the same, the example of such phenomena as Pol Pot, Khomeini, Amin, Bokassa, Castro might have shown Western observers that their assumptions were not necessarily valid as to the whole range of political motivation. Ideas based on unsubstantiated desk work, or even mere assumptions of "rationality," continued to undermine the West, and still apply in other contexts.

Every so often the Soviets did something that shook the world and showed them in their true colors even to the most myopic apologists and appeasers. For the time being, those who had been dangerously in error about Soviet motivations and intentions seem to have been shocked into facing reality. But when a year or two had passed, the same delusions reappeared.

7.

We have stressed, and in any other context could rightly be criticized as having overstressed, the misconceptions that to one degree or another affected sections of the Western public and of Western officialdom.

These have been put forward in the context of studying, and learning from, the ways of thinking that had such effects. But of course, in the long run a reasonably sound policy kept Western misunderstanding within limits, and, however shakily on occasion, sound policy prevailed.

On the Soviet side, the dynamic of ideological expansionism led to disaster. But in the West the end of the Cold War proper led to some remarkable claims, put forward in books by a largely anti-Western clerisy or advocacy.

These are concerned to show that the West did not "win" the Cold War, in one egregious case even asserting that the West and America "lost" it, not physically but "morally": the argument being that its psychological effects distorted what would otherwise presumably have been a better society here. Perhaps so, though the "otherwise" might have included the Stalinization of Europe, and not only Europe. And whatever may be urged in these ill-defined matters, it is clear that the Soviet Union lost the Cold War. To say so is, we are sometimes told, a reprehensible "triumphalism." Still, it does not seem out of place to insist, with all the reservations that could be made, on the central point that the West saved itself and its liberties, and that its totalitarian enemy faltered and failed.

We sometimes see a rather more serious view, that the Soviet Union would anyhow have collapsed sooner or later, and that the West's investment, or projected investment, in military technologies which Moscow could not match played no part. This is simplistic. Of course the various "causes" interacted, and cannot be crudely disentangled. But the failure of the economy was (as Gorbachev says) due in large part to its "militarization" beyond what it could stand. In this context, we may note Westerners who said at the time that the USSR was economically strong and could resist any suggested Western pressures, but who now say it was so weak that no such pressures were needed. This last view misses the point that a dog with rabies is in poor health, but that it would be a mistake to pat him: similarly with a "weak" Soviet Union disposing of a myriad warheads.

Details may be disputed, but the fallacy in question has on the whole only been accepted in certain Western circles, while rejected in Russia by those who had been at the center of Soviet policy. This was made clear on a number of occasions—one of the most striking being the contribution of former Soviet Foreign Minister Aleksandr Bessmertnykh and the almost equally influential Anatoly Chernayev at a conference on the Cold War held at Princeton early in 1993, both of whom stated flatly that President Reagan's Strategic Defense Initiative had played a major role in convincing the Soviet leadership that the USSR could not compete economically or technologically. (It was of course not only SDI that had this effect but the whole superiority in armament that it implied.) In much of the West, all this has largely been discussed at a low level of political partisanship rather than on its merits. (There are even books emerging from American academic circles which have no basis at all in Russian documentation: one of them, believe it or not, has its "study" proving that the Soviet Union made more concessions than the United States.)

The Soviet regime had ruined its economy by putting every possible resource into the arms effort, and this had failed. Within a few years the Cold War was over. But it has, or should have, given the West important lessons in understanding, and coping with, threats arising from intrinsically aggressive mind-sets.

Part II

FACING THE CONSEQUENCES

CHAPTER X

Scar Tissue:
A Note on
Post-Soviet Russia

I.

It is not our purpose to give a full description, let alone make a full analysis, of the breakdown of the Soviet system.

To transform such an inheritance as it left into a prosperous, democratic society seemed a simple task to some Western observers. A free market would release Economic Man; elections would install Democracy. The problems were clear and so were the solutions. There was no more to be said.

In fact, as we have seen, there was much more to be said.

Above all, we need to consider the nature of the distortions which were the main legacy of the Soviet regime. We do not seek to predict the country's particular future over the coming decade or two. A variety of well-informed but incompatible judgments on that future are now being put forward—which may imply that immediate prospects at least rest on a knife edge. We deal in a general way with, but do not "estimate," the complex forces that may determine the country's future.

Much that is said here applies, to a lesser degree (and not in detail), to the other post-Communist countries. We are concerned with Russia as the great exemplar of the post-Communist social and political order in all its difficulties, and at the same time the one country in that category which could still prove a serious danger to the world.

2.

The crucial decision was the launching of *glasnost* and *perestroika* in the late 1980s. Gorbachev and the brighter of his colleagues had at last seen that massive and continuous falsification was not only ruinous to morale but also incompatible with economic success, and even that the prevention of discussion was stultifying the whole political and social order. When your seas dry up, it is hard to stomach a fantasy of beaches and breakers. But as *glasnost* came, the struggle to attain reality grew ever more intense and faced major mental difficulties.

The newer technologies had proved inimical to the system. The foreign radios broke the state's monopoly of news and opinion and showed many Russians that the official truths were untenable. It is no wonder that Andrei Gromyko, then Soviet Foreign Minister, announced that to orbit a TV satellite broadcasting in Russian would be regarded as a hostile act and that the Soviets would shoot it down. Then the arrival of Xerox machines, even though they were in theory under strict control, gave the previously top-copy-and-five-carbons *samizdat* a great boost.

When *glasnost* hit Russia's own television, the effect was stunning. The televised debates in the Supreme Soviet, with Andrei Sakharov standing up to Mikhail Gorbachev and speaking for democracy, resulted in factories everywhere closing down, with workers clustered round the sets. More generally, in the Gorbachevite *glasnost*, the destruction of the Stalinist myth (and eventually of the Leninist one) came not in single refutations but in a massive, continual hammering in of the facts over months and years. This is how mental climates are changed.

The emergence of civic connections where a sort of atomization of the country had previously been seen was also much advanced by the new technology. Groups hitherto isolated were now in continual touch. During the August 1991 coup, fax machines ensured communication and copies of declarations from Pskov to Vladivostok were all over the lampposts of Moscow and Leningrad.

But the collapse of Communism had left a heritage of ruin, not only in the economy, the ecology, health, politics, but also—and above all— in the minds and psyches of its citizens. In 1987, well after the *glasnost* period started, the prominent Russian Academician D. S. Likhachev wrote of how Stalinism "spread deep roots in the mentality of several generations. . . . [T]he fear that it instilled in our minds and souls still shackles people's consciousness and paralyses it." A hundred similar comments on all the various mental and psychological scars could be quoted. In fact, in the words of the poet Fazil Iskander, "under the totalitarian regime, it was as if you were forced to live in the same room with a violently insane man," and such effects are long-lasting.

We cannot exactly speak of a *folie à deux cent millions*. Nevertheless, the whole population was deeply affected. At the lower intellectual level, the stultification was even more marked than the ideologization that accompanied it and caused it. In 1977 Andrei Sakharov was visiting a labor camp area in Mordovia, and one of the guards in charge seemed moved when listening to some poems being recited, Sakharov commented:

> Maybe I'm naive, but when I think of Vanya's face that day, and of similar encounters, I begin to believe that this wretched, downtrodden, corrupt, and drunken people—no longer even a *people* in any real sense of the word—is not yet entirely lost, not yet dead . . . and compassion for others and a thirst for spiritual fulfillment have not yet been utterly extinguished.

This gloomy generality and not very optimistic hope may have been an extreme view. But it dramatized, even if too sharply, a fairly widespread impression.

The first influential—though at the time secret—analysis came in 1983 from the official sociologist Tatyana Zaslavskaya, who later summed up:

> The primary reasons for the need for *perestroika* were not the sluggish economy and the rate of technological development but an underlying mass alienation of working people from significant social goals and values. This social alienation is rooted in the economic system formed in the 1930s, which made state property, run by a vast bureaucratic apparatus, the dominant form of ownership. . . . For 50 years it was said that this was public property and belonged to everyone, but no way was ever found to make workers feel they were the co-owners and masters of the factories, farms, and enterprises. They felt themselves to be cogs in a gigantic machine.

And again, as another Russian sociologist has written, "Decades of destitution have shaped in our people the psychology of poverty and want."

3.

In politics, we have seen, to put it mildly, something less than a rapid and painless modernization.

As the sociologist Andrei Bystritsky told David Remnick, "We wiped out the best and brightest in this country and, as a result, we sapped ourselves of intelligence and energy," with the concomitant result on the political plane that the present leaders could not be expected to be up to the level of "Washington or Madison or Hamilton or Lincoln."

In fact, no trained political class existed.

Again, institutional changes are in themselves only part of the problem. It has been said that the division of powers in Western countries leads to compromise, in Russia to civil war. Not quite, but as I write the executive and legislative branches are, as Fazil Iskander (again) put it, like two exhausted boxers locked in a clinch—and this at least gave time for compromise and adjustments to become habitual, though hardly irreversible.

As to economics, the USSR was unique in another way. It was an *overdeveloped* country, with too much industry (particularly heavy industry), producing useless or military goods. A similar point could be made about the extravagantly wasteful methods of oil production, compounded by enormous (and ecologically disastrous) leakages through improperly maintained pipelines. Again, roads and buildings are in a bad state. In fact, an enormous effort simply to retrieve the disasters inherited by the old regime is needed: an effort hard to bring the exhausted Russian people to face, especially after so many years of nonproductive effort forced upon them—with such meager results that their whole attitude to work became eroded. On the land, the old hardworking peasantry has virtually disappeared. In the factories, the watchword of "They pretend to pay us, we pretend to work" largely prevails.

The legacy of socialism was, in Mikhail Gorbachev's phrase, "collective responsibility and individual irresponsibility."

4.

The "creation" of a market economy is, however, to a great extent a misleading concept. Market economies have emerged rather than been decreed. Socialist economies are, of course, consciously set up by the state. The problem in Eastern Europe was to set up the conditions under which a market economy could come into being. First, naturally, the rule of law—in principle a simple thing, in practice not so.

It is not as if a country can, as it were, be put in dry dock and equipped with new institutions in a careful and considered way. The whole venture is more like trying to reequip a ship at sea, in stormy waters, with a new engine.

Vaclav Klaus, for some years Prime Minister of the Czech Republic, argued that reform is bound to be painful: "The systematic transformation is not an exercise in applied economics or applied political science," but a process involving the whole population and destroying "the former political, social and economic equilibrium." To succeed, it must be continually, carefully and credibly presented to the citizenry. This above all requires, he said, the formation of standard political parties, without which there is no scope for politicians and no "mechanisms" for democratic politics. It involves institutional changes—political, economic, fiscal and legal—together with changes in habits and customs. None of this can be "masterminded" by any a priori plan. And, he added, "the costs the people have to bear must be widely shared, otherwise the fragile political support is lost"—as indeed it was, at least temporarily, in his own country. Nor could the formal institutionalizing of "democracy" or the launching of a "market" form of economy provide the immediate attainment of Western standards.

With the Russians the position is, of course, far more difficult than with the Czechs. And to enlist the efforts of anything like the people as a whole faces huge difficulties. Even so, it is not so much the people, or political diversity, that is holding things up, as a justifiable lack of popular confidence in the political process. Again, the Russian bureaucracy has got into the habit of not fulfilling contracts, not fulfilling duties. In the democratic countries, contracts are enforced, delinquents fined or dismissed. When we speak of the rule of law, we mean contract law as well.

5.

By the 1980s the Soviet Union had already become a vast kleptocracy. As Alain Besançon noted, money had begun to play a major role, in addition to the long-standing perquisites of power, foreshadowing (as Besançon put it) a sort of "savage capitalism." The large-scale criminal element had, in fact, become almost institutionally intertwined with the bureaucracy.

There were stunning illegalities. Large amounts of caviar were sent west in tins labeled herring, with much of the top staff of the Ministry of Fisheries implicated. An export consignment of spades turned out to be made of titanium. A dozen tanks, crated as trucks, were barely stopped at a Black Sea port. On another tack, huge amounts of illicit vodka were distilled. And the ingenuity of some protocapitalists was astonishing: in one of the Central Asian republics a would-be entrepreneur discovered that no limit had been set for the delivery of cotton for therapeutic work to a local mental hospital. He bribed the director, who certified his patients as sane, then threw them out and replaced them with his own people, who soon had a profitable operation going (this, too, involving fixing the relevant local ministry).

As with the political scene, all this marked the post-Soviet heritage in the economic field. When the socialist order failed, the only class with access to and experience in economic matters was the state bureaucratic stratum, which went ahead and looked after its class interest in almost Marxist style. The leading or active elements used the emergence of the market to (as it is often put) "loot" the country's resources. The lesser bureaucracy continued to be parasitical on the economy, taking bribes for permits and so on.

The point here is that a subterranean, and risky, type of capitalism already existed—ready to man the abandoned bastions of semicriminal socialism. We should indeed note that there were people within the old economy who played a positive role, outside of and in principle contrary to the Plan—the *stolkachi*, or fixers, employed by factories to seek out and bargain for materials in short supply. And now, especially among younger people, a genuine entrepreneurial "small business" class began to emerge, while many others supplemented their incomes in various economically positive ways. Even as to the "biznes" class proper, Alexander Yakovlev tells us that though he had never expected anything like it, at least some of its members were providing some of the drive which had been absent from the old system.

6.

The responsibility for the abysmal level from which Russia has to raise itself lies with the Soviet regime. But a section of the population looks back on the Brezhnev era as one of comparative prosperity. So, in certain respects, it was—at the cost of using up the country's resources. But such nostalgia has its political and mental dangers.

The ex-Communist parties now or recently in power in Eastern Europe have lost their ideologies. Their tilt is etatist, but hardly more so than some Western trends. In Russia alone, the Communist Party, with probably less immediate chance of full power, keeps its name. Its younger leaders would like it to become "Socialist" or "Social Democratic." But the older traditionalists will not give it up. This is obviously a bad sign. Nor are political upsets in Russia impossible. Even so, reversion to the old economic, let alone political, system seems virtually impossible. One reason is that, except among this stratum of dinosaurs, Marxism is extinct—in the sense that it is simply mentioned with no more than a sneer in anything resembling intellectual debate, as is even more the case in Eastern Europe (though one philosophy professor at Prague University is said to be a "Marxist").

Yet—a peculiar anomaly—there are now voices in Russia who have given up Marx but kept Lenin!

7.

A cognate inheritance from Soviet times is, among some elements, its built-in xenophobia. The Communist system not only imposed its own ideologically based mental distortions on the population, it also encouraged and employed more archaic paranoid elements. The hatred directed against the West over forty years was indeed ideologically based: VAD (Praising American Democracy) and PZ (Abasement before the West) were official categories for arrest. But even at the higher Communist level, there still existed a more primitive xenophobia.

There is now wide support in Moscow's opinion polls for the idea that the West is consciously trying to ruin the Russian economy, with a view to converting the country into a backward source of raw materials.

At the same time, leading figures among the not-so-ex-Communists, such as Anatoly Lukyanov, often say, and apparently believe, that Gorbachev and Yakovlev were CIA agents entrusted with the destruction of the Soviet regime.

It need hardly be said that all such phenomena are signs of a diseased psychology, and that their political significance lies in whether, and to what extent, they can be used to fuel a politics of a revanchist type.

Russia is a country rich in raw materials. In fact, it was mainly profits from oil and natural gas which kept the Soviet economy from earlier collapse. These riches are not being properly exploited today—in part because crucial foreign investment is unwelcome for what one can only call paranoid reasons: this widespread Russian notion that foreigners will succeed in robbing the country. Such attitudes tend to cut Russia off from the world economically as well as politically, physically as well as culturally.

Western investment is necessary not only for the proper development of Russian resources but also as a sign that Russia has entered the world economy.

8.

On the positive side, Russia has now had eight years of pluralist politics—as one Russian said to me, this is not as good as a thousand years, but much better than none. It has had free, if not fair, elections, and a free or freeish press. The Swedish economist Anders Aslund remarked some years ago that for Russia to go through six months without disaster must be seen as a triumph. So far, disaster has been avoided.

The distortions of the public mind have none the less not been overcome. To write of post-Soviet Russia is to examine "rubble," as Solzhenitsyn put it. The collapse of the old structure has left a chaos that has not yet settled down into anything like normality. The immediate outlook is still confused—with nothing like a clear outcome in a situation without clearly defined parties, and a turbulence of conflicting and often self-destructive interests and sentiments.

It is in this context that a prominent Moscow liberal wrote, "We cannot go back to Stalin, but we could still become a second-class country—poor, cruel, and cut off from the West." An economic adviser to the Russian government, Lyudmila Piyasheva, summed up that the country is "a limited democracy with a semi-state, semi-privatized economy . . . anarchic, corrupt and oligarchic."

A further disquieting thought is that the political and economic order now prevailing in Russia strongly resembles in extreme form a corporatist-*étatiste* pseudocapitalism not unlike the negative phenomena now also emerging in the West and elsewhere.

The main point, especially from the Western point of view, is whether such a Russia could emerge as the bearer of an expansionist chauvinism, not indeed of the global and absolutist type, yet still a dangerous entity on the world scene.

The actual disintegration of the Russian state would be a disaster—and while nuclear weapons still abound, it would be a danger on a global scale. A truly despotic chauvinist Russia would be, if not quite as dangerous, still deplorable.

These are pessimistic scenarios, and even if they occur may not be irreversible. But history has often taken unlikely turns, and it is clearly incumbent on the West to do everything possible to help Russia, long devastated by a dangerous malady and still very far from being in good health, on the road to recovery. A reasonably peaceful, reasonably prosperous, reasonably civic Russia may be the crucial element in the crises that still threaten the world.

CHAPTER XI

◆

In a Wayward West

1.

W"estern" political culture implies nothing remotely resembling perfection, or even perfectibility. On the contrary, we can only look on it as the best and most hopeful arrangement available to us in the world of reality and enormously superior to its competitors past and present.

All real societies contain greed, power mania, sloth, incompetence, paranoia. All societies contain special interests, not only material ones but emotional ones too. And it may not be going too far to say that every consensual society experiences cycles of degeneration from which, when the results become clear, it pulls up sharply, often at the last moment—or fails to do so.

So the free society itself should not be Ideified: it is a system of compromise between the individual and the community, between the population and the state. This endlessly generates friction, myopia, corruption, faction, and perhaps always will. Nor shall we ever have politicians who understand every problem, who have appropriate plans for solving them, and who are able to put those plans into effect.

Meanwhile, many of our present-day problems arise from, or are greatly worsened by, mental attitudes that, though not usually ideological in the totalitarian sense, show a family resemblance. That is to say, they are usually the result of giving if not absolute, at any rate excessive, status to political or other concepts.

2.

All-encompassing theories of history and social change have indeed lost their luster. Serious economists and political scientists have abandoned, or are abandoning, the attempt to impose an unattainable rigor on their subjects.

Intellectually, one might have thought, most of the issues before us have, in fact, already been settled, or seen as without substance. The old absolute notions that environment counted for everything, and heredity for nothing; that liberty is possible without private property; that prosperity is achievable in the absence of what used to be called a middle class; that gender, and other matters, are a "social construct"—all these are crumbling away, or are no longer taken seriously *outside their sects*. The idea of a state-run economy is a marginal fad (one of the most interesting data in the moral comparison between social and individual effort, so often conceded to the former, comes when the critic Joseph Frank notes Dostoevsky's telling of his fellow convicts in Siberia that they were at their best when privately working to earn a few kopeks, which "guaranteed the individual a sense of self-possession and moral autonomy").

Again, the statistical basis of much social and economic argument is now known to be defective. And as to policy, it is now seen that, as Peter Drucker has remarked, no single piece of macroeconomic advice given by experts to their government has ever had the results predicted.

So far so good. But on the loss side, we have to note—and have noted—that the sects we speak of still pervade the less scholarly quarters of academe, and hence intrude from time to time on the real world. Worse, there has still been a failure to cope with the remnants of *étatiste* and other excesses in the mental atmosphere. In politics and administration these attitudes left over from earlier ideological pollution are still inhaled. This almost unwitting holdover from a past that those concerned have often repudiated in a superficial, conscious sense still pervades thought and policy to a surprising degree.

Moreover, it coincides with, and gives impetus and excuse to, a varied caste of bureaucracy, large-scale capitalism, and government, all tending to a new corporatism.

3.

Until recently there was rhetoric—even overblown rhetoric—in all political debate in the West, but the rhetoric was, in general, a sort of coloring on genuine and serious policy argument. Now the rhetoric, the oversimplified and emotional case, often tends to be almost all that is presented to the public mind.

This seems to be based on the assumption that the public is not prepared to listen to anything not brief and simple. Whether this is true seems doubtful: the public is capable of quite complicated thought in dealing with its own affairs. It is also capable of rejecting the extreme positions presented to it on issues (for instance, abortion) and taking a moderate stance.

Michael Oakeshott's definition of a civilized political scene as one in which the passions do not become overheated would not lead him, or anyone else, to imagine a politics of purely rational and cool debate. And even when a polity as a whole more or less answers Oakeshott's criterion, there are bound to be excesses: keeping these in check is the most we can expect.

When there are no real causes for faction, insubstantial ones have served, ever since those chariot-race fans nearly destroyed the Byzantine government. Opposition to particular governments in one or another Western country often generated factiousness of such intensity that in some cases it amounted to general support for the successive totalitarian aggressors. But naturally, examples of the more extreme factionalism came and still come from those who are actually committed to closed ideologies, or, less damagingly though still damagingly, victims of something like monomania on a single issue.

We now seem to meet perhaps not such extremes of partisanship, but still socially deleterious attitudes. These are, of course, to be found across the whole range of opinion, and among all sections of the population. But their pervasiveness among the "educated" is the crux. When Orwell saw the man in the street as both too sane and too stupid to hold some of the views to be found among intellectuals, he touched a nub, though of course a section of the less educated or uneducated is and has always been the prey, though not the originator, of ideologies—and "commitment" generally works against fairly amicable compromise or toleration.

One symptom is a reverence, as we have noted, for the "activist," who devotes much of his or her energy to securing the triumph of his or her political or other cause. Whether or not this is good depends, surely, on two things. First, is the cause good? Or if it sounds good, would its success in fact contribute to human happiness or advancement? Second, even if the cause is in this sense good, does the activist use methods that are destructive of other goods? (To which might be added, no doubt less importantly, does the activist gradually make a career of his activism, becoming part of a quasi-professional, even a profitable, political-type machine?)

The trouble is, again, a belief in various "certainties" accepted on insufficient grounds. We find this in such matters as global warming, recycling and related ecological themes, where—often enough—simplistic assertions have been accepted without serious consideration (and often transmitted in crude form to defenseless schoolchildren, who in some cases become priggish enforcers at home). On domestic issues, the activist themes represent exaggerated—even panicky—reactions to very genuine problems requiring careful thought and policy decisions. Unfortunately, such activist solutions too often project themselves into the political realm, and hence affect policy.

It has been argued—a century ago by Herbert Spencer, for example—that only people who are passionately devoted to reforming a social evil are effective. Clearly this is a worthwhile point. Still, such success has usually been mediated through compromise or teamwork with practical politicians—and these latter may also have a strong, even though less heated, moral commitment. Nowadays the trouble is that they may feel a need for activist political support and surrender their mediating role.

It is true that movements as such should not be judged by their more extreme adherents. The trouble is rather that it is precisely the sensationalist views that gain the public ear in best-sellers, articles, television programs, and, often, the status of a constituency.

One example of the result of these attitudes will suffice: the feministical arrangements now found in the American armed forces. Of course women can fill certain military posts—in World War II they were in action with Britain's antiaircraft batteries, handling the radar, but not the heavy ammunition or the guns: equally in action, equally in danger, but operating under different physical constraints (and not, incidentally, sharing billets). Now, in the United States, women have been "integrated" into infantry units. But since they are in general unable to pass the physical tests, these tests are lowered. Similarly with the fire departments in Los Angeles and elsewhere. If this trend persists, the United States will have infantry unable to match that of potential opponents. And so with the victims of fire in those cities who live up walls higher than the new criteria match. Similar demands are not made for women to enter the American football teams; nor that women's tennis championships should be assimilated to men's.

There are, of course, other reasons for not using women in infantry units. We are not here concerned to argue the whole case, since the above point alone is enough to destroy the concept (as I find whenever it is presented to remotely reasonable people of every political persuasion). But our purpose here is different: to note first that we have here a classic example of an idea in conflict with reality. And, worse, that it has been put into effect by government action—that is, by the effective political pressure of an ideological sect with the unseemly acquiescence of the political and military establishments.

Meanwhile, in Britain a more defensible admission of women to certain sections of the military was advanced by the minister concerned on the grounds that the armed forces "must reflect" their society. One may ask why, and what does this mean? But also, where does the "must" come from?

And this type of unconsidered reaction is, of course, found in many fields. Thus, to blame "capitalism" for pollution, except in the crude sense that some industry emits fumes, fails on a dozen obvious grounds—that it was far worse in the USSR; that it much improved in Britain following the end of state industries (this was in part because they had been old and inefficient, but also in part because they had "regulated" themselves). More generally, the whole environmental picture presented in schools and elsewhere is, to put it mildly, highly dubious. The trouble, as ever, seems to be that continuous misdirection is more effective—over the short run at least—than the frequent but not constant voices of critical argument.

Such aberrations are commonly accompanied by the notion of an enemy class, or sex, or race, determined to oppose all change. This is, as we have said, Marxism come again, a Manichaean view of politics. Passionate reformers have not only often blamed the whole social order for results which other and opposite social orders equally produce, they have often held that the despotic states must be good really, because their own opponents in the West attack them so strongly; or, by a similar process of thought, that the despotisms which criticize faults in the democracies so much must themselves be the representatives of reforming ideas. Besides, one's own grievances always appear larger than worse ones far away, unless one makes the effort required for any responsible comment. As Tennyson said in his "To One Who Ran Down the English":

You make our faults too gross, and thence maintain
Our darker future. May your fears be vain!

At times the small black fly upon the pane
May seem the black ox of the distant plain.

There is a smugness in "Look at me being pragmatic." But there are also dangers in the attitude, commoner outside than inside government, "Look at me being idealistic." To congratulate oneself on one's warm commitment to the environment, or to peace, or to the oppressed, and think no more is a profound moral fault. The true conscience includes an intellectual conscience. By their fruits ye shall know them, not just by their intentions.

4.

Most periods are characterized by a seepage of earlier general Ideas into their whole mental atmosphere, somewhat diluted but still pervasive.

A bureaucrat today does not think of himself as putting into effect part of a highly debatable idea. He takes the nature of his aims and methods for granted. As John Maynard Keynes once wrote, "I am sure that the power of vested interests is vastly exaggerated compared with the gradual encroachment of ideas"; but bureaucracy is often an interest group that is *also* the more or less conscious purveyor of a set of ideas. And of course even apart from the bureaucracy itself, we see the creation of a class of citizens who are, not temporarily but over years, dependent on government support and are a constituency for its continuance. (This should remind us of the problems of Russia.) Any increase in the number on the government payroll beyond a certain point is parasitical on society. Which is to say that every given increase in these numbers should be regarded as exceptional, and supported by arguments that are not merely strong but overwhelming.

As to bureaucracy itself, theories of its nature and development have been put forward. The only points that need making here are twofold. First, that in a consensual, civic and developing society, the state's role needs to be limited. Second, that in the purely economic field, state ownership or control cannot without actual disaster or decay exceed a proportion that is under debate but is usually held to be a maximum of some 30 percent of GNP.

Thus we are not faced with the choice between total governmental apathy and total governmental control. Hayek points out that all economies and social orders are to some degree "planned" in the sense that governments, or even groups of citizens, usually have general aims for advancing or adjusting the current condition of affairs.

"Bureaucracy" exists not only in governmental machinery but also in industrial firms, universities and other bodies. In part, bureaucratic proliferation is due to ever-increasing access to ever-increasing amounts of information. But while there is no theoretical limit to the amount of information that might be produced, there is a limit to the amount that can be handled or digested.

Again, success and promotion in the world of officialdom are now associated with achievement—by which is meant not successful administration as such but the launching of some new scheme. Nor do modest but viable improvements attract as much praise as sensational or attention-getting ventures. Moreover, as Weber points out, mistaken bureaucratic decisions do not undermine bureaucracy; on the contrary, the resulting trouble requires further bureaucratic effort.

Any government needs an administrative machinery; and though this needs to be kept as far as possible under public control, a civil service is in itself both worthy and useful. Its proliferation beyond a certain point, not readily definable, is another matter. Since it is not in principle governed by economic considerations the way most other jobs are, the built-in tendency to expand is not subject to more or less automatic constraints. We see the state as a mechanism for enforcing the legal order, maintaining the common defense, and such other activities that from time to time have appeared to be suitable to central authority. This notion of the state is wholly different from that of the totalitarian movements and regimes. For them the state is the possessor of total power over its subjects, and is the practical embodiment of the ideological fantasies and intentions of the rulers. For us the state can indeed be seen as the embodiment, for certain prescribed purposes and on certain prescribed conditions, of a country or a society. But respect for the state should be conditional on its not getting above itself with regard to the nation, or people, it in part represents.

What is clear is that the state, in most Western countries, has intervened both expensively and unsuccessfully in various social areas, under the political pressure of simplistic or erroneous notions.

5.

That other aspect of the state, the Law, is also crucial. Where but in the law can the speed limit or the rule of the road be determined? Trivial examples indeed, but nor could it be widely denied that there are more broadly social spheres where Law must be decisive, though the boundaries are matters of legitimate dispute.

Nowadays, thousands of laws are passed every year. As Giovanni Sartori has put it (in his *The Theory of Democracy Revisited*):

> Laws excessive in number and poor in quality not only discredit the law; they also undermine what our ancestors constructed, a relatively stable and spontaneous law of the land, common to all, and based on rules of general application.

For, inevitably,

> legislative bodies are generally indifferent to, or even ignorant of, the basic forms and consistencies of the legal pattern. They impose their will through muddled rules that cannot be applied in general terms; they seek sectional advantage in special rules that destroy the nature of law itself. And it is not only a matter of the generality of the law. Mass fabrication of laws ends by jeopardising the other fundamental requisite of law—certainty. Certainty does not consist only in a precise wording of laws or in their being written down: It is also the long-range certainty that the laws will be lasting. Nor is this all. In practice, the legislative conception of law accustoms those to whom the norms are addressed to accept any and all commands of the State.

Sartori comments that, pursued too far, this can result in something like a corporate state—a sort of velvet fascism (to be seen also in other political spheres).

A major flaw in this torrent of twentieth-century legislation was that while in earlier days there was time and opportunity for each law to be considered, understood and debated in a truly parliamentary fashion, this now became impossible. Then again, before a law was introduced at all, the problem it was designed to address had been a matter of public discussion.

It is also necessary, on the same grounds, that policies—and of course treaties—be comprehensible. Tax law in the United States (allegedly on the point of reform) is so complicated and so huge in detail that it is often not understood by the tax authorities themselves, even though its mere existence necessitates a huge employment of staff. It is in any case incomprehensible to the ordinary citizen without special advice. This should (of course) be illegal. "Ignorance of the law is no excuse"—

because, in John Selden's words, it is a plea anyone could put forward, and one that could seldom be rebutted. Fair enough. But the corollary is that laws should be easily understood, and at least reasonably concise.

Nor should regulations be so complex as to leave the citizen at a disadvantage vis-à-vis the regulators. They should also not be so broad as to allow the bureaucrat the wide powers of implementation that, in his strong position vis-à-vis the citizen, subjects the latter to caprice, and to expense.

W. B. Yeats pointed out in a speech to the Irish Senate in Free State days that a law then being proposed would give excessive power to the Minister of Justice concerned:

> The Government does not intend these things to happen, the Commission on whose report the Bill was founded did not intend these things to happen, but in legislation intention is nothing, and the letter of the law everything, and no government has the right, whether to flatter fanatics or in mere vagueness of mind, to forge an instrument of tyranny and say that it will never be used.

In fact, a common defect is that laws are interpreted by judges quite differently from what the legislators who proposed and passed them had explained as their intent. The judiciary is now in effect empowered, in the United States, to interpret general articles of the Constitution not as to borderline or hitherto uncertain matters, but in massive revision, on the one hand, and pettifogging detail on the other. Just as pressing egalitarianism too far ruins any economy, so pressing legalism too far ruins legality.

Moreover, it is hardly any longer even claimed that the Supreme Court merely interprets the law. Its members are openly selected on political grounds, and mostly on political grounds that encroach on social policy. Judges in the circuits of the U.S. Court of Appeals are often far worse examples.

Here, too, pushing ideas to an abstract level has had destructive effects. In America in particular, but also increasingly in Britain, the attempt to attain perfect legal equity, on the one hand, and compensation for troubles from any institution that has funds available on the other has been responsible for a deluge of litigation and a mass of judicial decisions based on enforcing claims to equity rather than justice—with results that have often been ludicrous (as in the case of the San Francisco burglar awarded damages for injuries against the householder through whose glass roof he had fallen) and, even more often, intrusive on the legislation already in place. Then again, in the United States, tort law, class actions, and general litigation are widely understood to be destructive of society. Of education we shall speak later; but one dreadful example is the inability of schools to discipline, remove or transfer disruptive pupils, one of whom can effectively ruin a class, but whose right to remain has in case after case been successfully pursued by antisocial parents through the delays, intricacies and idiocies of the courts.

As John Gray has put it, "Complex questions about restraint of liberty," which in most democratic countries "are treated as issues in legislative policy, involving a balance of interests and sometimes a compromise of ideals, have come to be treated in the United States, primarily or exclusively, as questions of fundamental rights." And this leads to extreme, that is to say absolute, positions being taken, with socially and politically fissiparous results.

As Philip K. Howard argues in his excellent *The Death of Common Sense*, with devastating illustrations, the "process" side of the law is by far the most unsound and oppressive part of the whole matter. It has many disadvantages. It is absurdly lengthy. And it is absurdly expensive. Magna Carta, it may be remembered, required that justice and right should not be sold, denied or *delayed*. Cases, especially in the United States, now often take so long that one is reminded of the fictional passage in Ernest Bramah's *The Wallet of Kai Lung*: "Doubtless the case in question can by various means be brought in the end before the Court of Final Settlement at Pekin, where it may indeed be judged in the manner you assert. But . . . such a process must infallibly consume the wealth of a province and the years of an ordinary lifetime."

6.

The American political and legal system, in its present form, might be compared to a rusty bicycle, which only American energy could keep going. However, it is argued that the various liberties guaranteed by the American Constitution, and interpreted by the American Supreme Court, are inherently superior to the liberties enjoyed in Britain. In particular, the Bill of Rights amendments, and above all the positive legal position of Freedom of Speech, are widely praised.

This is commonly presented in terms of the banality that anyone proposing any limits on it is "in favor of censorship." But in fact, everyone is in favor of some sort of censorship. The trouble has always been, as Dr. Johnson wrote, that "the danger of such unbounded liberty, and the danger of bounding it, have produced a problem in the science of government which human understanding seems hitherto unable to solve."

As ever, we have to choose, and while no one can be trusted with the task of censorship, it is equally true that someone will always try to go beyond any bounds set by public feeling. The judiciary, at least in the United States, has proved unable to cope. (And the intellectual-cum-media caste, needless to say, have expended much moral indignation on any attempt to limit certain types of free expression, while the electorate is too confused, and the political class too cowardly, to oppose this—until it burns itself out.)

7.

It is also urged that the faults seen in current politics in the West can be corrected by institutional reforms. Of course, well-thought-out changes are always possible. But institutions in themselves are not the central matter of consensual politics. As Aristotle wrote:

> There are plenty of instances of a constitution which according to its law is not democratic, but which owing to custom and way of upbringing is democratic in its workings; there are likewise others which according to law incline towards democracy, but by reason of custom and upbringing operate more like oligarchies.

Various constitutional changes are now being proposed in the United Kingdom on the grounds that they would make things "more democratic." But this is an inadequate criterion.

For example, there is the question of proportional representation. The various possible schemes are well known—though the Israeli complaint that it results in the smallest party dictating policy was matched by similar misadventure in Poland. New Zealand has had a parallel misfortune. And the Czech Republic is now working on a return to the first-past-the-post system. Other criticisms of such a change are well known; more important, though, after the election of 1992, when the Conservatives won power with a minority of the votes, polls afterwards showed that well over 50 percent of the electorate was content with the result. The point here is that British political habits were suited to the existing system. No doubt Britons would adapt to the changes suggested. The essential is, rather, that it is their habits of mind rather than particular institutional forms that really count.

Similarly, the notion that a republic in Britain would in some way be an improvement on constitutional monarchy is found in certain journalism but has no obvious merit except that of being, or appearing to be, more "democratic." There is little in, for example, West European experience to suggest that this notion has any substance. (Come to that, there is no formal reason against an elective monarchy, as in old Poland. Or in the selection or nomination of an heir, as in ancient times or in the origin of the present Swedish dynasty.)

Some of the constitutional improvements advanced in Britain and America have rather the air of Sir Boyle Roche, reported as saying in the Irish Parliament of 1775, "In the great cause of civil liberty, Mr. Speaker, I should be prepared to sacrifice not only a part of our glorious constitution but, if necessary, the whole of it—in order to preserve the remainder." The government is urged to take constitutional action in spheres in which, no doubt, it is theoretically competent, but in which its intervention in practice is destructive of civic society. The famous British parliamentary resolution of 1780, that the powers of the executive "have increased, are increasing and ought to be diminished," is once again applicable. For as Thomas Sowell has put it: "The grand delusion of contemporary liberals [I would say of contemporary *étatistes*] is that they have both the right and the ability to move their fellow creatures around like blocks of wood—and that the end results will be no different than if people had voluntarily chosen the same actions."

The problem in Britain is that in the legislature the party whips' control has got so out of hand that reform, properly speaking, seems more essential there than in the other spheres so often mentioned. When we speak of the executive, we should note that it is not distinguishable from the legislative in the same way that it used to be. The original role of Parliament was not to churn out legislation but to prevent unwelcome innovations and usurpations on the part of the executive by codifying (or interpreting in a particular way) the law, as it was supposed already to exist in principle. The problem now seems to be more one of changed political attitudes than of constitutions.

8.

We can hardly avoid another aspect of human society, the state of the Arts.

Historically, there has been little obvious link between admitted artistic achievement and the level of civilization. It is not rare to come across people in the West who are unable to believe that other cultures can be politically uncivilized or semicivilized if they can be shown to produce architecture, opera, ballet, drama and so forth on an impressive scale. Even in relations between modern states, we find "cultural exchange" sponsored or handled by Westerners who seem to imagine that a political amenity is thereby achieved.

We must distinguish between the various uses of the word "civilization." As is often pointed out, China has been "civilized" for millennia, but it never established a civic order. Cultures may win our admiration for the advanced development of their administrative arrangements, but political civilization proper is another matter. A state with a complex organization may yet be primitive at the level of articulation.

As to art, the paintings in the Altamira caves are as accomplished, as brilliant, as any that have been produced since. Yet there is a reasonable sense in which we may feel that the Stone Age hunters were all the same less "civilized" than at least some of their less brilliant successors on the same continent.

It is a common delusion of the generally educated that politicians they approve of are more cultured, or more concerned with culture, than their alternates. But political culture does not run pari passu with "culture" in the aesthetic sense. Abraham Lincoln was incomparably more advanced in political civilization than any Romanov or Hapsburg, in spite of all the ballet and opera of St. Petersburg and Vienna. Or, if we feel that some special exception should be made for the fan not only of Artemus Ward but even of the far worse Petroleum V. Nasby on the grounds that Saginaw County could hardly be expected to produce the culture of the old metropolises, we can retort first that Lincoln was extremely well read in the political culture, and we can anyhow destroy the dubious and shaky special plea by turning to England and noting that while the Tsars were at the Bolshoi, British prime ministers (Rosebery, for example) would be at the Derby. And it was Nero, was it not, rather than Vespasian, who was so keen on the arts?

I have suggested elsewhere that a curious little volume might be made of the poems of Stalin, Castro, Mao and Ho Chi Minh, with illustrations by A. Hitler: and this last name should remind us that the much touted slogan "When I hear the word 'culture,' I reach for my revolver" was uttered by a fictional member of the SA, the Nazi radical, egalitarian wing crushed in the blood purge of June 1934; and that, on the contrary, Hitlerism proper (like Kaiserism) swarmed over Europe to the accompaniment of vast claptrap about *Kultur* and its preservation from Anglo-Saxon and Slavonic hordes. If it comes to that, the first truly "cultured" man in English politics was the revolting John Tiptoft, Earl of Worcester, translator of Cicero, patron of humanists, the purity of whose Latin brought tears to the eyes of Aeneas Sylvius himself, but who is known to political history, according to different criteria, as "the Butcher Earl," owing to his record as impaler of prisoners and slaughterer of infants, new phenomena in medieval England. We have a horrid example to moderns in the incredible eulogy of him by William Caxton after his death as supreme "in science and moral virtue."

Nor can much in the way of a rigorous connection be made even between the forms of art and the political order. Mortimer Wheeler, the great archaeologist, has written that in Athens he

> could not help remarking upon the paradox: that the greatest monument of contented logic should survey so disturbed and uneasy a vista. And looking again upon the Parthenon, where every stone stands peacefully upon another and no stress exercises the mind of the beholder, one could not help reflecting, however irrelevantly, upon the paradox of another scene: that of Westminster Abbey, where stone fights Gothic stone in ceaseless unrest amidst a population whose traditional phlegm is an international gibe.

At any rate, it ought to be possible to dismiss the idea that any necessary correlation, individual or collective, exists between artistic culture and political maturity—though sometimes such a spread may be posited, as with Michelet's "invention" of the Renaissance, previously seen as merely the "rebirth" of learning, as a general revision of minds.

In any case, all such considerations presuppose, at least in modern times, some level of consensus on what art means—which, of course, may be from time to time amended by innovative artists.

To say something about current Western perceptions of the arts is thus hardly a digression from our main theme, since it is an area of the body politic or body social where strongly held theories and attitudes abound, but where, even more to our point, the very concept of Art in some minds has itself made a conceptual escape into the "intense inane."

The critic Arthur Danto argues that on a modern approach anything can be art. It would follow that the concept "art" has lost any meaning. Of course, nowadays it is presented as in practice anything an "artist" produces for which he or she secures a gallery—or poetry page or whatever. Meanwhile, its proponents make a dual, and self-contradictory, claim—that anything is art, and also that anything they produce is "Art" in the same sense as a painting by Velázquez. The answer is: the whole thing is demonstratively, and unanswerably, a deception, or self-deception. In part this seems to be due to the cutting-edge addiction found also in other fields. And similarly there is a far higher output of theorizing, or ideologizing, than even in the recent past. Gibbon noted of an earlier period that "A cloud of critics, of compilers, of commentators, darkened the face of learning, and the decline of genius was followed by the corruption of taste."

It is already some years since the Tate gave the Turner Prize to half a mother cow with half her calf, cut horizontally, in a glass case. (A friend phoned the Tate to tell them that the supposed mother was in fact a heifer—and a good sign was that the unfortunate Tate people laughed heartily.) And all this defended by the typically mind-scrubbed ex-financier in charge, Lord Palumbo, on the grounds that Turner, too, was rejected in his time. In fact, Turner was an ARA at twenty-four and a full RA at twenty-seven. Later Turner Prizes, some less "transgressive" than others, show a similar taste—the latest being smeared with elephant dung.

This art-quango establishmentarianism came to a head in the summer of 1998, when the whole drama advisory panel of the Arts Council resigned and it was also made clear that no tolerable figure would accept the directorship of the Victoria and Albert Museum.

The drama confrontation was due to an attempt to "streamline" the field, under a new chief with political and economic, but no artistic, experience. The Victoria and Albert row was similarly due to the museum's having been run into the ground for years under political or politico-business figures.

Establishmentarian input into the arts (found in America in slightly different form) has a variety of deleterious effects. Both the state and the financial institutions concerned teem with dilute attachment to fashion. And this attracts, and gives power to, a stratum of officialized "artists." The whole phenomenon is yet another example of the dire

effects of corporatism. In Britain there is a whole caste of semisuccess-
ful veterans of one or another section of the political-financial machine
who have achieved a tedious respectability and seek out, or have sought
out, culture instead of, or as well as, other fields of endeavor.

Meanwhile, like the Tate, the Royal Academy has sponsored an exhi-
bition of various entrails, busts in blood and so forth. Objections are
met with the suggestion that these only come from puritans with no
feeling for the arts.

The present writer was brought up on Cubism, Dada, Expressionism,
Surrealism in the plastic arts, on Kafka and Svevo, Lautréamont,
Cocteau and all in literature. That is to say that his view of certain sup-
posed artistic attitudes cannot receive the conventional shout-down of
"fuddy-duddy"; there is even a poem of his in the *Penguin Book of
Surrealist Verse.*

In this perspective, current schools owe their deadness and dreariness
not simply to an ever-diminishing shock effect in their raw materials,
but also to those materials *remaining* largely raw. There is no execution
unless at a very low and mechanical level. And this is even praised as
"conceptual." That is, there is no "artistry" that a bricklayer—or a
butcher and a glazier—could not do, assuming they could spare time
from their more useful occupations. Marcel Duchamp, before World
War I, was claiming that "intellectual expression" in the artist's mind
was more important than the resulting object. This has now become
ideologized.

Much of what we shall have to say about education also applies here:
art schools that have ceased to teach perspective, and have often also
abandoned human models, must surely be an objective criterion of
decadence. We find in this art world nothing that couldn't have been,
and probably was, done, if more tongue in cheek, by Dadaists eighty
years ago. Not a thing: the difference is merely in how solemn the new
lot are. I would have written "po-faced," but the last time I did that it
was printed in the United States as "po'-faced." The phrase has nothing
to do with being "poor" in Southern dialect: it refers to a facial expression like an old-fashioned chamber pot, used of people who talk nonsense with great solemnity.

This retro-Dada art activism imposes itself on the intelligentsia
rather in the vein of Koestler's remark about those thousands of
"painters and writers and doctors and lawyers and debutantes" spouting

a diluted version of the Stalinist line in the 1930s. And this time, at least in this context, it has entered the Establishment and "marched through" its institutions. Quangos and corporations fearful of being thought backward or (how dreadful) philistine go along. And here we are back with the mental and social problem.

I have painted a black picture (which sounds like one type of present-day artist's claim to renown); I have painted a blacker picture than the full story merits. But not much.

9.

That particular aberration, at least in its pervasiveness, is in part a peripheral projection of the corporatist tendency, which is more substantially apparent in the interlocking of government-bureaucratic and big capitalist enterprises.

This is what Vaclav Havel meant when he warned us that Soviet totalitarianism was only "an extreme manifestation . . . of a deep-seated problem that also finds expression in advanced Western society." For "there too, there is a trend toward impersonal power and rule by mega-machines or Colossi that escape human control." He added that these "juggernauts of impersonal power," whether "large-scale enterprises or faceless governments, represent the greatest threat to our present-day world."

Thus neither the state bureaucracy nor the trade unions are the only "interests" tending to disrupt the social order. Bureaucratism within many big companies is itself little more than a striking example of Parkinson's Law. But when it comes to the broader picture, we find in every country an excessive overlap (often actively corrupt, but anyhow an excess) of the private and public high bureaucracies.

The rise of a corporatist society in the West has been predicted for a long time. James Burnham set it forth in his *The Managerial Revolution* and Orwell argued about it. The tendencies that way are obvious. The measures to be taken against it, and in favor of the maintenance of a democratic polity and an entrepreneurial economy, should be equally obvious.

Corporatism as a tendency within "capitalism" was in its origins hardly a cerebral or conscious activity. Yet it, too, has to some degree become infected with an Idea. We get Managerialism—a supposedly superior, and completely rational, conception of organization, and not only in the strictly economic fields but also, by some overspill, in such areas as health care (usually with deleterious results, as always with premature conceptualization). In France, for example, as Emmanuel Todd put it in his *La Chute Finale*, "The personnel directing large enterprises . . . could rapidly become a bouillon of fascist culture (red or ordinary). In France, the appearance of pink upper cadres . . . is a very disturbing phenomenon."

In the United States Michael Kinsley, as editor of the *New Republic*, described how the phenomenon manifests itself:

> Peruse the annual Forbes 400 list of the richest Americans, and you'll see that a remarkable number got there through the growth in value of radio frequency spectrum space handed out for free by the FCC. Many others got rich from cable franchises given away by local governments. The scandal isn't that anyone in particular gets these deals, whether through political position, corruption or privileged minority status. The scandal is that anyone gets these deals at all.

Nor is this trend only to be seen on the "left." Noel Malcolm, in a perceptive essay in the *Spectator* some years ago, already saw that one tendency in the Conservative Party was in favor of a "Partnership" between business and government (with Michael Heseltine adducing the example of Japan!). This interpenetration of big capital and big bureaucracy has indeed flourished.

In addition, we notoriously find many of the big employers with huge salaries lacking humanity to their employees. The older notion that the workers were an investment and a responsibility has weakened. In the longer run, moreover, the corporatist trend is compatible with excess state spending. And a section of the public comes to accept the new order in return for bureaucratic jobs, or government subsidies. Another sign of this corporatist relationship with the state in America is that big corporations are unwilling to oppose bureaucratic interpretations of laws made by politicians under pressure from activist groups. This is in part because they feel vulnerable to boycotts, even if by comparatively few customers, and in part because the big firms can afford to pay what amounts to blackmail (as in the ridiculous Texaco case). Thus the smaller firms, which cannot afford such indulgences, are then left without anything like a "capitalist" defense.

Nor are these the only reasons why we are very probably going to see, sooner or later, a political realignment. Both a new left and a new right, for different reasons rejecting the established views, seem to be emerging, in what will eventually be a bloodless (one hopes) revolution to restore the civic order.

Meanwhile, many serious problems have simply not been solved, regardless of money or goodwill. We have not here argued over policies on many major issues. For example, "poverty" in the Western countries—which is not merely a matter of the poor in the earlier sense "but," as Geoffrey Wheatcroft has written, "a new form of relative poverty, of hopelessness and resentment, building up its own rage and bitterness, not because of the failure of free enterprise, but because of its very success, from which a minority are excluded."

For it is the exclusion more than the poverty, or even the relative poverty, as such, that is the crux. The new poor include those formerly employed in now obsolete or obsolescent industry, together with the younger ghettoized generation. That is, a very grave and harsh social wrenching has taken place—the concern of state and society as a whole. And even on a nonhumanitarian view, these millions in the West are voters the democratic governments and parties must take account of. And, as in the former Eastern Bloc, they are the potential and actual supporters of extremist parties. Tony Judt has pointed out that in France the groundswell for the National Front in the industrial areas is from former Communist voters: that is, the radical and alienated proletariat.

Perhaps populist, racist nationalism no longer has, or needs, an ideology like fascism or national socialism. The newer nationalist extremism may not have the staying power of the old ideologies and their parties. But Le Pen and Milosevic are trouble enough even if they are not set to be another almost unstoppable wave of the future.

10.

There is much more to be said about the failings of the West, both real and conceptual. This partial sketch may nevertheless indicate something of the nature of, and distinction between, these problems.

CHAPTER XII

"The Answer Is Education"

I.

It has often been said that the "answer" to most problems is "education."

But it is obvious that a high level of education in a general sense has often failed to protect twentieth-century minds from homicidal, or suicidal, aberrations. As we have seen, these have often been generated by men of high educational standing. And it has often been in colleges and universities that the bad seeds first bore fruit. Can anything more specific be urged?

Current instruction in the experiences and actualities of human society is, broadly speaking, not reassuring. But this is only part of a greater problem. The educational crux seems to be in saving minds, especially developing minds, from the habits of vogue or formula. That is to say, all teaching should actively encourage the critical treatment of all historical, social, literary and other doctrine in the humanities. This does not sound like much of what passes for teaching these days, which often implicitly discourages critical thought and explicitly conspires to inculcate the uncritical fashions of the moment.

It might be added that these, though often effectively political in a narrow sense, are not always so. There are formulae that are far from committing their proponents to political action or belief but nevertheless—like all formulae—often have a stultifying effect, and that, almost as much as their political counterparts, form "schools" of like-minded academics, assembling round parties and governments and taking over university departments in the interests of the supposed higher or more proven truths.

About education as the transmission of knowledge there is presumably no serious dispute. About education as a way of improving or exercising the mental capacity of those receiving it, there should hardly be much argument. No particular scheme of reform is advanced here. There are a number of these, but the main problem seems to be how to get the public, and the political, and the academic, minds to begin to accept the obvious (though not therefore readily digestible) need for fundamental rethinking.

A recent exchange of educational opinions had the "conservatives" urging that it was necessary to learn factual information, the "progressives" that it was necessary to encourage thought. But of course, data without thought are worthless, and so is thought without data. To stress the need for even a framework such as the dates of past events is not a mere boring formalism. To think so would be like objecting to a geographer needing a knowledge of latitude and longitude on the grounds that these are no more than tedious distractions from the real seas and continents. On the contrary, they help deploy the world for our minds to grasp. There should be nothing "left" or "right" in such a view. It would have been shared by Burke, Mill and Marx. As a result of ignoring it, a high proportion of the American population is now illiterate or semiliterate, not in any rhetorical sense but by the simplest tests.

2.

I imagine it is now almost everywhere agreed that stronger class discipline, more qualified teachers and better textbooks are minimal requirements for a revival of American, and to a large degree British, primary and secondary education. All this depends greatly on parental and public consciousness. But the attitudes—and even the curricula—of the school systems are in their turn to a large degree dependent on the cultural assumptions found in the universities. This is true even in the obvious sense that recommended curricula on (for example) high school history in the United States are set by commissions of "higher education" academics; and ideas about "modern" mathematics and the nonphonic teaching of reading derive from the seething pot of ideas emerging from an academic intelligentsia.

At any rate, we used to expect broad and comprehensive general education before going on to the special learning to be found, or sought, at universities.

The mere fact that a high proportion of freshmen at the University of California have to take "remedial English" is commentary enough on the high school system. But it also means that many of the young entry, even when not quite so obviously disqualified, are not suitable for academic work. They have not had, or have not absorbed, the general education that would enable them to pass on to a level of academic specialization. What proportion of entrants this is can hardly be stated with any sort of exactness. But it is too many. Numbers "drop out," and a good proportion of the remainder are instructed, or largely misinstructed, in subjects in which the material is either tenuous or obvious.

We often see complaints about the drain on the economy of supporting the no longer "productive" older section of the population. But a considerable part of the younger section of the population, from eighteen to twenty-two, or often for years longer, is equally "unproductive."

Even from the universities, at best, many emerge, as Churchill said of Hitler, "loosely educated." So, much of the population is uneducated, and much of the remainder is miseducated—which in modern circumstances may be worse. The humanities, in their university context, have to a considerable degree come under the influence of Ideas disconnected from education in the sense of extending our knowledge and improving our judgment. That is, we often see the semblance rather than the substance of education.

3.

The century's disasters have been due in a major way to ignorance of, or distortion of, history. Thomas Jefferson held that the basic education of the citizens of a democracy should be "chiefly historical." His reasoning was that history, "by apprising them of the past, will enable them to judge of the future; it will avail them of the experience of other times and other nations; it will qualify them as judges of the actions and designs of men."

Nowadays, too, the more that people are made properly aware of what happened in this century, and in previous centuries, the more likely they are to appraise present-day prospects in a sensible manner.

However, rather than cover, or even sketch, these problems, we may note a revealing example. When a history syllabus for fifteen-year-olds in high school, produced under official auspices by a commission of academic historians, is censured by a 99-to-1 vote of the U.S. Senate (the single vote against was on the grounds that the censure was not tough enough), we are clearly in trouble. A respectable academic com-mission exhibited a slant unacceptable even to the most liberal of the broader world. It was rightly pointed out that only certain sections of the report were objectionable (and that a revised version then pro-duced—though the report had been presented as final—was an improvement). But this partial defense was inadequate.

Its observed fault was that it misrepresented the West. In it, "robber baron" American capitalists of a century ago are antisocial. Slave-and-gold-trading African rulers represent glorious cultures. Etc. That is, the bad, or supposedly bad, sides of American history were stressed by stan-dards not used of others. Apart from the prejudicial aspect, this means that the coverage of the West—and of everywhere else—was inadequate in terms of breadth.

The commission's avowed, and on the face of it respectable, aim was to escape the constraints of too domestic a curriculum by covering the rest of the world. But it is impossible, especially at the school age to which the program is addressed, to give any but the roughest sketch of the variegat-ed histories of these cultures, even if not consciously distorted. A few selected areas scattered the world over cannot serve, though this was the result. From whatever point of view, a school-level world history could only be even minimally adequate on a much broader basis, as with H. G. Wells's, or even Hendrik Van Loon's. It is impossible, particularly at such an age, to absorb more than a clear and limited amount of history.

Then students cannot begin to approach the history of other cul-tures if they do not have a reasonable grasp of that of their own cul-ture—even a perverted, Marxist one is better than a handful of snapshots. Above all, there should be no blurring the fact that, as we have said, whatever the accomplishments and triumphs of other cul-tures, or civilizations, they lacked the distinctive and decisive character-istics of the Western culture—the rule of law, freedom of speech, political liberty.

I have found it easy enough to get this across to students initially unwilling to accept it.

"All cultures should be treated equally?"
"Yes."
"Then it is a good thing to be able to put forward the idea that they should be treated equally?"
"Obviously."

"Then a culture which allows this is, at least to that degree, superior to one that doesn't?"

"I see what you mean. . . ."

But even if not represented as a superiority, it is a point that should be made available to the student or schoolchild.

4.

This difference in cultural approaches has often been deplored. The organ of the American Association for the Advancement of Slavic Studies (of which I am a member) in Brezhnevian times published an article by a New York academic criticizing American correspondents in Moscow for looking at things from an American point of view and offering advice, and even therapy, to combat this vice.

But of course, everyone looks at things in some sense from the point of view of his own culture. The supranational, culturally neuter journalist or academic does not exist. Even American Stalinists looked at the USSR from an American point of view. They did not think (or at any rate did not say) hurrah for the terrorist dictator; they said, look at the Lincoln of today.

There are special difficulties, of course, in Soviet history, but the writing of history in general is in an unfortunate state. We find huge pop books with titles like *My Hundred Hours with Kennedy*. Then there are publications that are little more than mere arrays of theoreticized data, historiography (if that) rather than history. Unfortunately, particularly in the latter instance, one cannot tell what they are attempting to convey since one puts them down after a couple of pages, never to be touched again. However, they claim above all to have achieved objectivity through methodology.

But prejudices do not disappear because one is resorting to such "methodology"; they are merely disguised. It is not a question of opinions. Opinions, even strong ones, are compatible with the most conscientious treatment of the facts, as historians of any sense have long known. Gibbon wrote of the fanatical Jansenist Sébastien Le Nain de Tillemont that he was nevertheless completely "scrupulous" about evidence. G. M. Trevelyan saw that not "dispassionateness" but "good faith" was the real crux.

5.

A surprising number of midlife academics seem to have been trained in, or selected for, susceptibility to dogma. And most of these show one especial characteristic: an inability to believe that not everyone is driven by power lust, and that in the West those who are are held under some measure of control; that not everyone who wants more income is driven by insatiable greed, and that in the West those who are are as far as possible held in check by the legal, social and moral order.

These Marxist or semi-Marxist attitudes remind one that, if not so much in the United States and Britain, academe is a seedbed not merely of theory that is erroneous but also of theory that is positively dangerous. Peru's "Shining Path," perhaps the most vicious guerrilla movement in the world, was headed and founded by professors and mainly staffed by students. In Italy the Red Brigades drew most of their members from universities—especially from the so-called University of Trento, which consisted almost solely of a sociology department.

More generally, as John Maynard Keynes said even in his day, "Madmen in authority, who hear voices in the air, are distilling their frenzy from some academic scribbler of a few years back." Marxism proper has indeed largely given way either to simplistic terrorism or to a neo-Marxist current. As to the latter, it would seem that Marxism-Leninism is no longer in the realm of intellectual debate. Like creationism, it posited an immanent force in history. Like phrenology and Baconianism, it relied on complex calculation and analysis. Like astrology, it will persist in some minds—though in its pure form it looks as though it may soon only be found, like the spotted owl, in a few sanctuaries on the American Pacific Coast.

But the collapse of its old intellectual structure has also left a sort of residual sludge. Its main characteristic is a sub-Marxist detection, in every aspect of life and art and language, of mechanisms for safeguarding the existing order and suppressing a wide variety of social and other categories. When, under this rubric, logic and coherent thought are attacked as Eurocentric or androcentric, and the idea of good literature as an elitist power play, we must in all fairness put in a plea for the older Marxist tradition. Marx, Lenin, Trotsky, even Gramsci and Lukács, all understood that Aeschylus or Dante transcended any class context, that rational thought is possible, and so on. (And Marx himself—when not doing his imitation of an economist—had something of a style.) They may have been scholastics and fanatics and pseudoscientists, but they had not sunk into what Lenin, in a slightly different context, called "An Infantile Disorder"—though, coming at the end rather than the beginning of the Communist era, the present excesses might be better called "A Senile Disorder."

But though Marx and Lenin would have recoiled in distaste from their stepgrandchildren or step-great-grandchildren, two of their basic principles have been transmitted unchanged. First, that power is everybody's prime, even exclusive, concern. Second, that in every transaction there is a winner and a loser: that it is a zero-sum game, and that the idea of both sides or classes benefiting is impossible.

Such abuses tend to remove sound historical minds from political and general history. On the other side of the coin, academics of the middle generation whose political and general judgment was negligible were able to build reputations as experts by minor studies and then be consulted as to broader matters in which they had little competence, though much to say.

6.

One has only to look at the state of English departments at many universities to feel that a mental blight has descended, carrying, separately or blended together, the pretentiously meaningless and the politically vicious. As to the former, certain French theorists have a tradition of enjoying paradox, as is indeed understandable. When I was an eighteen-year-old student at a French university, this was taken for granted, even though one sometimes saw pushed to excessive, and obsessive, lengths what Bernard Shaw would have made the theme of passing dialogue, Swift a tongue-in-cheek tour de force. All the same, there was always an element of play. When exported to America and Britain, this saving residue disappears. At a recent seminar on the much resented influx of certain American movies in France, my old friend Alain Besançon remarked that a hundred soft-porn products of Hollywood did less harm in his country than a single French philosopher had done in the United States.

What is to our purpose is that this Idea (if such it can be called) rejects not only any specific value or meaning to works of literature but also any reality at all. This was, of course, seen in the famous 1996 hoax by physicist Alan Sokal, who had a spoof paper proving that physical "reality," no less than social "reality" is at bottom a social and linguistic "construct" accepted by, and published in, a major sociological journal. Again, some "students" at Williams College spoke of the Holocaust in terms of its not having occurred at all, but having "purchase, compared with the currency derived from other events," or, even if it did not happen, of its being "a perfectly reasonable conceptual hallucination."

The notion of a text and a subtext, or several subtexts, is a geological type of metaphor. At this sort of level, a work of literature might better be thought of as a large crystalline formation, within which one can see, at the same time, a corporate whole of visual variety—and then by careful squinting notice at first unrecognized detail, some of it contributing further to the whole, some of it irrelevant or misapprehended. And, of course, this, too, is merely a metaphor, though a less simplistic one.

At any rate, one thing obvious to adults is that, insofar as there is anything in the point that the effect of a poem or novel depends not only on the writer's intention but also on the reader's reception of it, it is so obvious as not to be worth saying; but that to make too much of it is to fall from the obvious into the inane.

In fact, to the degree that such things as the theses of deconstructionists and their heirs are not absurd, they are banal. The distinguished Anglo-Australian critic Clive James some years ago publicly described "deconstructionism" as nonsense without advancing any detailed arguments against it. When its proponents protested that he couldn't, he replied that, yes, he could. Such a position, on the face of it, is unfair. But that is to be formal. Clearly there are theories, even complex ones, so absurd as not to merit more than an abrupt dismissal. For example, pyramidology, which holds with a considerable accumulation of detail and concept that the future of humanity can be foreseen by a correct analysis of the measurements of the Giza pyramids. Or, for the last three centuries at least, astrology, again appearing in an impressive apparatus of mathematics. Nor need anyone be buffaloed by the fact that members of, or at least spokesmen for, such sects are often well informed as to details. Baconians are probably more "knowledgeable" about Shakespeare than you or I.

The present writer has had direct experience of how a set of irrelevant facts may be put together to support an absurd theory. My "Christian Symbolism in Lucky Jim," published originally in the Critical Quarterly, assembled dozens of extracts, character names and so on from the Amis novel, giving impressive, though spurious, credibility to the notion suggested in its title. This was so obviously fatuous that I hardly bothered to conceal its spoof character, giving reference to such unlikely books as *The Phallus Theme in Early Amis.* However, the journal had to print a note in its next issue disavowing serious intent because it had received numbers of letters from English teachers, students and so on taking it at face value (it still turned up years later in German journals). That is to say there were, and are, academic minds ready to treat any alleged *pattern* as credible.

More generally, we find professional unwillingness to be seen to criticize colleagues in the guild. Deconstruction-type thought, in close alliance with various sexual, social and racial attitudes, not only affects the academic establishment but also recruits new devotees. The present writer has actually spent a few days with the annual (American) Modern Language Association conference, not as a delegate but as a guest of a friend who was such a delegate. The mere experience, the faces of the thirty-year-olds who made up the majority of those attending, gave one a strong feeling that they knew only too well that they were caught up in something worthless or harmful, scuttling about like beetles in some Sartrean hell. They were, of course, doing what was necessary to secure employment.

It will hardly be denied that negative or harmful solidarities exist; that these are sometimes connected with interests; and that this is often partly or wholly obscured in the consciousness of those participants. Fads and fashions rise and subside in the fields of literary, social and political study. They have two destructive features: first, they are narrow, reductive, dogmatic; second, their adepts form sects and work together, even if not in a technically conspiratorial way, to take over or at least permeate major university departments—it is estimated that around 25 to 30 percent of such a department is enough to give effective control of its future recruitment.

So we find a closed-shop type of professional committment. The sort of pseudoscholarship in the Russian area, of which examples are given in Chapter VII, could only prosper, or even survive, in an unhealthy academic atmosphere. A recent and reasonably distinguished president of the American Association for the Advancement of Slavic Studies stated in a formal message that the debate on who had been right and who had been wrong about the fall of the Soviet Union should not be pursued, as it was "divisive" of the profession.

Such academic aberrations have over recent generations led to what can only be called intellectually scandalous results. Rather than welcome new approaches in anthropology, (another field with a higher charge of certainty than of knowledge), the professional associations tried to suppress the destructive, but eventually vindicated, critique of Margaret Mead's work; and tried to censure a colleague who had written about aggression in a tribe in Venezuela—indeed voted overwhelmingly to ban such research into that field.

Then, there are always academics or intellectuals whose temporary public *réclame* far outmatches the respect with which they and their opinions are held by what one might call responsible adults in their field. Yet the system has already to some degree extended from a miseducated academe into a badly educated citizenry.

These ephemeral orthodoxies come and go. The past century and a half has seen dozens of such claims, in psychology, anthropology, history, politics. They have always been an obstacle to serious work.

7.

And these days, jargon has to a large degree taken over in all the humanities. Indeed, one often finds "journalistic" used as a term of abuse in this milieu: it means written with a view to being read. Moreover, this academic jargoneering corrupts ordinary speech. As John Lukács has put it, "Our everyday language has become encumbered, Germanic, artificial, bureaucratic, inorganic. It may not be exaggerated to say that by now American writers face but two alternatives: write English, or write gobbledygook."

But the whole point of the latter dialect is to imply a mental superiority as against the ruck. And to master it, even fairly crudely, requires a certain mental effort, and a certain mental status. The theories and approaches thus presented are complex, and deploying them is often a complicated process, thus giving the illusion that it is a useful one.

8.

"The young," the objects of education, are not in themselves better or worse than any other age group. They are rawer, more easily imprintable, more susceptible to inadequately informed "idealism." We no longer find, at least to the same extent, the obsequiousness towards the young which flourished a few decades ago. But uncritical emotion over youth's idealism is still heard, with supposedly more mature voices encouraging their juniors to indulge.

The young and "ardent" are, in fact, the usual storm troops of any Idea. *Giovinezza! Giovinezza!* (Youth! Youth!) was the anthem of Italian Fascism. It was the *Hitlerjugend* leader, Baldur von Schirach, who asserted, "In a higher sense, the young are always right." And, as we have noted, the Nazis took over the German student organization before they mastered the German state. But the young are precisely those who, even in a civic society, have little or no experience of real politics. As Aristotle remarked in the *Ethics:*

> Every man is a good judge of what he understands; in special subjects the specialist, over the whole field of knowledge the man of general culture. This is the reason why political science is not a proper study for the young. The young man is not versed in the practical business of life from which politics draws its premises and its data.

The cult of young idealism becomes unfortunate above all when the young are encouraged to take their own primitive enthusiasms as generally true, without the normal abrasion of adult comment. Often at the age of eighteen or twenty, a student meets a glittering general Idea and, far from feeling any responsibility to submit it to serious questioning, henceforward follows it like a duckling imprinted with its mother. Is this adequately discouraged? The classic set piece of young idealism is Turgenev's:

> To you who desire to cross this threshold, do you know what awaits you?
>   I know, replied the girl.
>   Cold, hunger, abhorrence, derision, contempt, abuse, prison, disease and death!
>   I know, I am ready, I shall endure all blows.
>   Not from enemies alone, but also from relatives, from friends.
>   Yes, even from them . . .
>   Are you ready even to commit a crime?
>   I am ready for crime, too.
>   Do you know that you may be disillusioned in that which you believe, that you may discover that you were mistaken, that you ruined your young life in vain?
>   I know that, too.
>   Enter!

The girl crossed the threshold, and a heavy curtain fell behind her.
Fool! said someone, gnashing his teeth.
Saint! someone uttered in reply.

There are other words besides "saint" and "fool" which may be thought to apply to someone willing to commit crimes for an opinion he or she feels may turn out to be untenable after all. At any rate, to feel unstinted, or barely stinted, admiration for such a stance is surely to become an accomplice.

Once converted and incorporated into a bold brotherhood, such young people find themselves committed. I knew Georgi Markov, the Bulgarian writer later murdered in London by a Communist agent. A boy when the Communists took over his country, he had become one of the regime's most favored authors. His defection to the West sprang in part from his being commissioned to write a play about Bulgarian Communist partisans during World War II. He was given access to the files of those captured and shot by the then anti-Communist regime. They had been allowed to write last letters. He was expecting these (mostly by very young men) to be declarations of Party solidarity and defiance. Instead he found that most of them were letters to their parents regretting that they had failed to take their advice and asking forgiveness for thus harming them.

But this lack of experience applies in the West as well. It means that every five or ten years we get a new lot of enthusiasts to whom the real lessons of earlier action by the anti-Western totalitarianisms have never penetrated. The plausible fellow with the good line of talk may have the same name as the man who took in Daddy, but he's reformed, or he is only a relative, and anyway his offer to sell us the Holland Tunnel is quite a different proposition from that old deal about the Brooklyn Bridge.

In part this is because of a common enough fallacy: that if students are thought to be critical of the prevailing attitudes of their country or family, they have made an advance. This is true only if they are able to, and encouraged to, criticize the "new" idea with equal care and skepticism. As W. H. Auden wrote:

Yours, you say, were parents to avoid. Avoid then if you please.
Do reverse on each occasion till you catch the same disease.

That the "revolutionary" young are thus "reacting" against their parents may sometimes be true. It was not the impression formed by Dostoevsky or Turgenev about the nihilist young of the nineteenth century, whose parents were usually "progressive." Again, Edward Shils, who as Dean did much to save the University of Chicago from the worst of the student excesses of the 1960s by granting the few "demands" which made sense and expelling the leaders of disruption, told me that when the parents of these came to beg (or demand) pardons, they almost always held a diluted version of their offspring's credos.

The idealism (for want of a better word) of the young may be a powerful source of political or social energy. However, as we saw in the Communist and National Socialist cases, it can be misapplied. And nowadays in the West, as we have noted, it often seems harnessed to (say) ecological notions like recycling, of doubtful value even in that context—and sometimes instilled by well-meaning but ideologically imprinted teachers.

Not that one wants to be too sentimental about young idealism even at this level. A well-known American science fiction writer, with strong views on pollution, was addressing a large audience of students in a Western town some years ago. To loud applause, he said that every individual could help. (Yes! Hurrah! Hurrah!) So all of you stand and tear up your driver's licenses. (Stunned silence.)

One might think that young enthusiasts would take a serious look at the fact that as they become older, people just like themselves become ex-enthusiasts. The superficial ploys of blaming this on a seepage of idealism, the wear and tear of aging, corruption by the various bad elements of society, compromise with convention, might sound pretty simplistic even to a mind enchanted by its own idealism. They might take into consideration that, as the seventeenth-century sage Sir Thomas Browne put it, "We do but learn what our better advanced judgement will unlearn tomorrow."

Indeed, the young idealists might also take into consideration the evolution of their elders who remain unbourgeoisified. For these so often transfer their early enthusiasm into quite different channels— Yoga or calisthenics—while those who remain often become apparatchiks of tedious and moribund organizations (even Gus Hall was young once).

None of this is to deny the virtues of youth, though it does exemplify the contradictions, often learned too late, between ideas and real life. Nor is it necessarily the case that those of them who embrace more or less simplistic or utopian notions invariably forfeit their ability to profit from a cultural, critical and informed education. But we can hope for a reflux from the juvenile dead end of our culture.

9.

Not all young, or old, people are susceptible to education. The Emperor Marcus Aurelius, Gibbon tells us, had this trouble with his son and successor, Commodus:

> Nothing . . . was neglected by the anxious father, and by the men of learning and virtue he summoned to his assistance, to expand the narrow mind of young Commodus . . . but the power of instruction is seldom of much efficacy, except in those happy dispositions where it is almost superfluous. The influence of a polite age, and the labour of an attentive education, had never been able to infuse into his rude and brutish mind the least tincture of learning. . . . Commodus, from his earlier infancy, discovered an aversion to whatever was rational or liberal. The masters of every branch of learning, whom Marcus provided for his son, were heard with inattention and disgust.

That is to say, he was forced by family circumstances into a world to which he felt no attachment or inclination.

This is, perhaps, an exotic example. Still, young people are even now pressed by family expectations into a sphere that is alien to their personalities. All this is only to say that some, like Commodus, are more or less uneducable. Others have had a good education by the time they are eighteen, or even younger, but have neither the desire nor the bent for "higher" education.

For people can be educated, cultured and so forth without having been to university at all—as with dozens from Benjamin Franklin to Winston Churchill, from Shakespeare to Einstein, to say nothing of the great women writers of the nineteenth century. Nor is this only a matter of genius. Even erudition is possible outside academe, a point illustrated perfectly by Gibbon himself, the greatest of historians, who did indeed attend Oxford briefly when fifteen years old, from which (as he tells us) he got nothing. What all of them had was, in the first place, *reading*. We all know dozens of people, especially from an older generation, who are as much at home in these worlds—except in special fields—as their Bachelored and Mastered and Doctored acquaintances.

No doubt these were naturally inclined that way, or else brought up in circumstances where it was taken for granted. And, of course, they must have had some sort of preuniversity education that puts them above many university entrants, or exiters, these days. I think of such people (at random) as Julian Symons, or Roy Fuller, or V. S. Pritchett, or Iain Hamilton, the editor of the London *Spectator* (who left school at sixteen to work in a clothes shop), and of other major figures in literature and journalism.

All this is relevant, too, to the proliferation of business and management studies by which, in principle at least, a new business class emerges trained in all the expertises but deficient in education proper. When Leland Stanford, himself an outstandingly successful businessman, founded the university that bears his son's name, he commented that the humanities (then) were important "for the enlargement of the mind and for business capacity. I think I have noticed that technically educated boys do not make the best businessmen. The imagination needs to be cultivated and developed to ensure success in life."

10.

It has been argued, frequently, that a modern country, to be successful, needs a high proportion of educated inhabitants. A figure of one third of the young is often given in Britain. There is thus governmental pressure to produce the result. And with it comes societal pressure, and a new form of snobbery.

But the "modernity" point applies only to engineering, the hard sciences and so on, on the one hand, and training in vocational skills on the other—and even among these, quantity should not automatically be taken as quality.

A number of British writers on education, in both "conservative" and "liberal" journals, now take the view that there is a great excess of university graduates. Melanie Phillips, writing in the liberal London *Observer* (26 May 1996), pointed out that the inflation of universities has both devalued and diluted the vocational training that is now supposedly incorporated into them. She makes the devastating point that

Switzerland—a "successful" country by most criteria—has only about 12 percent of its young at universities, the others at vocational training. In Britain, she writes,

> The expansion of the university has meant degrees are increasingly being substituted for essential craft or skills training on the job. Instead of high quality training in how to do or make things, young people are being funnelled towards qualifications which mask their vocational deficiencies by increased social status. . . . Attempting to fuse the vocational and the academic is a continuation of the doomed attempt to use education to rid Britain of its class divisions. It has little to do with equipping young people or the country with what is needed. It damages both academic and vocational standards by diluting the one and devaluing the other. Academic courses become more and more skills-based and vocational, losing sight of the need to ring-fence a core of knowledge acquired for its own sake. At the same time, the drive for "professionalisation" means that the craft base is replaced by abstract theorising.

And, she adds, a great deal of what was genuinely academic is being degraded into pseudosubjects.

II.

Even apart from Marxism, the study of human society over much of this century was heavily distorted in the social, as against the human, direction. Durkheim held that no biological or psychological explanation of social behavior should be admitted if a sociological one was available—and this was accepted by most of the leadership of academic social science. Those who urged (like the liberal Lionel Tiger), from the empirical evidence, that certain human social traits seemed universal regardless of the particular social order, were long attacked as suggesting that minds are not all identical apart from social conditioning; and potentially that men and women act differently in the social sphere.

As the veteran Moscow sociologist Vladimir Kantorovich was able to write even in Soviet times, "Social sciences are not equipped to deal with individual behaviour." In an age of obsessed and erratic despots with major powers of decision, this is a fatal defect. The totalitarian state was, in one aspect, precisely the Archimedean lever with which a single man, or a small group, could "move the world." Again, more broadly, Montaigne wrote of human actions: "They commonly contradict each other so strongly." It has been pointed out of one of the recent social mathematizations—"risk aversion" theory—that it cannot account for the fact that the same people both gamble and insure themselves.

From the point of view of our subject here, this is not so much a matter of the philosophical limitations of the method, of the still persisting failure to refute Hume's views on cause and effect, or some of Kant's antinomies of pure reason. In the sphere of human activity, the objections are more immediate. In the first place, that the supposed purely rational and purely critical approach is a delusion; because all minds in fact start from, or include, some irrational elements and preferences. Second, that absolute critical dissection of human action and thought, if taken as a form of truth, leaves nothing but an infinite recession, and in political terms leads to what nineteenth-century Russians rightly called "nihilism"—the "nothing," however, being populated by primitive but unrecognized preconceptions. Third, in part because we have no science of psychology (as against a mixed bag of pragmatics), many important human activities have not proved amenable to more than a partial—and often superficial—analysis.

12.

The most damaging element in the study of humanity is the view that it can be done with the rigor of the true sciences.

This seems to be due to a confusion about the word "science," which in English carries the connotation of definable data, precise measurement and controlled experiment. Except at the cost of vast suffering, none of these is to be found in human studies, which are nevertheless subject to what Albert O. Hirschman wittily calls "physics envy."

In principle, the scientific approach is to advance a general theory with a view to testing it against every possible sort of evidence that might tell against it. In practice, even in the hard sciences, there are reservations to be made. Even good scientists who have risen right to the top of their profession become attached to, and partisan about, the theory they have created or helped create, and obstinate in defending it. Second, their students and acolytes at a lower level, while in a general sense "intelligent," are inclined to an acceptance of the last generation's breakthrough and novelty, and treat them as a barely criticizable orthodoxy. This is particularly true when academic advancement becomes dependent on validating the last theory.

It may be argued that the sciences have progressed through erroneous but fruitful theory, as with phlogiston and so on. Such errors, and the efforts necessary to correct them, did not affect questions of war and peace, of human survival or extinction, nor, unless in the most indirect way, those of property and poverty, of liberty and serfdom.

In the harder sciences, the experimental data eventually destroy fallacious general theory. In the humanities, most data are often hard to come by, or difficult to establish, or in any case lack definability. One might think that in such circumstances academic circles in the humanities would be particularly careful to avoid vaguely based general theories.

In any case, such approaches by supposed scientists in the human field have two aspects. First, devising ways to avoid thought themselves; and, second, suppressing thought in others. It is precisely the mind-set that accepted a "science" of politics that fueled the utopias of totalitarian systems; and was, as Michael Oakeshott diagnosed, "the assimilation of politics to engineering . . . what may be called the myth of rationalist politics."

Such thinking operates also by superficial analogies with the hard sciences, though such resemblances are usually of accidental features. As long ago as 1859 Oliver Wendell Holmes wrote, "A pseudo-science consists of a nomenclature, with a self-adjusting arrangement, by which all positive evidence, or such as favours its doctrine, is admitted, and all negative evidence, or such as tells against it is excluded." Or, as Emile Chartier (in his *Système des Beaux-Arts*) put it more recently, "We can prove anything we want to, the only real difficulty is to know what we want to prove."

An idea that has always been misleading is that mathematical theory is suitable to the analysis of society. Of course there are numerical data in such fields as economics and demography, though even there they need critical treatment. But we have long had a quite different phenomenon—the allocation of numerical figures to political and historical data. This goes so far as to give a "numerical value" to intangibles and abstractions.

The objections are obvious. First, the data most measurable and hence most appealing to mathematizations may not be the most significant. An American Professor of Philosophy was once approached by a researcher with the question, "How many pages of philosophy do your students of various grades have to read each semester?" "Well," he replied, "I suppose I could check that for you. But isn't there a difference between ten pages from a popular handbook and ten pages from Aristotle in the original?" "That's a matter of *opinion*. The number of pages is a matter of *fact*."

We have already spoken of the erratic nature of individuals, including rulers. I noted in the 1994–95 *Program of Meetings of the Society for the Promotion of Roman Studies* a lecture by J. J. Patterson on "Drink and Political Decision-Making in the Ancient World." How this would be covered in mathematical or schematic political science terms is a fascinating question: C_2H_5OH divided by ? = ??.

Already in the eighteenth century the notion of the omnicompetence or adequacy of "reason" deployed the concept of mathematically based politics. Condorcet (himself a mathematician as, of course, was Diderot) put forward the idea that given adequate statistical data, all social problems could be solved. This carries with it the implication that all who oppose such objectively based policies are sinning against the light; and so, again, it validates executive dictatorship, or at least authoritarianism.

It is reassuring to find that economists are beginning to abandon the idea of a mathematically predictive approach—which was, of course, rejected by Adam Smith, John Maynard Keynes and many of their other predecessors, but which had become widely accepted since. Douglas North, Nobel Prize winner in economics, has said, "The price you pay for precision is inability to deal with real-world questions" (*Wall Street Journal*, 29 July 1994).

As applied to politics, it is even less appropriate than in economics. Ironically enough, as the economists amend it, or open it to amendment by reality, political scientists who have taken it at second hand are still in the more primitive phase.

True research is not done on those lines. But much research these days also reminds one of Sir Flinders Petrie, who transformed antiquarianism into archaeology: "When an author collects together the opinions of as many others as he can and fills half of every page with footnotes this is known as 'scholarship.'" Or, even more broadly, Joshua Reynolds's comment that "a provision of endless apparatus, a bustle of infinite enquiry and research, may be employed to evade and shuffle off real labour—the real labour of thinking."

13.

An outstanding example of the failure of academic and theoretical expertise was to be found in Robert McNamara's conduct of the Vietnam War. In his recent apologia, he says that he failed to understand nationalism. No, what he failed to understand was Communism (though he no doubt misunderstood nationalism, too). He had no real idea of the motivations of the leadership on the "other side of the hill," that traditional essential to sound strategy. Bertram Wolfe, who worked with Ho Chi Minh in the Comintern in Paris in the 1920s, once told me that Ho never mentioned his home country: he was an international apparatchik with purely Leninist attitudes.

But McNamara's central error, which he still does not seem to understand, was that he undertook a responsibility involving the lives of scores of thousands of Americans and many more Vietnamese for which he was totally unqualified. This was true in the political sense adumbrated above, and in the military sense. Apart from what we can only call the cretinous body-count approach, for which perhaps the commanders he chose to rely on were at least partly responsible, we find (in our context) a complete apparatus of pseudoscientific lore. The whole approach of "signals and responses" was politically illiterate. And the military side had been penetrated by the then fashionable variant of inapplicable "scientific" approaches—"systems analysis."

The present writer, some years later, gave a talk at the Pentagon with the then Chief of Army Staff in the chair. Afterwards he said to me with a smile, of the strong criticism I had advanced against the use of systems analysis in such areas as war and politics, that probably two thirds of the majors and colonels who made up the audience were systems analysts. His smile grew even broader when I suggested that surely some use could be found for them in the ranks of labor battalions. At any rate, inappropriate schematicism cost us all a good deal. But McNamara moved on to further disaster at the World Bank.

14.

It might be thought that by the time this book appears, all such approaches, having reached their term, would be dying out. One would have to have a highly rationalistic idea of the human mind, and of professional committment, to take such a view.

Meanwhile, to the extent that these and similar Ideas subsist, universities will be providing to some degree, at least in the humanities, a classic type of miseducation. And the scientism of supposed experts on political, politico-economic and human themes is also associated, even in the West, with an excess of *étatiste* intervention with untested, unproven and often disastrous remedies.

"Intelligentsia," used in English, is a word with a foreign tang. It somehow, not unjustly, conveys a more bohemian milieu than that of the present-day "chattering classes" in America and Britain. I suggest (but will not irritate readers by overinsistence on it) "intelligentry."

Using the word in a general sense, it is not coterminous with Western academe. But it is much involved in what may be broadly called education. First, it is more or less the "educated" section of the community. Second, it establishes the habits of mind of the media and of public discussion in general—which of course seeps down from, and (if queried) is validated by, selected academe.

What is mentally reprehensible about this intelligentry is just what made the Russian intelligentsia a century and more ago so inimical to reality and to serious thought. But that intelligentsia, as Adam Ulam points out, was in its vast majority against academic success, or academic employment. It was, in fact, a culture of dropouts, and proud of it.

Its present equivalent, though also hostile to the real world, largely appears within (as a sort of parallel world) a career-conscious and stipend-competitive modern academic caste. Thus we have, in the "disciplines" that were not available for exploitation by the early Russian intelligentsia, a different social basis. One can certainly imagine Chernyshevsky as a present-day Professor of Political Science; but on the whole one feels that the intelligentsia would have maintained its poverty unviolated. One unfortunate result of this academicizing of the intelligentry is, as we have noted, that many of them are under institutional pressures to accept the Ideas of the prevailing sects. The old Russian intelligentsia bullied and blackmailed its converts, and anyone else susceptible to such tactics, but at least it lacked this powerful weapon.

15.

As Lionel Trilling once wrote: "This is the great vice of academicism, that it is concerned with ideas rather than with thinking," and, he adds, "Nowadays the errors of academicism do not stay in the academy: they make their way into the world and what begins as a failure of perception among intellectual specialists finds its fulfillment in policy and action."

The information that pervades intelligentry minds is "expert." In an interview some years ago, the young American actor Christopher Atkins described his first kiss. "I was horrified. I said to the girl, 'Do you have to slobber all over me?'" She replied that it was correct to use the tongue, took him all the way back to her house, found a book called *The Joy of Sex,* and showed him the procedure, laid down in the manual's appropriate page.

In this case, not much harm, if any, seems to emerge. But the way in which "informed" opinions may be considerably more misleading was demonstrated (in a way that horrifies one a good deal more than his date's kiss horrified the young man quoted above) in an article in *Scientific American* as early as February 1982. The writer, dealing with the effects of low-level radiation, printed a table of thirty causes, or possible causes, of death, first with the true results as determined actuarially, then as perceived by three groups of educated citizens—members of the League of Women Voters, Students and Businessmen.

Both the Women Voters and the Students ranked nuclear power as the cause of the most deaths, well ahead of motor vehicles, smoking, handguns and all the rest. The Businessmen not so high, but still eighth, ahead of surgery, aviation, railroads and so on. The actuarial figures showed that nuclear power ranked twentieth, above mountain climbing but below contraceptives, with approximately 100 deaths a year (mostly, of course, from nonnuclear accidents in the industry). Motor vehicles killed around 50,000, handguns around 17,000, surgery around 2,800, railroads around 1,950.

An even more striking revelation comes with the imagined and the true figures for pesticides. The Women Voters ranked them ninth, which would mean about 2,000 deaths; the Students made them fourth—that is, around 17,000 deaths; even the Businessmen made them fifteenth—at the 200 level. The true figure was too small to register, but at any rate less than 10. (And spray cans, actually thirtieth of the thirty, were ranked as fourteenth and thirteenth, respectively, by the first two categories.)

And this is how, in America at least, the citizenry, and more especially those supposed to be among the better-educated or most concerned with public policy, envisaged important facts. They were thus totally misinformed. Their state of mind was stuck among the panics of the

Middle Ages, when rumors that the wells had been poisoned by the Jews or the Gypsies swept whole populations of illiterate and backward peasants. When the California fruit crop was threatened by the pestiferous Medfly, it became necessary to spray large areas from the air with chemicals long proven to have no effect whatever on human beings. The state nearly let it go till too late, owing to protests not from the farmers but from the sophisticated townships of Silicon Valley. Similarly with the recent protests against a few pounds of plutonium in a spacecraft. A horrifying primitivism persists.

But Ug at least had no pretensions to be an Educated Man or an Informed Citizen. The problem is not so much that these nourish primitive fantasies as that they make no effort to correct these by means of the discriminating forebrains of which they are so proud; that they do not, when faced with a danger, take the rational course of seeking out the facts. As it is, they build up a picture of the facts— often a fallacious one—from what they find around; that is, in the media, which is to say the eye-catching mixture of fact, factiousness, guesswork and invention which forms the most readily available store of public wisdom.

It may be said that the public gets the media it deserves. Still, one may surely feel some repugnance for the new caste of cheap demagogues battening on the new superstitiousness. The Headmaster of Malvern wrote a few years ago that his boys, while highly skeptical about religion, were highly credulous about Chariots of the Gods. Unless there is a change in the public mind, the world is in trouble. The kiss of death may be dry rather than slobbery, but it is pretty unpleasant all the same.

16.

Not only the natural enough misunderstanding of historical happenings, but the falsification of recent events in a more or less conscious propaganda direction is also common.

The most notorious example was the Oliver Stone film, *JFK*, about the assassination of John Kennedy. This was based on what, as had been made clear to the producer, was a pack of falsehoods. Now, of course, the right to tell lies is inherent in the right to free speech. But the right to expose such lies, to bring discredit on their sponsors, to make their name a hissing and a byword is also contained in that right. The Kennedy film was indeed savaged in the "serious" press, both left and right. But this was not enough to shame, or even shake, the promoters.

Anti-British, or anti-English, films are as common as the anti-American variety, and have had an effect in (for example) Australia. Nor, as the world-famous critic John Gross has pointed out, can much good have come of a recent allegedly historical film about the Irish leader Michael Collins which shows a—completely inauthentic—scene of a British armored car firing on a football crowd.

At a less scandalous level, Gross also censures the film *Braveheart*, a largely mythical account of William Wallace, in which the English are the worst—indeed the only—ravagers. It is hard to say how much Anglophobia (the only permissible xenophobia) it may have stirred up. But on the positive side, one of my sons tells me that he was lately in Texas with a group of Americans who asked a visiting Scot what he thought of the film, doubtless expecting an anti-English outburst. But he answered: "Tairrible! It's no' but a haggis Western."

Even worse, of course, is the recent Ted Turner series on the Cold War, much of it ludicrously tilted against the West—and now seeking acceptance as a teaching tool in the American educational system.

17.

Overlapping all this we find in the intelligentry a section that is Idea-prone in a more abysmal way. These are not necessarily complete or conscious devotees of an ideology; but, starting with the notion that defects of society are due to class or racial oppression, they absorb more than enough of that. This stratum is noted for its irreconcilability, its intensity. As to self-righteousness, as I write I have just seen, parked in its slot outside an academic flat on an "elite" campus, a smart little sports car with stickers on its bumpers:

Ignore the Dominant Paradigm

and

Silence Is Complicity.

The latter is, of course, an incitement to yell something about smug, self-satisfied, blinkered bourgeois.

It is only in a contradictory spirit that I quote Deng Xiaoping, then General Secretary of the Chinese Communist Party, in a report to the Chinese Central Committee of 23 September 1957, where he says that "the bourgeois intelligentsia, in addition to the fact that a small segment of it adheres to right-wing views, also suffers from other seriously mistaken views, specifically individualism, liberalism, anarchism, leveling and nationalism."

One might feel that some of our own bourgeois intelligentsia has not such a good record.

◆

CHAPTER XIII

Halfway to One World:
Imperialism, Anti-imperialism

I.

With all its faults, hardly anyone really doubts that "the West," in a general way, is the progenitor and center of what world community or world political culture now exists. There are of course those who resent this, and even ideological-interest groups who deny it, or much of it. We may note, however, that even extreme opponents of "the West," or many of them, are devoted to perverse products of Western thought.

For capitalism, socialism, industrialization, modern technology and science, the nation-state are, broadly speaking, Western inventions. But above all, the idea and practice of the fairly consensual society, of the element of criticism within it, and of the rule of law are the foundations of the Anglo-Celtic culture, and constitute in the long run—imperfectly, improvably—both its source of power and its usefulness in the evolution of a stable world community.

None of this is to suggest any racial superiorities. It was all a matter of historical chance. As we noted in Chapter II, some of its characteristics have arisen in other areas and may evolve without too much stress into the broader concept. Indeed, it is precisely because the West can in the long run pervade and be pervaded by the world at large (and so cease to be "Western") that it is valuable to humanity as a whole.

And saying all this is not, of course, to deny the achievements of other cultures and other civilizations—in the arts and architecture, in administration and imagination, in literature and philosophy.

2.

The linkage of the continents into a potentially single world was of course the result of European explorers, followed by European trade and European colonization—and European ideas.

We have heard a lot lately about the decline of empires. This is usually a set of false parallels designed to show that America is inevitably heading for a fall. The Roman Empire fell; the British Empire fell; so the American Empire will also go—thus runs the argument when stripped of its trappings. The objections are obvious. The Roman and British empires were radically different from each other. A great historian of the period, J. B. Bury, after a careful and detailed analysis, came to the conclusion that the fall of the Western Empire was due to accident. In any case, the end of Britain's empire was in every respect different from that of Rome (not merely that London was not sacked by Afghans!). And, except under some different usage, there is no such thing as an American Empire. As it is, we use the word "Empire" of a variety of polities. The Roman Empire, the Macedonian, Assyrian, Persian and other ancient states qualify. Earlier on the rulers of what we now call "empires," Sargon or Xerxes, were simply "the great king," with the implication of superiority if not universal supremacy. Alexander, too:

> Daroosh is dead and I am king
> Of everywhere and everything

exaggerates. But some such claim or share of a claim is implied right through the Lower Empire, Charlemagne and so on; and, of course, by the Mongol and Chinese rulers.

Then such oddities as Napoleon's Empire. And the Holy Roman Empire ("of the German Nation"), which, as Voltaire pointed out, was neither Holy nor Roman nor an Empire. The term is applied, too, to such states as the Japanese Empire, which now rules no foreigners at all, since this is the formal usage. And the then British Empire, which, on the contrary, did not formally exist. The King of the United Kingdom and "his other realms and territories" had no title as British Emperor, and the

Empire only turned up formally in a few minor contexts—the Imperial General Staff, the Order of the British Empire—or as a practical formula, though, as the report of the Imperial Conference in 1926 put it,

> Nothing would have been gained by attempting to lay down a Constitution for the British Empire. Its widely scattered parts have very different characteristics, and are at very different stages of evolution; while, considered as a whole, it defies classification and bears no real resemblance to any other political organization which now exists or has ever yet been tried.

The king was indeed also "Emperor of India," a different thing (the last Empress of India is still alive as I write).

3.

Empire and its concomitant—Imperialism—are now almost exclusively used of British and other European rule over territories overseas. But before we consider these still highly controversial matters, we should note, of Empire in general, that four generations ago the whole of the vast territory between the Belgian border and the Bering Straits, between the Belt and the Arabian Sea, was ruled by four empires—German, Austro-Hungarian, Turkish and Russian. This area is now divided between some thirty-five sovereign states. Nor was the term "Imperialism" commonly used of these empires, other than Russia's (apart from Germany's overseas adventures).

But in all these contiguous subject areas, the nationalism which we have discussed earlier became in the twentieth century, as it had not been previously, a dominant historical force.

The nature of the "new nations'" relationship with their foreign rulers and with each other requires consideration of the varied history of the empires concerned. Meanwhile, let us note that (at the present count) sixteen of the subject nations in this area which later emerged into independence were European.

The German Empire proper, though containing major border minorities, was not in the normal sense multinational, although it tried to become so in 1914–18. The Turkish Empire had not in principle considered its subjects in nationality terms, dividing them rather by religious communities; but, particularly in its European part, nationalities were arising until its dissolution in 1919. Austria-Hungary was indeed multi-national, and had begun an attempt to reconcile its various nationalities, or at least some of them, in a way still, or again, relevant, in that there is now a consciously similar movement in Central Europe. For, unlike what has to some extent happened in regard to the old spheres of Britain, France and the others, the former subjects of Austria have little in the way of resentment of Vienna. Even the countries more recently ravaged by Germany are supposed to forgive, if not quite forget. And it is true that localized national rivalries, where the peoples involved are still there around the frontiers, are in some ways more persistent than the anti-imperialisms directed against a vanished power and a fading history.

That leaves us with the largest, and longest-lasting, land empire—that of Russia.

The Russian Empire spread over quite disparate territories, at different times. Eastward, the whole of northern Siberia had been brought under Russian rule in the seventeenth century, and was and is largely populated by Russians—though leaving major enclaves of earlier peoples, mostly Finnic and Turkic, who are now demanding autonomy or sovereignty.

The Slavic, Baltic and Finnic peoples to the west and south of Russia were conquered in the eighteenth and early nineteenth centuries; the peoples of the Caucasus mainly in the first half of the nineteenth century, at a time when the British were completing their hold over India; the Turkic and Iranian peoples of Central Asia in the last part of the nineteenth century, when European rule over Africa was being established. These territories to the south were thus comparable to the other colonial empires. The Siberian expansion was more like the movement across Canada. And the expansion into Europe compares only with those of the other intra-European imperial powers that perished in 1918.

By the time the First World War broke out, national feelings in the Russian Empire had emerged, or revived, in all these disparate populations.

From the earliest years of the Bolshevik Party, Lenin and his colleagues had been in favor of taking over the old Russia as a centralized state, with no more than a grant of cultural rights to the subject peoples. In the revolutionary period they sought support among local nationalities in the immediate struggle, with no thought of any long-term commitments. But their victory was such a near thing, and so precarious, that in the end they organized the new state on the basis of giving national feeling the maximum *apparent* role compatible with the *reality* of Soviet centralization. The Union of Soviet Socialist Republics, formed in 1922, defined its members as "sovereign states" with the constitutional right of secession. The new republics were to be "national in form, socialist in content"—sometimes defined as the freedom to be Communist in your own language. This, to some degree, at least for a few years, took the edge off national resentment.

But all in all it was fraud, and the populations soon began to resent Moscow rule as not just communist but also imperial. In the West, though, and to an astonishing degree among the anti-imperialistic in the Western colonies, the new system was seen by many as solving the national question. As we now know, it did nothing of the sort. The Soviet Union remained in practice just another empire, and one particularly unpleasing to its subjects. It was clear, too, that any prospect of a future "liberalized" Soviet Union was impossible—since if liberty were granted, the peripheral nations would vote for independence. This was not difficult to see even a third of a century ago, when I observed (in *Russia after Khrushchev*):

> If the Soviet Union is to deal with its colonial problem in even the most superficially adequate way, it has no real choice but to turn itself into a genuine federation. But if the unity so created were voluntary, it might be temporary and precarious. The present rulers would certainly make no move in such a direction if they could possibly help it. But they may yet find themselves constrained by forces outside their control to make concessions—which could only lead to bigger demands, put forward from positions of increased strength. The question is critical, and not only is it unsolved, but it is probably insoluble under the present system. That is to say, it is one of the elements in the present general crisis of the Soviet system, and one that could lead to future changes which may now appear remote and extravagant. Here, again, we should remember that the Soviet future is unlikely to comprise an easy and evolutionary development, and that any too cautious or conservative view of its potentialities is certain to be wrong.

Meanwhile, the last and largest multinational empire has belatedly gone the way of the others. Its legacy, as we have said, is the eruption of long-suppressed nationalist forces, both Russian and non-Russian. It will take some time before they settle into reasonably stable conditions. The detail of the Russian and Soviet colonial past and the post-Soviet present is indeed complex. On the general position, one can only say that so far there has been less friction between the successor states than we might have feared; but that the exceptions—in the Caucasus and the Crimea and on the Dniester in particular—could in certain circumstances be the forerunners of trouble elsewhere, and that Western policy should be ready to encourage stability and discourage instability as one of its more urgent tasks.

At any rate, the main lesson of the Soviet Union's breakdown is that in the modern age of national consciousness multinational arrangements are precarious, as with Yugoslavia as well as the USSR. In our time at least, the closer nations come together, the looser the ties that unite them must be.

4.

"Imperialism," not only in the British case, is a fairly modern concept, usually in a hostile sense. It is, in any case, as with other wordings we have noted, often used as though it were first a single scarcely differentiated phenomenon and, second, a conscious 'ideology" of those seen as practicing it. In reality, things were different.

First, in the British case, broadly speaking the empire preceded the idea, and "Imperialism" as an aim and concept only emerged in the late nineteenth century and even then by no means dominated London's thinking. Its main proponents (as also in the United States' lesser expansion) were "liberal imperialists" who saw themselves as emancipators. More generally, the Empire remained, as it always had been, pragmatic—a matter of piecemeal expansion and with frequent retreats.

The French overseas empire was, in the main, a far more conscious effort. The German was almost entirely so—with "a place in the sun" claptrap. If we confine ourselves to such empires, in which a metropolitan center rules over other countries, we are at least positing a structural resemblance. But even these empires, which have vanished, or all but vanished, in the post–World War II period, differed enormously.

Anton Chekhov made the point. He was much impressed by the British role in Hong Kong. In a passage omitted from the otherwise scholarly twenty-volume Soviet edition of his *Complete Works and Letters*, he says he is "indignant" at fellow Russians who criticize the Briton for "exploiting" the locals. He says, yes he may, but in return he gives them various benefits, while the Russians "also exploit, but what do you give?"

5.

The new nations arising over this century emerged out of, but also against, the empires.

V. S. Naipaul has written in moving terms of how bitter it was for an Indian that his country's entry into the broader world—mentally as well as physically—was brought about by foreign rulers, and yet how vital it was. Reading a dispassionate Briton's account of India a hundred and forty years ago, Naipaul finds that the Muslim had no duties to anyone outside his faith, the Hindu none to anyone outside his "clan," neither having the general idea of the responsibility of man to his fellows:

> And because of that missing large idea of human association, the country works blindly on, and all the bravery and skills of its people lead to nothing.
>
> It is hard for an Indian not to feel humiliated by Russell's book [William Howard Russell's *My Diary in the Year 1858–9*]. Part of the humiliation the Indian feels comes from the ambiguity of his response, his recognition that the Indian system that is being overthrown has come to the end of its possibilities, that its survival can lead only to more of what has gone before, that the India that will come into being at the end of the period of British rule will be better educated, more creative and full of possibility than the India of a century before; that it will have a larger idea of human association, and that out of this larger idea, and out of the encompassing humiliation of British rule, there will come to India the ideas of country and pride and historical self-analysis, things that seem impossibly remote from the India of Russell's march.

Thus, Naipaul adds, "for every Indian the British period in India is full of ambiguities."

Rather similarly, Nirad Chaudhuri, veteran critic of both Britain and India, dedicates his book *The Autobiography of an Unknown Indian*,

> to the memory of the British Empire in India which conferred subjecthood on us but withheld citizenship; to which yet every one of us threw out the challenge: "Civis Brittanicus Sum" because all that was good and living within us was made, shaped, and quickened by the same British rule.

As we noted, imperialism as a conscious concept of a section of the British ruling class only emerged long after the rise of actual empire.

Opposition to the whole expansion, let alone to the Idea, was widespread in Britain (and conquered territories were frequently given up for such reasons). Anti-imperialism among the subject peoples was also a late development. Until this point was reached, there was no special resentment against British rule as such. The rising Indian intellectual class supported the repression of the "Indian Mutiny." In fact, the mere substitution of overseas rulers for local, or Afghan, power was widely accepted.

Chaudhuri comments that this remained largely so until World War I, but that from then on national feeling and national resentment began to take over. As resentments and aspirations arose, there was plenty to fuel them. It was not so much that it is easy to compile a list of imperial excesses and oppressions, in particular the spectacular example of the 1919 Amritsar Massacre. These in themselves pale compared with those committed over most of world history over a greater part of the world, including the area of the empire before and after British rule; but committed on behalf of what was now increasingly seen as alien power, they greatly shook, though they did not destroy, the long and often interrupted Indian-British dialogue that led, a generation later, to independence.

It is not only that even occasional wounds inflicted by alien rulers are always harder to take. As is clear from all the leading analyses from Kedourie and Gellner to the more direct evidence of Chaudhuri and others, the leading offense given by the British was that they only sporadically and belatedly admitted the colonized, even as they became qualified by every other criterion of the West, to full partnership.

It has been rightly stressed by many from every side that—not only in India—British condescension, even when it did not degenerate (as it too often did) into gross offensiveness, was greatly resented. A representative of Fiji at a "Third World" conference in Beijing soon after its independence caused a minor ideological scandal by saying that British rule in his country had not been bad, but that the "colonialists" had been far too standoffish.

As Orwell says, it is perhaps inevitable that a ruling nation sees itself as superior, otherwise why is it ruling? Still, in this context at least, the British seem to have been far worse offenders than the French. But the mere "humiliation" (as Naipaul puts it) was felt more deeply, the psychological wounds of implied inferiority being in some ways more lasting, than violence (as de Gaulle said, "Blood dries quickly"). Still, the negative side has been lavishly exposed and attacked, especially over recent years. And a serious view needs to take in the positives—not only in themselves but as compared with the other European empires.

6.

It is an odd circumstance that the "racial" attitude on the British side did not really emerge until well after the establishment of British rule in India. As Percival Spear shows in his *The Nabobs*, private letters between prominent British officials in Warren Hastings's time speak of local worthies (and not merely rajahs and such) in the most soundly equal terms. And, of course, much of India was already under what for the populations was foreign rule, while the divisions of caste and religion far overshadowed race as such. It was not until Lord Cornwallis became Governor-General at the end of the eighteenth century that the downgrading of Indians both officially and socially began (so that this figure can, in a sense, be held responsible for two great failures).

Still, even a century later the atmosphere was not unrelievedly deplorable. My maternal grandfather, in the Indian civil service over a century ago, collected with his friend S. T. Shaligram and published in Bombay in Marathi (and later in an English translation in London) the Marathi ballads, hitherto found only in oral form (and in some cases on the brink of being lost). My point, however, is to quote a passage from his introduction:

> I had known for a long time of the existence of the noble ballad in this volume which tells of the famous escalade of Singhur by Tannaji Maloosray, and had for months, or even years, been pushing enquiries in the Deccan with the view of discovering the man who knew it. It happened quite by accident at Satara that Dajirao Shirke, a gentleman on the establishment of Sirdar Rajaram Bhonsle (both of whom will, I hope, excuse me for mentioning their names), learnt what Mr. Shaligram and I were about

—and gave the necessary help. Again we find in a footnote: "I am much indebted to my friend Mr. Purshotam B. Joshi for help in this description of the Gondhalis." This is not the language of Nazis on Slavs, let alone Jews. (Sometime after independence his other grandson attended the unveiling of a bust to him at the leper colony he had founded.)

On another note, my great-great-uncle Captain (later Admiral) Francis Close had a command in the 1850s in the anti-slave-trade patrol maintained by the Royal Navy off the West African coast. I still have his notebooks of that time. We used to see the name plate he had taken from a captured slaver: the *Lydia Gibbs* of Salem.

Attitudes like my grandfather's seem not to have been uncommon in official circles. The period we are speaking of was before the national movement really began. The Indian National Congress had only been founded—hosted by an Englishman—five years before, and was to take a very gradualist stance for a generation to come. But later, too, that attitude was not uncommon. One humiliation is not to be compensated for by a thousand instances of amenity. All the same, these are worth registering if only to correct false conceptions of the whole picture.

7.

Naipaul argues that the long "British Peace" of the late nineteenth and early twentieth centuries gave India the chance to mature. And this may be said of the whole empire: over most of it, nations in the sense of self-defining entities developed mainly through the import of Western ideas, and it was always foreseen—by Macaulay, even by Kipling—that they would devolve from London's control. Which indeed they did, without much trouble from Britain (though a fair amount among themselves). We may thus see the Empire, with all its negative features, as an institution in withdrawal as and when nations developed. In fact, a number of the new nations in the Third World had gradually reached a cultural self-consciousness learned by their elites at Western universities.

A statistical analysis by Seymour Martin Lipset, Kyoung-Ryung Seong and John Charles Torres, recently found that the variable having a higher relation to democracy than any other the world over was "having been a British colony." They—none of them of British origin incidentally—attribute this to the fact that many of the old British colonies had had "elections, parties and the rule of law before independence," so that, unlike in the French, Dutch, Soviet and other empires, "out groups" were gradually "incorporated into the polity."

Again, Orwell, himself a devoted opponent of British rule in the subcontinent and elsewhere, points out that "over the whole of its vast extent, a quarter of the world's surface, there were fewer armed men than would be thought necessary by a small Balkan state." In what is now Ghana, there were fewer than a hundred armed Europeans. In what is now Zambia, a country the size of France, there was one battalion of local troops, with a few dozen British officers and others; while the police only carried truncheons.

8.

Naipaul is, of course, of Hindu origin, from Trinidad, so has a double perspective on the old empire. His broad verdict, in an American interview, gives the impression, as do his other comments, of having been, as it were, wrung from him: he calls the British imperial record "pretty terrific. It would be churlish to say otherwise. It would be foolish to say otherwise. It would be unhistorical to say otherwise."

The British version of empire has, moreover, left some notable signs of the survival of the good side of the relationship. In particular the Commonwealth, joined by almost all except the admitted imperial failures like Burma and Ireland. And there is little anti-imperialism in the tone of the 1997 application by the government and opposition in Fiji to *rejoin* it, "and, in this way, re-establish cherished and treasured links with the British Crown."

Nevertheless, resentments at empire are reasonable and inevitable. Part of its legacy is, naturally, some level of hostility against the former colonial power. This emerges in its more extreme form as an obsessive Idea, historically a distortion and currently a diversion from real problems. And this latter comes in two modes. First, in the politics of the former colonial countries themselves; but second, in the West, and in particular the United States, where a lack of direct experience and a tendency to simplify views has allowed overcrude conceptions to flourish.

American intellectual opinion, even among those with no particular political attitudes, often sees imperialism in terms of E. M. Forster's *A Passage to India* and Joseph Conrad's *Heart of Darkness*. As Chaudhuri points out, Forster was wrong on almost all counts, but particularly in giving the impression that the failure of contact took place on the administrative side. On the contrary, as Chaudhuri notes, it was in the administration that the best relations existed; it was the social barriers that caused the trouble.

Heart of Darkness is based on Conrad's experiences in the Congo, where fearful chaos and misery and death had resulted under Belgian rule, or rather absence of effective rule. Conrad specifically attacked the Belgian experience, and also that of the Spanish in the Philippines and the Dutch in Indonesia, and commented of the latter's Boer offshoot that it was "a fact that they have no idea of liberty, which can only be found under the British flag all over the world."

9.

In the ex-colonial countries, to a considerable degree, the "anti-imperialist" Idea persists in ritualistic form, or as an increasingly unpersuasive way of transferring some of the responsibility for present troubles from the local political leadership—nothing to be either shocked or surprised at.

But this natural sentiment is also a basis for a view of all Western influence as a continuation of imperialism—with "colonialism" replaced by "neocolonialism"; under this rubric, any local politician who can claim to be less subservient to the West can accumulate some ideological capital.

This approach thus sees current relations between the ex-colonies and "advanced" countries as still of an essentially imperial type, with the United States in the major imperial role.

The United States is, true enough, the only surviving superpower. As such, its "interests" include a worldwide foreign policy and commitments. To call such arrangements "imperialistic" is a natural demagogy in anticivic circles. And that implies an American "Empire"—which is indeed a phrase sometimes used; but, as we have said, the image is metaphorical. Nor does the hoped-for civilization and democratization of the world mean its subjection to American power. On the contrary, it implies the withdrawal of American power in favor of a congeries of mutually friendly nations.

Sensitivity to the charge of "imperialism" has led to a reluctance to "interfere" in the affairs of Third World countries in the hands of kleptocratic dictatorships. That is, not to insist on credible internal economic policies as a condition for aid. This ruinous attitude has now worn thin but is still trouble enough.

However, the American historical tradition seems to generate "anti-imperialist" misapprehensions (just as the American Irish—or their politically active spokesmen—have been far more anti-British than the Irish Irish). A well-known American science magazine a few years ago carried a letter from an Indian scientist resident in the United States stating (among other misleading matters) that famine had ceased since the British left India. I remember the former leader of the opposition in the Lok Sabha, Mr. Minoo Masani, telling me how the legal definition of famine, that is, the conditions requiring a state of famine to be declared, had been changed, not the reality. Once more, words. (And the context may remind us that a conscious falsehood about the fearful Irish famine has been inserted into New York school texts.)

The Idea of Anti-imperialism is thus to be considered on several grounds. First, it is traditionally pervasive in the United States, though given its most extreme form in anti-Western academe. Second, it is used as a negative label for any effort by the United States, or the West, to encourage liberties, to block fanaticisms, and to make aid dependent on positive economic policies. Those concerned with the future development of their countries, and of the world, cannot afford to let obsolete resentments distort their aims.

So what purpose is served by the usual employment nowadays of the words "imperialism" and "colonialism"? First, it implies a malign force with no program but the subjugation and exploitation of innocent peoples. Second, it implies that this is something like a single undifferentiated entity. Third, it implies that there were in no case ever any real benefits, to the world or to the colonized regions. Fourth, it implies that the continuing troubles of the former colonies are due not merely to the heritage of foreign rule but also to its continuation, or revival in a new but essentially indistinguishable form, after the disappearance of the former rulers.

Only the second part of the fourth proposition is at least arguable, but if so, it requires a reformulation. The rest of the implications are untenable, with the terms "imperialism" and "colonialism" serving mainly to confuse, and of course to replace, the complex and needed process of understanding with the simple and unneeded process of inflammation.

All this is only to say that "imperialist" and "colonialist" are nowadays to a large degree mind-blockers and thought-extinguishers comparable to "sexist" and so on in internal polemics.

CHAPTER XIV

◆

The "Europe" Idea

I.

It is sometimes argued that Britain and other former colonial powers, having lost their empires, should make up for it by abandoning their independence. And "Europe," in the sense of a prospective political and economic union of some of the countries of that continent, is nowadays much promoted.

Geographically speaking, Europe is a somewhat hazy concept—an ill-defined peninsula of Eurasia, with its eastern frontiers on the Urals and the Emba River, its southeastern along the Kuzma-Manych depression (the traditional line of the Caucasus having been largely abandoned). Europe, in encyclopedias, is described as including Ireland, Madeira and other Atlantic islands, but not Cyprus. The Trans-Emban villager is, of course, no different from the Cis-Emban: Russia is not readily divisible into such continental categories (nor, of course, is Turkey). In practice, it has been usual to define Europe in the historico-political sense as the area to the west of Russia—though this has involved certain changes as frontiers have moved. Still, it is in this narrower and more homogeneous sphere that a specifically European political and general culture is nowadays conventionally located.

This faces two obvious objections. First, that to the degree that a European tradition exists, it is not confined to the geographical limits of this Little Europe, but also extends, in all but an absurdly restrictive sense, to its transoceanic transplants.

Second, that Europe, or European thought, has generated a wide variety of political notions; and that the linguistic, legal and administrative traditions of the countries of that part of Europe usually considered representative of its civilization are notably dissimilar.

The concept of "Europe" as nevertheless a political, or politico-economic, entity has been supported by a variety of more or less pragmatic arguments. But in principle it is plainly something different—an Idea. This in the sense that it implies the imposition of an agenda unjustified by historical or other realities. In Russia the authorities are officially seeking a new credo or idea for the nation. In the states of Western Europe a somewhat similar moral void seems to have emerged with the defeat of the socialist, let alone the communist, idea. "Europe" seems to emerge, in many minds, as a sort of substitute.

And, as argued earlier, to be put into effect an Idea requires an abnormal proliferation of bureaucracy. Though the bureaucratic trend can subsist without a sustaining Idea, it does so with weaker morale and greater vulnerability. The previous excesses of Western bureaucracy were morally justified in terms of the humanistic benefit of nationalization and etatization to the population. This is now largely abandoned; so the bureaucratic trend was left mentally unprotected. On this view, the Europe Idea played an important psychological role.

And, as has long since been pointed out, European federalism has another of the most definitive characteristics of the Idea—every event, whatever way it turns out, supports the thesis; when it prospers, that proves its case; when it falters, that proves it should do the same, only more so. The European Federationist arguments are mainly two. First, in terms of sentiment, of a supposed European feeling. Second, in terms of hardheadedness, this-is-the-future and so on.

The notion of a European allegiance, emerging after World War II, was, at a superficial level, in some ways an honorable and appealing one. What it missed and misses, above all, is how the feel of citizenship arises—that it cannot simply be elicited by appeals or compulsions on behalf of a supranational entity. This crucial point has been evaded by even the most effective apologists (such as the Labour MP Giles Radice). And this is to say nothing of the noncivic histories of many European nations. Fifty years is not a long time, and we are still in a period where it is difficult enough to get Fleming to lie down with Walloon, let alone Croat with Serb. The "European" answer to this is that there is indeed a danger of strife, and that a supranational European state or federation will be a vehicle by which the forces of goodwill can prevent nationalist eruptions. But how? To say that the larger federal unit will provide so much of a counterattraction, as against nationalism, that it will win in the political field is speculation—and a speculation not justified by the experience of other multinational federations. The world has seen many such arrangements break up—not only the USSR, Yugoslavia and Czechoslovakia but also the United Arab Republic, the Federation of the West Indies, and Malaysia. Indeed one might add in this century the union of Sweden and Norway, and of Austria and Hungary; and, earlier, two separate attempts to form a Central American union.

2.

The "European" attitude has something in common with the short-sightedness, and too great reliance simply on political willpower, of the revolutionaries. Like them—though of course to nothing like the same degree—there is excessive stress on easily graspable, or generally fine-sounding, ideas and too little on the real structure of our cultures. Certainly the drift of events can be mastered by conscious action. But we should not think in terms of government decisions that our broadest and deepest cultural attitudes would simply follow. Nothing could be shallower. The political leader who wishes to carve out the forms of the future is likely to be more successful if he goes with the deep-seated traditions of a civilization rather than across them. And if the Dover-Calais day-tripper is to replace Drake as a British culture hero, at least let him not set up as a man of broader horizons.

A ponderous section of the British establishment, or political-financial-media class, has been imbued with the Europe Idea. There is of course now, as ever, a great deal of lively intellectual critique and a minority (as yet!) of less superficial politicians who have had an effect on the momentum; and there will be more. But meanwhile, the position is, mutatis mutandis, not unlike that of the 1930s, when the same political-establishment stratum, left and right, favored the ill-considered policies of appeasement.

We are told that both Michael Heseltine and Kenneth Clark were struck, when "over there," with what a fine idea the United States of America was, and thought a United States of Europe would be an equally good thing. At any rate, some of the "arguments" seem to be at this level. In fact, no serious reasons (properly speaking) have ever been advanced for British membership of the EU. It has been urged on the grounds that it is economically desirable; this is demonstrably untrue of certain of the EU's policies, and insofar as a single market is in principle helpful, it is only so if it does not become a protectionist zone against the rest of the world. Then, the political unity of "Europe" is represented as in itself a good thing. This is supported by various subsidiary arguments, but these either present various advantages obtainable without political unity or make such assertions as that political unification alone will prevent Franco-German wars—though if that is the case, it seems that it would emerge without British submission to an authority supposedly organized for that purpose. But more generally, few specific, and no general, advantages are put forward. Indeed, when the economic claims are made, this is said to be the reason for the transfer of power to Brussels; but when the economic burdens are conceded, as with unilateral ruin of the British fishing industry, this is said to be worthwhile on the grounds that the political unification is so eminently desirable. As Kingsley Amis once put it, the argument often amounts to saying, "Britain will suffer economically, but at least it will lose its independence" (or vice versa).

Such being the case, this writer may perhaps be excused a certain acerbity in some of the comments that follow: a change, at least, from the continual labeling of British "Euroskeptics" as chauvinistic, insular, regressive, shortsighted, trogloditic and all the rest.

To have one or two bad arguments advanced in its favor does not destroy a case. But anyone examining the arguments for and against the supranational Europe is struck by the preponderance of thought and evidence on the more skeptical side—and the absence of clarity not merely in the public arguments but in the treaties and regulations of the federalists.

3.

There is indeed what may be defined as a European culture: contributions both to a great broadening of our thought on philosophical and political matters and to a more "aesthetic" broadening of our feeling about the human individual in his (or her) personal autonomy and social dependency. In part, this is due to the accident of proximity, and we have long been aware of the older Chinese philosophy, the Japanese biographical subtleties, the religious and erotic arts of India and so on.

But just as Eastern thought did not translate itself into political liberty, so the rich compost of European thought only exceptionally nourished the civic or consensual order. In fact, some of the products of the European liberation of thought were dead ends, with "dead" the operative word: too many of the humanist minds of the Continent, from

André Chénier to Osip Mandelshtam, were victims of these fatal aberrations. At any rate, European culture cannot be enlisted on the side of the European denationalized corporate state.

The British journalist Alan Watkins once noted at a conference in Germany that "the more convinced supporters of the EEC among us—Mr David Marquand, Mr Peter Jenkins, Mr David Watt, the late John Mackintosh—could hardly order a glass of wine in German," unlike Richard Crossman, who opposed the EEC. Similarly Edward Heath's vile French in favor of the EEC ("Wee, wee, noo som tooss Yuropayong") had earlier been in marked contrast to Enoch Powell's polished French, Italian and German criticisms of it in Paris, Rome and Bonn.

Political and emotional ties with Europe will not be severed by retreat from the full rigors of the EU. As by no means a unique example, I myself lived for years in France as a child and went to university there. My trilingual (American) father won the Croix at Verdun in 1916 with the 65th Division d'Infanterie. One (English) grandfather was born in Nice; one grandmother was brought up in Germany, the other lived for years in Italy. I speak or read half a dozen European languages (three well enough to appear live on their TV). I have translated Pasternak and Lamartine and written on Stendhal and Rimbaud. I have several continental relations-by-marriage. I lived on the Continent for a number of years. It might be argued that real knowledge of, even affection for, continental Europe makes one reject a light-minded and premature political unity.

The cultural aspect in its literary-artistic sense hardly seems important in that context. Our cultural relations with France do not depend upon state or economic measures, and never have done. (Come to that, we did not have to federate with the Soviet Union in order to read Tolstoy; on the contrary, such a federation would have involved our being unable to read Solzhenitsyn.) Indeed Britain and France were culturally closer in the eighteenth and early nineteenth centuries, when they were not merely politically divergent but often actually at war. The Duke of Wellington spoke excellent French. It is precisely when special political arrangements have to be made for cultural cross-fertilization that we know that mutual antipathies prevail.

4.

Except in a very general sense, the European political culture cannot be regarded as a unity. We have already stressed that there is no identity of political and legal practice, custom and traditions, at the level now implied; no real basis for federalism.

The United Kingdom is a particularly alien element in any such projected synthesis. Its natural links, as Pompidou put it, are over the "open seas," to the countries that emerged from a similar legal and political history. The idea of the state inherited in many Continental countries from despotic or from revolutionary times is very different. Bureaucracy, regarded as rational and acceptable rather than as dubious and unsympathetic, is part of its essence. The French political figure Pierre Lellouche has analyzed his country's problems in his *La République Immobile.* He finds it increasingly a model of the *étatiste* decline, with overpayment to state employees and to trade-union leaders who demand it. He strikingly illustrates the power of the bureaucratic forces by pointing out that of 577 members of the National Assembly, 249 are "public servants" whose posts are meanwhile held for them: that is to say the bureaucracy dominates the very legislature!

The current condition of "Europe" thus contains *étatiste* elements of a particularly intrusive kind. Supposedly to promote a fair marketplace, regulations on a large—and petty—scale have emerged, whose purpose is to produce a "level playing field" with such things as the absurd centralization of criteria for sausages or strawberries. The leveling is not of unfair obstacles, merely of healthy variations.

The EU is thus far from being a group of nations in general and flexible agreement, operating policies and programs agreeable to each other, but each suited to its own circumstances and history. On the contrary, it long since became excessively centralized, heavily bureaucratized, grossly overproductive of regulation, and intrusive in one thousand irritating ways—as in attempts to unify, for no reason except uniformity for its own sake, mildly different dates of the bird-shooting season.

Indeed, "Europe" now has or claims larger powers over its members in some fields (such as labor law) than the federal government in Washington has over the states.

The creeping federalization of Europe has involved a series of deceptions. The British were originally told that it was only to be a matter of a Common Market. The Heath government, having said it would only seek membership with the "wholehearted" support of the country, got a key proviso through the House of Commons by only three votes. The

French referendum, at which Maastricht obtained a bare majority, was run with so much one-sidedness from the state media that it would have been invalid in most countries.

The establishment, political, financial and industrial, in Switzerland urged a "Yes" vote in the 1992 referendum on Europe. They warned that a "No" would be economically disastrous. The Swiss electorate gave a "No." The stock exchange boomed, interest rates sank, and the economy in general flourished as before.

Economic predictions seldom work out. But in the Swiss case—as in the Danish and other cases—one may suspect that the establishmentari-an Europeanists were more or less consciously crying wolf simply to obtain a result they wanted on ideological rather than economic grounds.

As a successful confederative democracy Switzerland offers, indeed, a remarkable lesson. In the eighteenth century, when the League had been in existence for nearly five hundred years, there was no common coinage, system of weights and measures, army or courts. Even when the country became a "federation" in 1848 and much of this was amended, foreign affairs becoming the concern of the federation, the cantons yet could, with federal approval, make nonpolitical agreements with each other and with foreign states. And there was no federal legislation, properly speaking, until 1874. A lesson to Brussels!

5.

The Maastricht and Euro phenomenon can be even more usefully com-pared with the negotiations for a federal union in the fledgling United States in the 1780s. There the issues were discussed in public, clearly, intelligently, fairly and at length; and the Constitution, though in some respects capable of various interpretation—and well understood as such—was also clear and comprehensible. Maastricht was debated, if that is the right word, in terms of verbalisms, slogans and vague threats; and this on the basis of a document both incomprehensible (even to the Foreign Ministries concerned) and full of misleading anodyne phrases.

In fact, by the standards of John Jay and James Madison, recent European negotiations have been extremely defective, to the point in some cases of deception.

It might be argued that the process of amending the U.S. Constitution is a difficult one. But when we turn to Europe we find major constitutional changes carried out on the basis of the most meager temporary majorities, as with the French near rejection of Maastricht, or the Welsh near rejection of devolution. Worse still, the referenda are repeated (as in Denmark) until the desired result is obtained—then represented as irreversible!

6.

But above all, "Europe" is divisive of the West, and is in effect anti-American. The former chief foreign policy adviser to Chancellor Helmut Koch, Herr Horst Teltschik, has put it more bluntly than some, but well expresses the moral:

> It is a good thing for every superpower to have a rival of equal strength, keeping the scales in balance. The history of the last few decades shows that there are many on this planet who favour having a counter-weight to the USA or an alternative. As a European, I say that a Europe in the process of integration should take on that role.

Wilhelm II in his day also advocated a "United States of Europe" against America.

As we have said, Europe, taken in the valid sense of a very general congeries of tradition, is not limited to geographical definition but includes the "Europes Overseas." Without them it is not unitive but divisive of the true Europe. Federal Europe cuts across the deeper unity, and does not promote its realization.

7.

It is not merely that the Treaties of Rome and Maastricht are far too detailed and intrusive for a preliminary step towards unification; not even that under them interferences contrary to established British law are imposed on Britain, of a type both pettifogging and guaranteed to cause the maximum irritation for the minimum outlay. But Britain was also trapped by a "cultural" point. When Britain puts an economic or other undertaking into domestic law, it is, by and large, enforced; this is untrue of France, and even more untrue of Italy and Greece. On a cruder, though less deceptive, note, an "irreversible" decision taken in 1995 to abolish checkpoints between member countries was reversed by the French after five weeks.

The EU's regulations seem on the face of it to be tight *beyond all rea-*

son. The tactical feeling behind them, apart from the obvious calculation that more rules mean more bureaucrats, seems to be that the more numerous the bonds, the more difficult they will be to get out of. But this ignores the fact that the more infuriating the bonds, the stronger the urge to be rid of them. Even genuine social improvements may be unacceptable if imposed. Frau Heydrich once told us (*Sunday Express*, 8 August 1965) that her husband had "introduced higher education and health insurance and raised the standard of living," and that the British had killed him because he was, in this way, winning over the Czechs. Similar errors are being made today.

8.

We may sum up what appears to be wrong with the EU as a matter of general principle. That is, the facts that it ignores deeper tradition, that it is divisive of the West, and that its scope is based on an extremely limited (and in modern times obsolete) geographical conception. But even if it had been conceptually impeccable, we may think that its merely organizational defects have been well worth examining in any discussion of internationalist action.

In one aspect, what all this amounts to is a thoughtless and inadequately prepared attempt to impose a certain type of unfamiliar (and justifiably unfamiliar) bureaucratic style on new member countries. And this again implies, in the heart of the EU organization, an ignorance of, or ignoring of, the deepest civic traditions and habits, the cultural psychology of the various states. Rupert Brooke felt able, in full security, to think, when in Germany, of an England where "blooms the unofficial rose." Even though British society has tightened and coarsened in this respect since then, the feeling remains general, and he was expressing a national rather than an idiosyncratic view.

Again, Britain is unsuited to this form of bureaucratic regulationism for several reasons. One of these is, as we have said, that in Britain, unlike in France or Italy, laws and regulations are actually enforced. But this sort of corporatism is only, if at all, tolerable when there is acceptance of fixing, or bribery, or mere effective noncompliance. These methods could, perhaps, evolve in Britain, too: they have always accompanied corporatism, in both its totalitarian and its weaker forms. Not that cronyism is lacking in Anglo-America-Australia-etc.: County Durham under Old Labour was as pettily "corrupt" in this sense as New York under Tammany: what was not to be found was anything like the mass evading or ignoring of all legal requirements.

9.

The "European" institutions that produced both such petty nuisances as we have noted and such major disasters as the Common Agricultural Policy are seldom defended except in the most general terms. The European Council of heads of governments meets privately two or three times a year and delegates most decisions to Councils of the European Ministers of the various departments. These also conduct their affairs in secret, in effect decide policies, and pass these decisions to the European Commission of twenty-one appointed members, who initiate the actual legislation. Under them are over twenty thousand bureaucrats (with tax-free salaries) who manufacture regulations. Several hundred standing committees meet daily. There is virtually no public responsibility all through this apparatus. There is no proper accounting for the EU's $90 billion budget; in 1995 some $10 billion had disappeared through fraud or incompetence—plus a fair percentage through "error." This was public knowledge, but the supposedly supervisory European Parliament only took cognizance of it, amidst explosive scandal, in 1998–99.

John Laughland, David Pryce-Jones and others have examined in more detailed fashion, and against a gradient of obstruction and deception, the way in which the whole structure is repugnant to both democracy and common sense.

10.

The EU is above all in contradiction to the principles of "firm leadership and light rule" which have traditionally been successful in Britain from medieval times. Most of the Continent has a somewhat different tradition—though even here the British lesson may be thought to apply indirectly, in that British arms were able to destroy the succession of Sun Kings who attempted to export their system.

The noneconomic reasons given for British identification with Europe are highly general, and lacking in any serious verifiability. As we have noted, much has been said about Britain having lost an empire, and so needing to project itself though a larger entity. Why? And if this mythical necessity were indeed valid, it is odd to compensate for empire by submission to a small share in a large bureaucracy. Even economically, as D. Hannan points out (in his *Towards 1996: Britain in a Multi-Speed Europe*), Britain's natural trends are clear from such facts as that most of British overseas investment is in non-EU countries, as is, in spite of all pressures and inducements, about half of British trade.

It is possible to point to certain economic advantages under the EU, though none under Maastricht or the Euro. Those that have accrued are precisely the ones that are compatible with no political assimilation. And even economically, they do not balance out the disadvantages incurred from other parts of the bargain.

But even on the narrowly economic argument we may have reservations about the present structure of the EU. The successes of the Common Market have been in its role of free-trade area (and to the degree that this role has not been distorted by its other concerns). One can envisage the EU's evolution into an abandonment of its less successful or sound roles.

In any case, let us insist that political aims must have priority. That is, the whole civic culture and its defense must come before any question of mere economic advantage. This is, of course, obvious unless to those subjected to so much current talk about the overriding importance of the GNP. As Margaret Thatcher once said, "My country faces severe economic difficulties. But I sometimes feel that the political debate in Britain, as in Europe as a whole, is too much dominated by economic argument. It is too easy to be trapped in a web of economic statistics. If we keep our eyes fixed too long on the balance sheet, we may lose the habit of looking up at the 'broad sunlit uplands' of freedom."

When the idealization of "productivity" becomes the original and central theme of what is supposed to be a major political development of our time in Europe, the results are almost bound to be deplorable. We were originally told that Europe would unite for defense, for democracy, and other desirable aims. But if standards of living and GNP are the top priorities, and for all parties in the state, then the issue of defense (for example) loses a great deal of its due importance. Rome fell, to put it briefly, because the economically dominant classes would not pay for the army.

II.

So a federal Europe is, we are promised, just round the corner institutionally, though in effect bereft of such characteristics as any foreign or defense policy, good or bad. As to anything resembling such policies, we need only note European feet-dragging on the Falkland issue, German refusal to help in Iraq, and so on. Again, Anthony Hartley, himself long an official of the EEC, has written of the confusion and inanity of "Europe"'s reaction to the war in Bosnia:

> The German proposal to recognise the republics of Croatia and Slovenia might have acted as a disincentive to the Serbian army, if it had been adopted sooner. But it was rejected, largely as a result of British and French opposition, and Germany rendered its own plan unworkable by advocating a peace-keeping force without being willing to take part in it. German insistence on recognition eventually prevailed, but at a time when it was likely to make matters worse by simultaneously disrupting the proposed UN peace-keeping force and infuriating the Serbian army without, however, providing Croatia and Slovenia with any practical guarantee of security.

Why is it that on this and other issues Western Europe, with a larger manpower and a comparable GNP, bobs militarily in the wake of a weakening United States like a dinghy—a dinghy, moreover, manned by febrile, catatonic or mutinous sailors? As soon as one asks, one has the answer. Recent American weaknesses, however dangerous and depressing, are as nothing compared with the vacuity of the whole "European" defense pretension.

There are those who feel that NATO remains adequate, if no more, in a military sense, to some degree compensating for political weakness, or at least forming a link and a commitment which mobilizes Europe within the present possibilities. After the Kosovo events, it clearly needs reordering and revivifying, with a purge of the incompetence in political and politico-military circles, both American and European, resulting from deeply institutionalized misconceptions.

There are a number of Americans who have been strongly in favor of the United Kingdom's membership of the EU. One member of a recent administration expressed this idea to me several years ago. In fact, the enthusiasm was then greater than is commonly found in Britain itself. The idea behind it was that an ally of the United States, comparable in power, would emerge, and thus assume some of the responsibility which has, unfairly enough, weighed down so heavily and uniquely on America for the last few decades. Moreover, this view in Washington is often associated with the notion of a federal Europe as easier to handle than a lot of little countries—as though multinational federation has proved efficacious in the Soviet and Yugoslav cases. But we may also note that we hear no similar insistence on the unification of the North American members of NATO, two countries far closer in tradition and language than those of "Europe"; nor is the Americo a currency to be found in Ottawa. Or again, we find the notion, held by some in Washington, that Germany should be backed because it is, or could be, the "biggest" of the European states, or that Germany can be "contained" through a "united" Europe—it might just as easily (if we must think in these categories) project itself through such a Europe.

12.

The European Union is, as we have said, to an important degree a forced creation. It constitutes a bloc hindering the development of world free trade, being from the global point of view a large-scale special interest (or set of special interests). And it has proved inadequate to finding a joint foreign policy with the rest of the democratic world, or even as yet within its own councils.

The "idealism" of the sponsors of United Europe has the frequent faults of idealism: excessive devotion to an aim, disregard of legitimate public feelings, implicit falsification of particular moves. A supranational, though in this case nonuniversal, ideology cannot really be a substitute for a progressive, balanced pragmatism. As to its supposed "democratic" future, at a recent conference I listened with astonishment to a German politician urging that no one could complain of a lack of democracy in the forthcoming united Europe, since majorities would be required in the European parliament—which of course begs the whole question. (His previous record included leading the opposition to the stationing of U.S. cruise missiles in Germany at a critical period of the Cold War.)

Through a combination of myopic calculation and commitment to a poorly conceived Idea, the European Union's present form is seen above all on the record, and on general considerations, as a poor contribution to a reasonable future. Meanwhile, its divisiveness of the West and its runaway bureaucraticism must surely be confronted as best we can not merely as unlovely in themselves but also as distortive—even corruptive—of the West's culture.

In Britain, France, Germany and elsewhere—but especially in

Britain—developments in the EU are unpopular. In the general Western revulsion against the political establishments, this can be expected to show itself in pressures that will reverse the centralizing, bureaucratizing trend and, at a minimum, leave a Europe of sovereign states, free to develop their other connections.

In any case, whatever the nature of any settlement in continental Europe, from the British point of view a major change of direction is indicated.

The European Idea is both obsolete and premature. It is obsolete in the sense that the physical propinquity, the cartological tidiness, on which the whole idea so largely rests is no longer as real as it might have been in the days of Sully. It is premature in the sense that the political cultures involved are not yet similar, or assimilable, enough for what is intended, while there are other more closely related cultures whose con- nection should take precedence.

Nothing in this chapter is to be taken as implying that Britain, or the United States, should have any but the warmest relations with the conti- nental countries. On the contrary, these would be greatly improved by the elimination of the negative phenomena cited here.

In a larger perspective, a uniting of Europe is only tolerable within a uniting of the civilized world—and eventually of the whole world.

CHAPTER XV

◆

A More Fruitful Unity
(The Oceanic Perspective)

I.

We face what is still a dangerous period. The forces of peace and progress are still in disarray. Yet all attempts to produce anything like a united will among the free nations have been at best partial or local successes, often not even that.

Everywhere there is today a great questioning of current international arrangements, and often also of internal constitutional and other arrangements relevant to that broader problem. Better policies can yet save the situation—if the necessary political will and political unity are present.

Elan and effort may seem to some degree to be exhausted, disappointment and disenchantment to be piling up. But we are in a position to consolidate, gain our second wind, and start on the next stage upward—or to begin a decline.

For the greater unity of our democratic culture and the eventual erosion of the surviving despotisms are desirable not merely in their own right, but as the best prospect of emerging from the twin dangers of barbarism and of nuclear war which have threatened this generation and are still not eliminated.

But if we need to struggle for greater unity, this is to say that the political arrangements of our Western culture are defective. The European Union is not proving to be the factor of strength expected by some. NATO, even at its best, is inadequate to coordinate the political will of our nations, and is anyhow too limited in geographical scope to face planetary challenges.

Such forces of solidarity, even if shaky and often inadequate, can to some degree be improved by a continuous process of make and mend, which is the ordinary way of politics. But some of the seams appear a little threadbare, some of the patches a trifle worn.

It is, in fact, a moment for regrouping. The very disintegration we see is producing an urge for action to create greater and more reliable forms of union.

2.

The decline of the truly international attitude in both America and Europe, and the increase in local nationalism, must certainly be in part due to a failure of all the international bodies to present living, fresh, attractive alternatives. The EU, the Commonwealth, the UN, GATT, are all seen in their different ways as faded, exhausted, fallen from their original promise and inspiration.

The internationalist idealism in the United States, in particular, was for a long time directed to the United Nations and its agencies. Though this may continue to make sense in specific fields, politically speaking that body shows few signs of any ability to be a supranational unifying force, as against a useful mechanism for international adjustment. Indeed, it may be argued that too strong a devotion to the United Nations encourages acceptance of majority decisions by dubious regimes of a type indefensible in principle.

The United Nations will be seen, at best, except by those who remain exceptionally impressed with the potentiality of what is still the only global body in existence, as no more than an area where adjustments can (to a limited degree) be effected; a facility for certain international acts at a technical level; and a scene of confrontation and political warfare: a forum, rather than a step forward to world unity, at least at present. To the extent that appearances of unanimity are sometimes achieved, this has been largely due to a Western unwillingness to stick to our principles. On the other hand, it retains a measure of legitimization, as in the case of Kosovo.

Britain indeed, like the United States, belongs to several international bodies. The United Nations—and not as part of a joint European delegation; the Commonwealth. It will be argued that the latter is so loose a grouping that little friction between British membership in it and other organizations is to be expected. That is true, though there is in fact some friction. And Commonwealth membership does involve certain obligations in principle if not in law.

The Commonwealth still has, for many Britons, something of the vague idealistic appeal which the idea of the United Nations has for many Americans. As a means of cultural and to some extent economic association, many of its components are, of course, in the Western tradition. And there seems no reason why contact should not be maintained on the present basis without interfering with more serious political reorganization of the West.

On the other hand, the Commonwealth's unity, and indeed its continuance, depends on its being loose—and only peripherally effective in the strictly political sense.

When I was young, London was still "the great city that hath a kingdom over the kings of the earth," if you want to put it that way. In the period since the British divested themselves of empire, they have stuck for one reason or another to horizons narrow not merely politically but also perhaps morally, though a European assimilation would narrow them further still. At any rate, the energy and experience of the British people now have little in the way of credible outlets in the politics of a world to which they clearly have a contribution to make.

But Britain has never been or tried to be one of the two "great powers." A former permanent head of the Foreign Office (himself a Catholic Southern Irishman) put it to me soon after the war, when Britain still held a quarter of the world, that she had never been one of the leading military powers and had always resisted aggression as part of an alliance. Nowadays even the alliances seem inadequate.

It is natural for non-Britons to think that empire, and later loss of empire, dominated British attitudes. However, empire at its highest only sporadically (and decreasingly) engaged or interested most of the population. Nor was British self-confidence, and even sense of superiority, greatly affected by the end of empire, (and internal problems were incomparably more crucial to a vast majority). Nor had it ever been the case that the main concerns of British foreign policy were about the old empire. The Pax Britannica which covered much of the world was peripheral; the battles that engaged the whole population and threatened the survivors were fought in the surrounding seas, in the air above, and on the landmass that starts little more than twenty miles south of Dover. And it is on that front that America's greatest problems, too, have been faced—and the world's.

Nor, though the Continent now looms less urgently, has it ceased to be a source of bureaucracy and bureaulatry, of rejection of the Anglo-American concept of law and liberty, of protectionism, of anti-Americanism. Britain, and America, must be vitally concerned with Europe. That is no reason for Britain to, or America to encourage Britain to, submit to or be merged in what can only be paradoxically described as an insular Europe.

3.

If we seek something better, it seems sensible to turn to a grouping which would be natural rather than artificial, going with the cultural grain rather than cutting across it. It hardly needs saying that what comes to mind is some form of unity between the countries of the same legal and political tradition: that is to say an Association of the United States, the United Kingdom and Canada, with Australia and New Zealand and, it is to be hoped, Ireland, the nations of the Caribbean and the Pacific Ocean, perhaps others. Such an international grouping could in the long run lead to a world order, and in the short run be a valid entity. It will not come into being tomorrow. Here we can only adumbrate a future, sketch out problems and possibilities. A political change, a change in our peoples' consciousness, is needed. The time seems ripe, our countries to be awaiting an initiative which can lead them out of today's inadequacies and dangers.

Within the West, it is above all the English-speaking community which has over the centuries maintained the middle way between anarchy and despotism. For most of the rest of the world, in the past as now, this balance has failed. (A great Chinese historian once despairingly wrote of his countrymen that their history alternated between periods when they were enslaved and periods when they wished they were.)

Necker's praise of the British constitution, that it was (then) the only government in the world "which united public strength with individual security," is the defining point of the system we now describe loosely as democracy. And the same could be said of the United States. We are used to our inheritances. We think it natural and normal that we enjoy the civil and other liberties common to our countries, and we rightly complain about their defects or inadequacies. But our order is not that which has commonly or widely prevailed—as a look at the present-day world should be enough to remind us. We are, through the luck of our history, the main bastion against the various barbarisms and worse which have reared their heads so devastatingly in the past half century. Nor need we forget that in World War II those areas of Europe and Asia which were indeed liberated, and not turned over to a later despotism, were liberated in the European case largely by the combined arms of the United States, Britain and Canada; in the Asian case largely by the combined arms of the United States, Britain, Australia and New Zealand.

In spite of everything that has been said against it, of all the announcements of its demise, the "special relationship" between Britain and the United States remains. There are, indeed, misunderstandings; there are those in each country concerned to exacerbate these. But at a profounder level, the word "foreigner" is never used in Britain of an American (and, in the United States, even at the Vietnam nadir of disillusion and isolationism, Gallup polls showed Britain as the only overseas country to which a majority of Americans would still send troops for defense against "Communist-backed forces"). Meanwhile, Britons emigrate to California rather than Calabria, to Vancouver rather than Valencia.

The Declaration of Independence speaks only of dissolving the then political connection with Britain. As an American historian comments, "No one in the new nation, high or low, expressed a desire to repudiate the social, intellectual, cultural, and moral heritage" (Arthur Schlesinger, Sr., in *The Birth of the Nation*). Moreover, as another remarked, "It is not even certain that the political separation of Britain and America which took place in the eighteenth century is a permanent one" (Professor John R. Alden in the introduction to his *A History of the American Revolution*).

The English-speaking countries have diverged indeed, but not too much. It is true that, even within our tradition, in many parts of the world there is lost ground to be made up. Since the establishment of the EEC, for example, in both Australia and New Zealand we have seen not only a disruption of economic links formerly existing between them and Britain but a concurrent political alienation, though not yet to the point of resentment on the decisive scale.

The sentiment for greater unity remains, but it lacks a program: the high prospects of a grand Association could supply this.

What I am thus putting forward is a flexibly conceived Association of the countries of the same language, legal tradition and general political culture, as the natural way in which the greater unity can develop: a unity that matches our history and feelings, and is not an artificial cutting across them.

4.

The difficulties of bringing these countries into Association are clearly great. But they are, in principle, petty difficulties, a tangle of detailed interests, thoughts and habits. Though of course there are many differences, the situation resembles that which faced the American Federalists in the 1780s. At the lower level, everything was against them. It seemed almost impossible that, in spite of their common heritage of law and liberty, a general unity could prevail in thirteen democracies over so various and so tangled a mesh of legalisms and local interests as then existed.

The weaknesses, the disintegrative tendencies of the United States in the period immediately following the Revolution were in fact obvious, and they provided material for countless Cassandras. But a man like Benjamin Franklin could see through this to the basic strength. And, just as it was precisely the crumbling of the old American confederation, the backbiting and worse between the states, that induced the Federalists to make the effort for unity, so our own problems present the same sort of challenge.

It is a mistake to imagine that only revolutionaries and utopians are capable of strong and radical action. Where great changes are needed in the interest of stability and progress, men of vision have not seldom been available to press them through. In the 1780s events in America were *not* allowed to drift on in an unsatisfactory fashion, in the direction of disintegration and impoverishment. The difficulties were diagnosed and opportunities seized.

It is surprising, too, to find it argued that the distances separating North America, Australasia and Britain are too great for political union; and to have a unity of Britain and Continental Western Europe urged (as we have noted) on grounds of geography. Britain's political links have for centuries been across the oceans.

But in any case the argument by distance fails. The thousand-mile spread of the American States in the eighteenth century was, in fact, effectively far greater than the twelve-thousand-mile spread of the countries of our culture today. Caesar Rodney rode through the whole night to arrive in Philadelphia to cast the vital vote for the Declaration of Independence. Today a helicopter would have got him there in a fraction of the time. At that period it took two days to get from New York merely to Philadelphia by John Barnell's "flying machine," and five to Baltimore; while other connections were worse still. The alternative sea routes took nearly as long and were even more subject to delays. Nowadays, statesmen and businessmen can get to Canberra in much shorter times, while communication by telephone and so on is an additional effective shrinker of space.

Again, the British had the closest political connections right across the globe to New Zealand in the farthest antipodes at a time when it took weeks and months to maintain contact. Now, when London can speak to Auckland or Adelaide instantaneously, when they can be reached in person in a couple of days, the British are told that their natural political contacts are with Europe. Europe is indeed nearer, in the crudest physical sense, but ours is precisely the era when travel and communication have made this ever less and less significant for practical purposes. Moreover, this has been increasingly so. In the past twenty years the time of travel between mid-London and mid-Washington has decreased far more rapidly in proportion than that between mid-London and mid-Rome.

The obstacles of geography are in fact exaggerated. What about the obstacles of nationalism and ethnicity?

First, there is no racial implication in the fact that our political culture is the most advanced, and the most promising. This style of political and civic organization happens to have emerged and to have survived most importantly in Britain, and to have spread most widely from that center. This historical chance, needless to say, does not mean that our form of society is exclusive in principle, or attached to any particular genetic group.

Great Britain itself has several "nationalities." No one who knows the English, Scots and Welsh could believe for a moment that they are really much the same. The cultural, temperamental and other differences are very great indeed. But the political and civic tradition, the elements of unity, transcend them.

There are, of course, nationalist movements in Scotland and Wales—

to some extent as a well-founded revulsion against state centralization. We now have major constitutional devolution. But there are strong arguments against extreme nationalisms which have so far prevailed upon the electorate (and it does seem a little dated to—as a Scottish non-Nationalist allegedly put it—urge that Scotland take her rightful place at the United Nations between Saudi Arabia and Senegal). Nevertheless, it is arguable that Scotland and Wales might feel a richer liberty within a larger Association.

If the British population is itself fairly heterogeneous, the American is more so. In their economic interests and their social structure, even the original United States were, as we have said, a variegated lot. As Thomas Paine pointed out, the populace were by no means entirely of the same stock: even if the black element was then largely excluded from the civic culture, the New York Dutch, the Germans and Swedes in the middle colonies, the important Huguenot element, let alone the Irish, were far from negligible—and the Germans were about a tenth of the population, the Scotch-Irish about three quarters of a tenth.

What the colonies had in common was first, of course, a main language, but second and more important, the institutions and habits of the legal and civic culture.

Some American and other writers have taken the view that "national identity" in the sense in which it is found among the European peoples is to some degree weaker in the United States; and that, for this reason, there is a tendency to substitute general principles or supposed general principles for the deeper and less conscious bonds.

It may be true that some such substitution takes place, at least in certain minds. But it would be hard to assert that an American identity, starting in Revolutionary times, did not get a firm hold. The argument that the huge influx of immigrants from various nations to some degree diluted this may appear plausible on the surface. But to what degree? The astonishing thing, until very recently at least, was the effectiveness of the "melting pot." But the fact of maintaining the older national, religious or cultural traditions of the countries from which the Americans derive (or in recent years of a notable return to them) need not in any way affect the general national feeling. For in the first place, with us the state does not aspire to be the center of all public aspiration. We can include communities of different internal loyalties. In Britain loyalty to a Scottish clan, or to the Jewish community, does not in any way compete with loyalty to the country. America's ethnic diversity, in fact, may yet promote greater national pride.

It was said of Disraeli, "At but one remove by birth from Southern Europe and the East, he was an Englishman in nothing but his devotion to England and his solicitude for her honour and prosperity," and this would apply to many originating outside our culture, but temperamentally within it. Some of the most prominent and devoted adherents of the ideas involved—statesmen, judges and others—have been immigrants, like Felix Frankfurter, or been black, like leaders in both the United States and the Caribbean countries—and elsewhere. Some 30 million people of African descent have English as their native tongue, and generally regard our political tradition as their own. Most are in the United States, but they include majorities or important minorities in a number of independent states, largely in the Caribbean, together with a major community in Britain. No doubt there are racial problems in most of our countries. But more decisively, polls in the United States show that a great majority of blacks see their country as worth defending. It would be up to the Association to give even greater reason for, and scope to, such feelings.

5.

Meanwhile, let us again assert that the links between the various countries of which we speak are not merely historical—though here, too, the connection is powerful. More powerful yet is the commitment to its concepts of Law and Liberty, in a way that is not shared to anything like the same degree by other countries within the general democratic sphere.

Then again, the closer our various countries are brought together politically, the more we can learn even as regards our internal arrangements from our fellow confederates. We all face economic and social and legal problems, and it is reasonably clear that in most cases some could have learned from the previous experience of others—and didn't. A closer means of direct consultation might be helpful. Formal differences in the legal systems as such are no impediment. The Scottish and English legal systems within the United Kingdom are greatly different; while in the United States Louisiana's laws differ importantly from those of the rest of the country. Again, in Britain, Canada and the United States there are constitutional issues now coming to the fore, and some of them are ones in which the experience of one side of the

Atlantic is directly instructive to the other. In Canada such questions affect the whole future of the federation. Such problems might in the long run be easier to cope with under a larger union.

6.

The United States nowadays has less wish to undertake the enormously preponderant role in the West's foreign and military arrangements and responsibilities which has fallen to it since the war. A unity with the other countries of the same tradition would both ease the American task and spread some of the American responsibility. Countries that have, however unintendingly, relied on the Americans, and themselves been inadequately faced with either the responsibilities or the decisions of world power, should be brought into the central processes.

But it is not only that the United States, still the most powerful of democracies, may no longer feel capable of bearing the burden on its own. Countries such as the United Kingdom, Canada and Australia have the skills, but they do not have the power, to act wholly autonomously with any but local effect. Yet their interests, too, are deeply involved in the world scene, and there are contributions they can make far outside their own areas which could help the whole free community. A recent American tendency to make unilateral decisions, and then complain that its allies are not backing it up, is relevant to the present world troubles. But unilateral American actions are of less benefit to the United States itself than if they had been properly concerted. On the other hand, the Americans may in turn rightly complain that it is possible for their allies to commit them, against their own judgment. The power of the small states to involve the larger ones has been illustrated many times over. Under closer Association, countries such as the United Kingdom, which have not seldom felt themselves committed by American decisions tending to the unilateral, would fully share not only the responsibility of decision but also that of military or other action.

Nor is it true that—as some British left-wing circles would certainly declare—the United Kingdom would come more directly under American control or influence. Precisely the opposite, it would no longer find major confrontations, or lesser decisions on weaponry or local commitment, taken without its participation. At present it is possible for a confrontation to occur in many parts of the world in which, though some sort of formal consultation might take place, decisions would in practice be taken in Washington, which would inevitably commit Britain too; or alternatively the United States would have to face a crisis alone—to the benefit, in either case, of none of us. Nor, in stressing the negative side, should we forget that in the Iraq confrontations in 1998 it was Britain—and Canada and Australia—that supported the United States: which is to say that a de facto trend to united policies already exists. The policies themselves are, of course, open to severe criticism.

7.

In the whole stretch of the British Isles, from Muckle Flugga to La Maitresse, the feeling is that Britain's internal difficulties (as well as international) are refractory enough to call for some quite new initiative—such as might and should emerge in a greater union.

On Australia and New Zealand, there is little to say that is not obvious. As with Britain in Europe, the defense of the Southwest Pacific depends on the support of the United States—or, in the broader view, of the whole Anglo-Oceanic community. In two wars Australia and New Zealand militantly supported their European progenitor, the United Kingdom. The fissiparous tendencies we have noted above are largely to be blamed on isolationist moods and even more on the "European" aberrations of the British. At any rate, there are now anti-British feelings in both countries—and, in Australia, republicanism. All the same, both countries still send their elites predominantly to London. A removal of London's disastrous anti-antipodean (and now anti-Caribbean) food-import policies must, in time, ease resentments. And, in spite of a routine anti-Americanism of the worldwide type, a general realization of the necessity in Pacific circumstances of the American alliance predominates.

In North America, one profound constitutional change has already taken place this century by public vote. This was in 1949 when Newfoundland, then an independent Dominion, united with Canada after a plebiscite. As to the present Canadian situation, some polls have shown that in the case of a secession by Quebec, majorities in a number of the western provinces might wish actually to accede to the United States. Resistance to such an extension simply of the United States is nevertheless strong. On an Association basis, the former trend might be muted and the latter still largely satisfied.

If Quebec were indeed to secede, clearly the whole situation in

Canada—and hence in the relations between the United States and all the "British" countries—would become fluid. In such a situation it would be necessary for any real statesman to have his policies ready. But even apart from that (and one would naturally hope that a whole Canada might play its part in an Association), it is plain that minds are ripe for broader solutions.

It would be premature to consider in any detail many of the problems of the Caribbean or Pacific worlds: the position of Puerto Rico, for example, is already anomalous—and why not? Yet, membership in the Association of the Caribbean and Pacific and other island territories that are linked in a political, historical tradition is a desirable prospect.

In an Association one of whose principles would be a repudiation of racial prejudices, and acceptance of the will of populations everywhere, the membership of these "ex-colonial" countries would, as we have suggested, be morally significant. The considerable non-Caucasian population of the United States and the United Kingdom—and to a lesser extent of New Zealand, Australia and even Canada—should in any case be represented in the delegations to any Intercontinental Congress. And one would expect the active cooperation of Jamaica and other states of the Caribbean—a true area of black power—to have a sensible effect in its turn upon both white and black in the United States and England. At this level of state cooperation, Association decisions might be expected to carry special weight—unlike those of majority "white" governments' vague vote-catching, or of the rhetorical antagonisms of the United Nations. In the Caribbean, tendencies to local nationalism and even racialism are opposed by powerful forces. The strengthening of friendly links with the other countries of similar political civic and linguistic tradition, giving Jamaica, Trinidad and the others a real say in the policies of the whole community, must fortify this spirit.

In the Pacific, too, there is a range of these island states whose inhabitants have, through temperamental sympathy and attitude, accepted the Western consensual tradition—or rather melded their own earlier and similar traditions with ours. The peoples of Tonga, Fiji, Western Samoa, Tuvalu, Kiribati, the Solomon Islands, Papua New Guinea, the three territories of Micronesia, as also the residual British, American and New Zealand territories proper, all accept the principles for which we stand. And when it comes to detail, one can see in this greater unity such adjustments as—in effect—a reunification of Samoa. Over the whole area, membership in the Association could mediate not too obtrusive local unities, some of them already in place.

To turn to the European area of the Association, it is to be hoped on a number of grounds that the Republic of Ireland might also accede, even if not at once. The Irish tradition of neutrality would, it is true, tell against this—even though a partial, nonmilitary association status might possibly form a temporary bridge. If so, the great Irish administrative and military talent, once available to the British Empire, would again have a role on the world stage. Ireland, the Irish both North and South, and their problems, constitute a special case. Here it would only be appropriate to say that their contributions to both Britain and America have been great and that they could easily find a valuable place in our Association.

8.

Could Britain be a member both of such an Association *and* of the European Union? Be that part of the Association which is also in Europe, or, looked at another way, that part of the EU which is also in an outside Association? Could Britain remain in a looser EU, serving in rather different form in the way a Labour Foreign Secretary, Dennis Healey, urged—as "America's Trojan horse"?

It must be allowed that a revision of the Treaties of Rome and Maastricht—whose main general defect is in any case an excessive spelling out of detail—would probably be required, or at least a suitable interpretation hammered out on certain points. For if we accept that the EU in its present form is psychologically and politically premature, the only available solution (short of total secession, which would at least be preferable to total acceptance) must be in the first place to loosen it institutionally. But there should be no insoluble problem. When we consider the constitutional arrangements that are to be found throughout history, we discover ways in which ingenuity has provided a diversity of precedents.

In feudal times proper, all sorts of variations were seen, with the English king being a vassal of France for territories like Aquitaine, but for other purposes sovereign on equal terms. More recently, some of the relationships established within the old Indian Empire showed similar flexibility. Elsewhere, too, an extraordinary array of modes of political association can be found, suggesting that in a reasonably loose and undogmatic unity various types of associate membership, treaties of protection, observer status and so forth can be devised for particular countries. In the Holy Roman Empire a number of states were partly in and partly out, so that the Hapsburg rulers were in it in respect of Austria, but not in their capacity as Kings of Hungary, and the Hohenzollerns were in as Electors of Brandenburg and out as Kings of Prussia. It contained Free Cities, Prince-Bishoprics and hereditary Monarchies, with the Emperor elected by the heads of the leading states. In the German Confederation (1815–66), similarly, large states outside, with small properties inside the boundaries, were represented—for example, the Netherlands (by Luxemburg) and Denmark (by Holstein).

Many modern arrangements demonstrate a similar flexibility, far from what perfect logic would seem to require. India is a Republic and a member of an admittedly ramshackle Commonwealth of which a Queen is Head. More practically, Malaysia is a federation of monarchies and non-monarchies, of which the Head of State is one of the monarchs. Andorra had as one of its coprinces the President of France. Federations within federations are known. Switzerland has "half cantons."

9.

If we are not yet agreed on specific solutions, there is increasing accord on the nature of the problems, and on the failure of previous diagnosis and treatment.

It would be premature to do more than outline the perspectives. And though it would not yet be appropriate to define the precise degree of unity institutionalized in such a grouping, the word "Association" implies—let us say—something weaker than a federation, but stronger than an alliance. It is not that the reins would be looser than in the EU, but that there would be no reins.

This proposal, it may be thought, combines grandeur with modesty. It presents advantages and attractions to both left and right; to both nationalist and internationalist; to the United States, the United Kingdom and the other countries concerned.

It is a move that can carry the whole middle ground. It falls neither into the narrowness of petty and local economic interests nor into the vacuity of utopian fantasy.

It cannot be attained without a serious political struggle. But such a struggle would itself be revivifying—as in the United States in the 1780s.

Imagination will be needed, as it always is, to effect such a great political transformation. Against it will be ranged, not merely opposition of various sorts but also the forces of apathy, and even more of established habit and interest.

10.

Evolution to a united and peaceful world is not something that can be undertaken in an abstract way. Those like H. G. Wells, who simply advocated a World State, seemed to imagine that the mere concept was so obviously demanded by progress and efficiency that intelligent people everywhere would accept it and then, in one way or another, impose it.

The natural evolution would be, as we have said, a progressive uniting of the traditional civic cultures, attracting to that established center cultures less similar but converging in their direction, and finally cultures initially highly alien but, over a longer or shorter period, evolving their own forms of civic order.

Generally speaking, closer integration of the (in the main) English-speaking countries, can create a center of power attractive to the other countries with a democratic tradition and form the basis for a yet broader political unity in the longer run. And this in turn could eventually be the foundation for a full unity of a democratized world.

For from the point of view of the world at large, we can view a greater Association both in the short and in the long term. In the short term in defining political civilization, in opening a great part of the world to joint solutions of economic and social problems; and in the long term in securing world peace, transforming the politically backward areas, and creating the conditions for a genuine world community.

A unity of the United States, the United Kingdom, Canada, Australia and New Zealand would itself be a viable hyperpower and, if no more could be done in the first phase, would suffice for a start. But it is to be hoped that all, or as many as possible, of the other countries having partly or entirely the same system might again conjoin at a more fruitful level.

A closer Association of the United States and Britain and the other democracies of our tradition would not affect the principles of NATO. On the contrary, some such means of infusing a new spirit seem necessary. For if NATO is to avoid the two perils of European apathy or parochialism and American disenchantment, the best way would be to

have at least Britain committed unreservedly to a joint *global* policy and
strategy, over which she would have more say than at present and in
which she would equally undertake greater responsibility. On the one
hand, this would undermine any American isolationist tendencies; and
on the other, the fact of American involvement in this new and expan-
sive manner would offer the shakier allies on the European continent a
guarantee and a rallying point from which they could develop fresh
strength and morale.

It can be argued that France and Germany, for example, will be alienated from the Oceanic countries and NATO by such an "English-
speaking" union. I believe this to be false. It is the present unsatisfactory
arrangements that have encouraged or allowed tergiversation in Berlin
and Paris. These have most obviously *not* been stopped by membership
of NATO or the EU. And GATT, again fine in principle, is in practice
hampered by various narrow interests—particularly those of the
"Europeans"—acting, almost always, contrary to British interests.

Germany, Italy, Spain, even France have in generations not long past
seen highly disturbing developments, to say the least of it. It is true that
democracy has in a general way maintained or reestablished itself
against the various threats in most of these areas. And all help possible
should be given to carry this yet further. But the notion that British
membership in Europe must certainly have this effect seems dubious.
One can argue that greater influence could be brought to bear from an
"Oceanic" Association, but also that, to look at it another way, Britain
could mediate the Association's policies towards Europe.

Judged in this deeper perspective, then, the EU looms small: either as
an irrelevance that can be adapted and encysted, or as an aberration that
can be corrected. None of what has been said here is to denigrate all the
hopes and the energies behind the EU. The EU itself, in the period
since Britain's entry, can hardly be said to have stood up to the strains. It
is now, of course, unpopular in Britain, though not only in Britain. And
there seems no doubt as to the results of a poll put in the following
form: "Given the choice, Britain's future will be with the United States,
Australia, Canada and New Zealand—or with Europe?" Many EU supporters are not perhaps necessarily wedded to the European solution as
such; but they had it presented to them as the only way to keep Britain
from becoming an isolated backwater. Our point here is that the scope
and enthusiasm behind the drive for Europe might readily be diverted

towards the even broader horizons of the Association.

It will be noted, too, that our scheme for an Association provides a larger unity than the narrower European Union; but that it also (being of a more organic type) needs less rigidity, and so gives more scope to the lesser local unities and their interests. The refusal of the EEC, already in July 1971, to make special provision for the Isle of Man and the Channel Islands (whose voters were not consulted at all in the negotiations) may be compared with the more flexible arrangements we have in mind.

But above all, far from the struggle for a great "Oceanic" Association implying any weakening of ties with the less powerful European and other allies, it should be accompanied by, and indeed imply, an energetic effort to strengthen the world alliance between democratic states. It is clear that the other forms, even if partially effective, are not in themselves adequate. They may continue to perform useful functions in limited spheres, encouraged rather than disrupted by the greater power of the Association.

II.

But suppose that the often stated aim of some "Europeans" to create a political and economic and even a military force roughly equal in power to the United States were feasible. This proposed division of the West into two more or less balanced centers or power is far more radically divisive, for numerical reasons alone, than a proposal greatly to strengthen the center. Confidence and unity in such a grouping as the Association should in fact revive rather than reduce the morale of other allies in Europe—and Japan. Such a reconcentration of power, far from repelling the other democracies, would be a center, a fulcrum. And similarly, far from a large concentration of political liberty in such an Association being a barrier to its arising elsewhere, such a central and easily deployed strength would form a rallying point for an eventual triumph of world democracy. For a strengthening of what is recognizably the core of the alliance automatically implies—and in practice has always gone with—a reinforcement of the centripetal element throughout the democratic world. Europe would be forced to come to terms rather than compete. And if the EU has proved to be in the interests of neither the United States nor Britain, and is proving a handicap to the development of worldwide policies for the democratic cultures, a different approach is clearly required from the Europeans themselves.

The perspective of an Association opens up eventually to a free market of the entire "Western" world. The EU on the other hand, is more or less openly concerned with a narrower autarchy in competition with the United States.

There seems to be several things to be learned from the experience of the EU. That is, quite apart from the creation of a Little Europe mentality. The mere mechanics of the supposed unification of Western Europe were wrongly conceived, and are certainly a lesson to any greater association.

First, as we have said, it was believed that economic unity could or should precede and produce political unity. But in general, as we have said, the broader and higher attitudes that constitute politics must always prevail; or, to put it another way, the economy can only be a component, important but never decisive, of the political. Of course it goes without saying that certain minimum economic matters must be adequately dealt with or a polity will collapse. That is far from making economics determinative—just as in a house the plumbing must work, but equally none of us would choose a house for its plumbing.

Economically, though, such an Association as we speak of, or at least its North Atlantic component, is not a new idea. A respectable school of economists has long preferred the Transatlantic option on economic grounds alone. Douglas Jay, President of the Board of Trade in the Labour government from 1964 to 1967, urged instead of the EEC the idea of a North Atlantic Free Trade Association. In his original conception, this would have consisted of Canada, the United Kingdom, the United States and the old European Free Trade Area. As he pointed out as early as 1968, this would have saved Britain from the expensive food policy of the Common Market and would have provided a duty-free market without rises in export costs. He noted also the advantages to Canada, at the time the country with the smallest tariff-free market of any leading industrial nation.

In America, Congress was told by President Lyndon Johnson's Trade Representative, William Ross, that the project was receiving serious consideration. A conference at New York University between members of the business, trade-union and university worlds of Britain, Canada and the United States, including United Kingdom Trade Union leader Frank Cousins, the economist Roy Harrod, Senator Javits and Professor Schlesinger, and representatives of the Canadian Conservative and

Liberal Parties, welcomed the proposal. This particular initiative—this particular variant—did not lead to results, but at the very least it shows a potentially receptive mood to the idea of a closer approach in the direction we have suggested.

And now we see the New Atlantic Initiative, supported by a far broader spectrum of statesmen and thinkers in Europe and North America. At the same time, American political thinking in this direction emerged again in 1998 with the suggestion from several Washington sources that the United Kingdom might join NAFTA. To say that there will be difficulties and obstacles is to state the obvious. If the process is worth pursuing, they can be overcome, however striking some of them may appear at a given moment.

Most of these initiatives have been in terms of a joint Euro-American approach. But this is hardly possible until the grotesque rigors of the European Union are abated. Meanwhile, as we have suggested, a British move into a transatlantic, or rather transoceanic, association—while retaining membership in a less overweening "Europe"—could prepare the way for a later coherence of the entire "West," and its allies elsewhere.

We have both the physical power and the moral prestige first to preserve the precarious peace of the world and, for the longer term, be the focus and example for a liberalization of the problem areas in their turn, and a genuine world community. If we grasp our opportunity, we may be in a position, to paraphrase the Younger Pitt, to save ourselves by our exertions and the world by our example.

12.

At present we can only speak of a change of direction, and anything like a realization of the suggested Association will take time. On the other hand, the public in all the Western countries, including the United States and Britain, is in a readily understandable mood of resentment at, and rejection of, bankrupt policies—and not only in international affairs. We seem, in fact, to be at one of those moods seen later as the occasions of radical change.

Arrangements that might result from the long and complex negotiations necessary before an Association could in fact be formed might differ in all sorts of inessential ways from any first sketch, as in all such cases. The union of the American colonies that was proposed, and unan-

imously accepted, at the Albany Congress of six of them in 1754, envisaged a President-General, appointed by the British Crown, and a Grand
Council elected by the colonial assemblies, with power to raise troops
and fleets and levy taxes and duties. This was premature, and things had
changed by the time a union was actually effected. But it was the basis of
much that followed—and within a comparatively short time.

The precise detail of closer arrangements between our component
states, at a given stage, seems less important than making some progress
in establishing the direction in which we are to move. Once started, the
momentum toward closer union would carry us forward, though at a
rate one cannot determine in the abstract.

13.

There will, of course, be opposition to these proposals. It will come
from various sources. In some Third World countries, the cry of neocolonialism or neo-imperialism will go up. Nor should we underestimate
its effect—even though there is also much sentiment for closer collaboration with the former colonial powers: indeed the two feelings may be
found in the same person. We must do everything to avoid the appearance, but even more any trace of the reality, of such a phenomenon.

In Britain, those of the left who wish to use British political insulari-
ty to turn the island into a sort of fogbound Cuba will see our suggestions as something that will make their schemes impossible.

Then there are many who have emotional capital invested in present
arrangements, in particular the extreme "Europeans" in Britain. And
some have institutional or career capital invested, too. There will be
those who point to the difficulties of such a change. But of course all
great advances have difficulties to overcome.

Chauvinist Americans, on the other hand, will deplore it as a method
of impeding America's ability to act independently. And a major block
is the existence of protectionist instincts in the United States. But if
there are protectionist moods in America, there are also moods favoring
broader international trade and competition. Moreover, to argue thus is
simply to present the problem. There were narrow States' Rights moods,
and interests too, in New York when Hamilton and Jay were conducting
their campaign.

14.

Formally speaking, the actual powers devolved to an Association, at any rate until a further stage may be reached, will be small. No derogation of sovereignty will arise. The task will be coordination and cooperation, to the extent that is not so much ideal as necessary.

Sovereignty is in many cases not susceptible of clear-cut definition, particularly when states associate in any way. Each of the United States is still technically speaking sovereign, and the degree of that sovereignty was not settled until ninety years after the Declaration of Independence. Originally, the Union, let alone the preceding Confederation of that period, was a coming together for reasons both practical and ideal, on the basis of what pragmatic politicians felt could be agreed to at the time. That is, a good deal was left undefined, or inadequately defined, to be developed by later generations. With us, too, instead of being faced with the vast set pieces of the Treaties of Rome and Maastricht and just arguing for adjustment within them (as who should say, do loosen this straitjacket at the elbows), there would be a period of flexible negotiation with no preconceptions about the stage to be reached within a given time.

At every point, negotiators would be committed, having learned from the errors of "Europe," to oppose bureaucratization, to avoid regulationism, above all to insist on—what "Europe" paid lip service to but betrayed—the true principles of subsidiarity.

It is not my purpose to lay down the ways in which this change might come about. Clearly, a political and publicity movement in our countries would have to develop. One can envisage a start made by committees of politicians from all the democratic parties, and of others in public life, emerging from the New Atlantic Initiative, which has already opened serious and urgent debate among all those concerned with the problem of Western unity in the face of the dangers of the present day.

In fact, the new perspectives of an Association constituting at once a plausible internationalism and (in a sense) a broader nationalism, with promise in every sphere, should prove a new stimulus to those who seek a better future.

The time is perhaps not too far off for something like a Declaration of Interdependence, and the election of an Intercontinental Congress—with, from the start, no more than a small and flexible permanent staff and a coordination of foreign, military and trade policy. We can meanwhile present the substance of such an arrangement—one that has breadth and scope and yet avoids the spurious breadth and scope of dogma or artificiality.

And similarly, let us repeat, far from a large concentration of political liberty in such an Association being a barrier to its arising elsewhere, such a central and easily deployed strength would form a rallying point for an eventual triumph of world democracy.

The internationalist idea and internationalist ideas in general may thus be channeled into the construction of a community with a genuine cultural unity and, though not world-embracing, fit to act as a model and center from which the eventual progress of the whole world may proceed; for as President Kennedy said in his message to Congress on 11 January 1962, "Our basic goal remains the same: a peaceful world community of free and independent states—free to choose their own future and their own system, as long as it does not threaten the freedom of others."

In that context, what is here proposed is not a solution so much as a direction. It is one that is in accord with both our reasons and our feelings.

◆

Afterword

I.

Iam well aware that there is much more to be said on the themes I have covered; and that there are important issues which I have passed by, or barely touched on.

In the foreign policy field, I have considered little more than the question of the unity of the civic culture in facing such problems. But, of course, that unity is needed today above all because of the threats to present world peace and future world survival and progress. It would not be within the scope of this book to present solutions to the particular perils facing us. However, it would be inappropriate to finish without a brief rehearsal of the main cruxes.

There are major countries equipped with large nuclear arsenals which are, or may be, under the control of leaderships hostile to the West to one degree or another and not easily to be included in a world order. There are, too, smaller pirate states with at least some nuclear (or biological or other) weaponry, and others that have that potential. This may obviously bring about major crises and immense destruction if not coped with by clear understanding backed by determined countermeasures. Some of these states support international terrorist activity, itself bad enough, but it also implies terrorist access to nuclear (or bacteriological, etc.) weapons.

And the West may not, though it may and should, maintain and develop the requisite military as well as political deterrence. This must mean strong investment both in the necessary research and in its deployment as weaponry (it is no good being ahead in the research if others develop the actual weaponry first). Opposition to this is inherent among those who believe, or feel, that arms are deplorable in themselves—a natural feeling, but the usual result is not to disarm completely but to reduce arms (and research) to a dangerously low level—though it used to be said in a similar context that nothing was as expensive as the second best navy. This is an absolutely crucial issue.

2.

Russian foreign policy even before Kosovo seemed based on rallying states hostile to the Western world into a sort of reactionary alliance. This is perhaps to put it strongly, and other options are being kept open in Moscow. This troublesome attitude is not the same as the ideology-driven unappeasable hostility of Soviet times. All the same, it has its dangers.

Russians based it in part on the expansion of NATO. It is clear that this expansion was not properly thought out; and if it were still in the idea stage, it would be sensible to oppose it. But while the plans to expand infuriated many in the political class in Russia, to oppose it once launched would have been to signal to the more chauvinist of them that they could thwart Western designs, and merely to encourage such attitudes. (I find that this view—that we had no need to do it, but that it would be even worse to abandon it once started—is widely held in Western informed circles, both left and right.)

Of course NATO was a military guarantee or defense against Soviet aggression. And, of course, it is predominantly seen in the East European countries joining it as a guarantee or defense against any possibly aggressive regime emerging in a future Russia. But, equally of course, a Russia irrevocably and clearly settled down as a peaceable member of the world scene would itself be a welcome component perhaps of NATO, certainly of an alliance for a less localized world stability. A best case. The worst case would be if the United States withdrew from, or enfeebled, NATO. Then Europe—and the world—would become danger zones, with bad, possibly disastrous, consequences for the United States.

Russian strength internationally speaking, as indeed under the Soviet regime, lies in a vast nuclear armament. Its weaknesses are obvious. Of course, we must hope for—and work for, insofar as that is possible—a Russia recovered or recovering from its economic, political and mental crises. And so, in its different circumstances, with China—of which we have hardly treated, except by implication. Just as Russia is unpredictable in international, as in internal, affairs, China is also unpredictable, and also armed with nuclear weapons (and working to produce more and better). It is easy to say that the West should balance its incentives to bringing both countries into the world order, and disincentives to their reverting to dangerous threats to such an order. Such a balance, far from being achieved, seems to be swaying somewhat erratically.

China is, moreover, an example of the world trend to a merger of state and corporations (with the state firmly in charge). This is a phenomenon we have so far dealt with in the context of corporationist bureaucracies, operating, in this sphere, not so much from ideological motives proper as from habits picked up from defunct ideas—a problem for the democratic populations everywhere. In the Chinese case, as elsewhere, it shows itself compatible with an expansionist attitude. China may evolve into a democratic and peaceable condition, as some think. Or it may reach that stage through revolutionary crisis, as others think. But there is also the possibility that something like the present system may persist longer than is desirable from the point of view of world peace.

Moves to integrate Russia, China and other such states into a world order include, and have long included, the idea of financial links which will, it is hoped, tie them into the world economy. In that connection, an element in any sound foreign policy must be a reasonably thought-out attitude to loans by private, state or international bodies. Over the past decades, as we have seen, vast sums have in effect been poured down ratholes. That is, the money was not used as advertised, to improve the economy, but went into apparatchik pockets. Nothing was achieved (and this was true of all *étatiste* kleptocracies, not only the Communist ones).

These huge outlays were made by famed institutions on the basis of advice from highly paid professionals. The results are more in accord with David Pryce-Jones's note on the qualities involved: "Greed, callousness, indifference and frivolity."

3.

Again, the human rights issue, as we have argued, is germane to Western foreign policy, in that suppression of the free movement of people and ideas is an obvious hindrance to progress towards a civic world. Moreover, such suppression, even occurring in states making no international trouble, may be the precursor of more virulent regimes.

In a different sense, human rights in the developing world, too, is an issue not merely of humanitarianism but also of hardheaded policy. Civil strife in the Third World, when it continues, causes cultural regress into a bandit mentality. Generations of young men, even boys, depend on gang loyalties and Kalashnikov rifles. The economy is ruined. Politics dies out.

In this and other contexts, an endemic fallacy that has colored Western diplomacy in the United Nations and elsewhere has been the notion of winning support by ignoring gross slanders by not only Communist but also other hostile states. Daniel Patrick Moynihan, when representing the United States at the UN, took the opposite view, always answering, and strongly counterattacking, such assaults. As he then pointed out, far from alienating the uncommitted, if anything this won them over. Forthrightness, and an insistence on truth, proved as effective as it was desirable—desirable, above all, in the long run, as a recognition that the international debate must, in our fundamental interests, not let our good case go by default. And firmness and clarity do not mean gross provocation or counterprovocation.

On the other hand, a general consistency of approach should not mean an adherence to any *theory* of negotiation as now found among some academics and sometimes spilling over into foreign policy professionals. In his inaugural lecture as Regius Professor of Modern History at Oxford, Michael Howard remarked of the "real lessons of history" that these apply to "people often of masterful intelligence, trained usually in law or economics or perhaps political science, who have led their governments into disastrous miscalculations because they have no awareness whatever of the historical background, the cultural universe of the foreign societies with which they have to deal. It is an awareness for which no amount of strategic or economic analysis, no techniques of crisis management or conflict resolution . . . can provide a substitute."

The Western miscalculations over Kosovo seem to have been based on the attitudes Howard cites. NATO, designed to fight Russia, could hardly have failed to defeat Serbia. But its initial politico-military approach, as John Keegan noted at the time, "reeks of the seminar," of experts who were expert in expertise rather than reality.

Again, the popular foundations of foreign policy are also not as strong or as soundly based as they should be. In part this is because the media coverage of world events has been inadequate. As Michael Ignatieff has pointed out, one of the results of current ethnic conflicts and the presentation of their horrors on Western TV may be "the feeling that the world has become too crazy to deserve serious attention."

4.

It is impossible to predict the effects of various crises not only in Russia or China but also elsewhere. Each crisis is unique in its range and combination of objective and subjective factors. And in any case, populations react differently to what seem to be parallel events. We have noted this in the failure of the stresses of the Industrial Revolution to lead to systemic crisis in Britain. The Marxist historian E. P. Thompson saw that, for one thing, class analysis fails to show how the British classes had a certain social balance and mutual understanding, and interpenetration, interrelation and humanity. Peter Vansittart, in his recent and fascinating *In Memory of England*, gives many illustrations of this social spread, so different from that of much of the Continent. (He also, though far from imperialist, provides many illuminating details of the human realities of the old Empire.)

To have a reasonable chance of handling our problems, we need to learn from this and other history. Meanwhile, a certain degeneration of our own civic order has been accompanied by a substitution of vague sentiment, or pretentious sophistry, for the understanding and training needed to sustain it in the world. Above all, successful policy is strongly dependent on the willpower, and the unity, of the democratic nations. Not that perfection can be expected in either. As to the willpower, that depends on informed and firm leadership for which no formal criterion can be devised.

It is hard to define a country or a culture's self-confidence. Lytton Strachey, the most skeptical of historical writers, once described England in the 1720s, at the time of Voltaire's stay:

> The great achievement of the Revolution and the splendid triumphs of Marlborough had brought to England freedom, power, wealth, and that sense of high exhilaration which springs from victory and self-confidence. Her destiny was in the hands of an aristocracy which was not only capable and enlightened, like most successful aristocracies, but which possessed the peculiar attribute of being deep-rooted in popular sympathies and of drawing its life-blood from the popular will.

Change aristocracy to "the political class," and ask ourselves whether such an assessment applies to any country in the West. It is true, as Strachey says, that "stagnation" set in soon afterwards; but if we are to seek the cause of the incomparably lower morale of our countries at present, we must surely seek it, at least in part, in the cancer of the clerisy.

We have not attempted to cover the whole range of foreign policy, nor have we sought to examine the whole range of Western domestic affairs. Thus we have said little about environmental problems. Many of these are obvious—pollution is there for all to see, and in some areas to breathe and drink. We have already suggested that some people actively involved in seeking solutions are temperamentally directed into misplaced activism based on false or dubious information. We find in the highly respectable *Economist* (20 December 1997) an article arguing at length that all the (extreme) environmental and similar scares of the past few decades—with the sole exception of the effects of pesticides on the fauna—have been of this type (including global warming, except marginally). Pollution can surely be combated for its own sake; indeed a serious approach must be hindered by distraction on to imaginary or greatly exaggerated targets.

The new corporatism and the bureaucratic caste it generates are, as we have suggested, negative features enough. One should add, first, that the computerization and the quasi-instant transfer of economic data and knowledge has an inbuilt tendency to promote "maximization" of profit—not so much on the productive as on the financial side. And second, that among not so much entrepreneurs proper, or even rentiers, as in this managerial stratum, a notable dehumanization of traditional "capitalism" has taken place, accompanied by the notorious excesses of salary and perks. Western governments, themselves entangled with this stratum, are coping inadequately; and the question is one for the public, left and right.

In this context, though also more generally, we have not dealt with technologies as such, let alone their probable or possible future development. But we should not for a moment fail to realize that the future lies before the human race in terms of thousands and millions of years, far longer than Homo sapiens's past, and far longer still than that of civilization. We are, nevertheless, at a major crux in that almost endless perspective of possibility.

5.

Looking back on these pages, I see, too, that I have not given enough attention to, for example, the persistence to this day of an adolescent revolutionary romanticism, as one of the unfortunate afflictions to which the human mind was and is prone. This is now being demonstrated yet again with (hardly credible though it may be) a revival of the cult of the totalitarian terrorist Che Guevara. It may (just) be worth recording that Adam Watson, a former British ambassador to Havana, told me that while he regarded Fidel Castro as an amiable rogue, he had found Guevara "a cold-blooded hypocrite." This reference was to his lifestyle and not, unfortunately, to his doubtless "sincere" destructive drives.

On a rather different, though not unconnected, note, readers will have come across criticism of the British Marxist historian Eric Hobsbawm. The point is not Hobsbawm's faults or merits—and some of his earlier work indeed has merits—but that an intellectual tendency in progressive establishment circles has evidently been brought, perhaps in student days, to regard these with a good deal more awe than most in the field would credit: a bad sign. Well, good luck to him (though bad luck for the British intelligentsia). We might, however, note as a contrary influence the frank and tormented abjuration by the no less influential writer Doris Lessing of her long-lasting Communist obsessions, a real human being abreacting what she now understands as an emotional and intellectual trap.

Among similar points I have not stressed in the mental sphere is the coarsening of the social and intellectual atmosphere in the West, in addition to—or together with—its dumbing down. The striking thing is that this is not the emergence of what in Britain would be called a yob culture from some uneducated antisocial stratum so much as the conscious adoption—even invention—of such standards, and their imposition on the rest, by an alienated intelligentsia whose aim seems to be to make Mick Jagger look like Lord Chesterfield. This can perhaps be viewed as a somewhat degraded version of the proletarian pose we noted in earlier Marxists—now become lumpen.

Another negative symptom is the fairly recent emergence of a validation of novelty as such. Half a dozen recent advertisements for jobs in local authorities in Britain are quoted (*Private Eye*, 24 July 1998): all in terms of "innovative," "breakthrough," "cutting edge," "groundbreaking." One example, for a post with the Birmingham City Council: "right at the forefront of cutting edge service—pushing forward change that will be seminal in this fast changing context." That is, it might also be described as—almost—an ideology in utero. The notion of administrative ability or other less shallow qualifications has gone. This is a fairly small-scale example, but of course activity for the sake of activity, or for the sake of the public appearance of activity, is to be found throughout British and American politics.

And, of course, in the arts. Marxist aesthetics were bad enough. Adam Slonimski, when head of the Polish Writers Union in his country's brief "liberalization" in 1956, said of "socialist realism" that it could prove that Notre-Dame was progressive, or alternatively that it wasn't beautiful.

And now, in a slightly different mode, advanced cutting-edge thinking on art can prove that a pail of bodily fluids and solids is beautiful, or alternatively that ugliness is aesthetically superior. This evokes such comments as (from the *Guardian*): "These days an artist cannot just be a good artist, but must be a loud artist as well." Or instead.

In themselves such art, such criticism, do not prove that a nadir has been reached and things can only improve. But it is worth registering more substantial grounds for such a hope. In the 1960s Kenneth Tynan announced that Noël Coward was now gone and forgotten. Coward has reemerged but where is Tynan? Arnold Bennett was patronized as not up to Bloomsbury chic; now he is recognized as a better novelist than Virginia Woolf (who survives largely on her letters and criticism). Sargent: swing; but the list is long—and perhaps indicative of a more general revulsion.

6.

We live in a world where the ideologies proper have suffered material and intellectual defeat.

For several generations, after 1917, a series of states existed that secured the emotional allegiance of many Western intellectuals as embodiments of their own utopian fantasies. When Stalin's USSR lost some of its appeal, the icon was transferred to Maoist Asia, then to Vietnam, Cuba, and finally the Sandinistas. No such center of attraction now exists.

But the demise of their greatest, and most irrational, competitors has plainly not left the societies and economies of the West (let alone of the Third World) in great condition.

Moreover, for some, the collapse of ideology has left an aching void. Even in the United Kingdom, with socialism gone, there has been a move to provide the Labour Party with a new Idea, with meetings and discussions run by think tanks about a Third Way and so on. Meanwhile, in Russia there has been public and high-level discussion on constructing, or reconstructing, the Russian Idea. In antidemocratic circles, this often amounts to the mental dregs of Marxism-Leninism being mixed with a premodern mishmash of nationalism and exclusionist religion.

More profoundly, the whole culture of civilization is at question not only in Russia, if especially in Russia. The nonagenarian Academician Dmitri Likhachev, since Andrei Sakharov's death Russia's most respected scholar, had told us of the cultural and psychological crisis still affecting Russian minds. Of the Stalin period he notes, "[T]hese psychological diseases are contagious, and the infection he started is still spreading. For seventy years they have been squeezing out of us feelings like sympathy, kindness, warmth."

He sees the institutions that nourished and preserved the cultural side crumbling away, and with it Russia's status as a contributor to, and member of, civilization. "Everyone wants Russia to be a stable European country, with European freedom and thought, rationality, recognition of other cultures as equals. . . . If European culture in our country is not preserved, then it will be replaced by some sort of perversion. It's extremely dangerous to the nation itself and to surrounding nations as well." That is, he sees the problem as not one of replacing a ruined ideology with a new one, but of the revivification of a broadly civilized mentality.

In fact, a Cold War must always subsist between the principles of pluralism and those of ideological despotism. It is a struggle that has lasted two centuries. Before France's then greatest poet André Chénier went to the guillotine in 1794, he wrote a splendid attack on the Jacobins who "presume to confer *Certificates of correct thinking.*" And that attitude persists.

7.

More generally, this book is an overview, an attempt to present in a reasonably coherent way the crucial causes of past disaster, and so of the problems still facing us in our hopes for a reasonably peaceful and consensual world.

It will be seen that I believe that only the eventual evolution of a civic type of order the world over will save us from the dangers that still threaten.

That various cultures, or cultural attitudes, will persist is obvious enough, and their contribution to a loosely united world is a very positive thing—broad variety not being the same as mutual antipathy. But we cannot in the long run accept the supposed corollary—that rogue regimes and movements produced in these cultures can be tolerated in principle, any more than could the National Socialist equivalent produced in the Western culture. On the contrary, only pluralist versions, or versions incorporating or evolving toward pluralism, can be seen as real components of a future world. None of this is to say that the complex tactical problems of foreign policy can be solved by simplistic confrontations. But a long-term strategy must maintain this general aim, nor dismiss it as impossible.

So we now have the opportunity of creating a worldwide political order based on the unity and power of the democratic culture. But the opportunity is not the same as the certainty. The past is full of eras of progress that ended in darkness. Success depends on several factors, but in major part on our learning to avoid, in the West as in the East, the mental distortions that were the main source of our earlier troubles. We are in something of the position of France at the time of Montaigne, when the extremists of religious wars were discredited and moderation had its political and intellectual opportunity—which faded. The power of fanaticism and of misunderstanding is by no means extinct.

Can the negative trends we have noted be reversed? Yes, they can. Can an intelligentsia shake off its delusions? Over the long haul, yes, it can. Can the civic culture prevail and create a peaceful world? Yes, it can. But we need to remember Churchill's words, at the crisis of the Battle of the Atlantic, "all the great struggles of history have been won by superior will-power wresting victory in the teeth of odds or upon the narrowest of margins."

We can improve the odds by a careful consideration of what needs to be learned, and unlearned.

Select Bibliography

Abramovitch, Raphael. *The Soviet Revolution, 1917–1939.* New York: International Universities Press, 1962.

Alden, John. *A History of the American Revolution.* New York: Knopf, 1969.

Almond, Mark. *Revolution.* London: De Agostine Editions, 1996.

Applebaum, Anne. *Between East and West: Across the Borderlands of Europe.* New York: Pantheon Books, 1994.

Aristotle. *The Ethics.* Baltimore: Penguin, 1955.

Aron, Raymond. *Democracy and Totalitarianism.* London: Weidenfeld & Nicolson, 1968.

———. *The Opium of the Intellectuals.* Garden City, N.Y.: Doubleday, 1957.

Auden, W. H. *Forewords and Afterwords.* New York: Vintage Books, 1974.

Beauvoir, Simone de. *The Prime of Life.* Cleveland: World Pub. Co., 1962.

Becker, Jasper. *Hungry Ghosts: China's Secret Famine.* London: J. Murray, 1996.

Berger, Joseph. *Shipwreck of a Generation.* London: Harvill, 1971.

Besançon, Alain. *La falsification du bien.* Paris: Julliard, 1984.

———. *The Intellectual Origins of Leninism.* Oxford: Basil Blackwell, 1981.

Brovkin, Vladimir. *Behind the Front Lines of the Civil War: Political Parties and Social Movements in Russia, 1918–1922.* Princeton, N.J.: Princeton University Press, 1994.

———. *The Mensheviks after October.* Ithaca, N.Y.: Cornell University Press, 1987.

Brown, J. A. C. *Freud and the Post-Freudians.* London: Cassell, 1963.

Bullock, Alan. *Hitler and Stalin: Parallel Lives.* London: HarperCollins, 1991.

Burckhardt, Jacob. *The Greeks and Greek Civilization.* London: HarperCollins, 1998.

Burnham, James. *The Managerial Revolution.* New York: The John Day Company, 1941.

Caute, David. *The Great Fear: The Anti-Communist Purge under Truman and Eisenhower.* New York: Simon and Schuster, 1978.

Chaudhuri, Nirad. *The Autobiography of an Unknown Indian.* London: Macmillan, 1951.

———. *Thy Hand, Great Anarch!: India, 1921–1952.* London: Chatto & Windus, 1987.

Chekhov, Anton. *Polnoe Sobranie Sochinenii* [*Complete works*]. St. Petersburg: A. F. Marks, 1903–1911.

Chernyshevsky, Nikolai. *What Is to Be Done?* Ithaca, N.Y.: Cornell University Press, 1989.

Churchill, Winston. *Winston Churchill's Secret Session Speeches.* New York: Simon and Schuster, 1946.

Ciliga, Anton. *The Russian Enigma.* London: Ink-Links, 1979.

Cohn, Norman. *The Pursuit of the Millenium,* rev. and expanded ed. New York: Oxford University Press, 1970.

————. *Warrant for Genocide.* New York: Harper & Row, 1967.

Conquest, Robert. *The Great Terror: A Reassessment.* New York: Oxford University Press, 1990.

————. *Present Danger: Towards a Foreign Policy.* Stanford, Calif.: Hoover Institution Press, 1979.

————. *Russia after Khrushchev.* New York: Praeger, 1965.

Courtois, Stephane [et al.], with the collaboration of Rémi Kauffer [et al.]. *Le livre noir du communisme: Crimes, terreurs et repression.* Paris: Robert Laffont, 1997.

Crankshaw, Edward. *Putting Up with the Russians.* London: Macmillan, 1984.

The Dark Side of the Moon. Preface by T. S. Eliot. London: Faber and Faber Ltd., 1946.

Djilas, Milovan. *Conversations with Stalin.* New York: Harcourt, Brace & World, 1962.

————. *The New Class.* New York: Praeger, 1957.

Dostoyevsky, Fyodor. *The Possessed.* London: Dent; New York: Dutton, 1931.

Ehrenburg, Ilia. *Den vtoroi; roman* [*The second day; A novel*]. Moscow: Khudozhestvennaia literatura, 1934.

Eliot, T. S. *The Rock.* London: Faber, 1934.

Ellis, John M. *Literature Lost.* New Haven, Conn.: Yale University Press, 1997.

Fermor, Patrick Leigh. *A Time of Gifts.* New York: Harper & Row, 1977.

Feshbach, Murray. *Ecocide in the USSR: Health and Nature under Siege.* New York: Basic Books, 1992.

Feuer, Lewis. *Ideology and the Ideologists.* New York: Harper & Row, 1975.

Frankel, Charles. *Human Rights and Foreign Policy.* New York: Foreign Policy Association, 1978.

Furet, Francois. *Le passé d'une illusion.* Paris: Robert Laffont, 1995.

Gellner, Ernest. *Encounters with Nationalism.* Oxford: Blackwell, 1994.

————. *Nations and Nationalism.* Oxford: Blackwell, 1983.

————. *State and Society in Soviet Thought.* Oxford: Blackwell, 1988.

Gentile, Giovanni. *Origini e dottrina del fascismo.* Rome: Istituto Nazionale Fascista di Cultura, 1934.

Gibbon, Edward. *The Decline and Fall of the Roman Empire.* London: D. Campbell, 1993–1994.

Gildea, Robert. *The Past in French History.* New Haven, Conn.: Yale University Press, 1994.

Gliksman, Jerzy. *Tell the West.* New York: Gresham Press, 1948.

Gromyko, Anatolii. *Vneshniaia Politika Sovetskogo Soiuza* [*The foreign policy of the Soviet Union*]. Moscow: Politizdat, 1975.

Grossman, Vasilii. *Forever Flowing.* New York: Harper & Row, 1972.

———. *Life and Fate.* London: Harvill Press, 1995.

Guevara, Ernesto. *Man and Socialism in Cuba.* Havana: Guairas Book Institute, 1967.

Hannan, D. *Towards 1996: Britain in a Multi-Speed Europe.* London: Alliance Publishers Ltd., 1994.

Haskell, Francis. *History and Its Images: Art and the Interpretation of the Past.* New Haven, Conn.: Yale University Press, 1993.

Haynes, John, and Harvey Klehr. *Venona: Soviet Espionage in America in the Stalin Era.* New Haven, Conn.: Yale University Press, 1999.

Hillary, Richard. *The Last Enemy.* London: Macmillan, 1950.

Himmelfarb, Gertrude. *The New History and the Old.* Cambridge, Mass.: Harvard University Press, Belknap Press, 1987.

Hingley, Ronald. *The Russian Mind.* New York: Scribner, 1977.

Hobsbawm, E. J. *The Age of Extremes.* New York: Vintage Books, 1996.

———. *On History.* London: Weidenfeld & Nicolson, 1997.

Hoffer, Eric. *The True Believer.* New York: Harper & Row, 1951.

Hollander, Paul. *Political Pilgrims.* New York: Oxford University Press, 1981.

Holloway, David. *Stalin and the Bomb.* New Haven, Conn.: Yale University Press, 1994.

Hope, Christopher. *Moscow! Moscow!* London: Heinemann, 1990.

Hough, Jerry, and Merle Fainsod. *How the Soviet Union Is Governed.* Cambridge, Mass.: Harvard University Press, 1979.

Howard, Philip K. *The Death of Common Sense.* New York: Random House, 1994.

Jackson, Henry M. *Henry M. Jackson and World Affairs: Selected Speeches, 1953–1983.* Seattle: University of Washington Press, 1990.

Kedourie, Elie. *Nationalism.* London: Hutchinson University Library, 1961.

Kennan, George. *Memoirs, 1925–1950.* Boston: Little, Brown 1967.

Khilnani, Sunil. *Arguing Revolution.* New Haven, Conn.: Yale University Press, 1993.

Koestler, Arthur. *Arrow in the Blue, An Autobiography.* London: Collins, with H. Hamilton, 1952–54.

———. *Darkness at Noon.* New York: Macmillan, 1941.

Kolakowski, Leszek. *Main Currents of Marxism.* Oxford: Clarendon Press, 1978.

Kramer, Hilton, and Roger Kimball, eds. *The Future of the European Past.* Chicago: Ivan R. Dee, 1997.

Kravchenko, Victor. *I Chose Justice.* London: Robert Hale Ltd., 1951.

Landes, David S. *The Wealth and Poverty of Nations.* New York: W.W. Norton, 1998.

Laqueur, Walter. *Fascism.* New York: Oxford University Press, 1996.

Larina, Anna. *This I Cannot Forget.* New York: W.W. Norton, 1993.

Lellouche, Pierre. *La republique immobile.* Paris: B. Grasset, 1998.

Lenin, Vladimir. *Collected Works.* Moscow: Foreign Languages Publishing House, 1960–70.

Le Roy Ladurie, Emmanuel. *The Mind and Method of the Historian.* Chicago: University of Chicago Press, 1981.

Lichtheim, George. *A Short History of Socialism.* New York: Praeger Publishers, 1970.

Macaulay, Thomas. *Critical and Historical Essays.* London: J. M. Dent, 1961.

———. *History of England from the Accession of James the Second.* London: Macmillan and Co., 1913–15.

Macfarlane, Alan. *The Origins of English Individualism: The Family, Property and Social Transition.* Oxford: Blackwell, 1978.

Mandelshtam, Nadezhda. *Hope Abandoned.* New York: Atheneum, 1974.

———. *Hope Against Hope.* New York: Atheneum, 1970.

Marx, Karl. *Karl Marx, Frederick Engels: Collected Works.* London: Lawrence & Wishart, 1975–.

Matthews, Mervyn. *Privilege in the Soviet Union: A Study of Elite Life-Styles under Communism.* London: G. Allen & Unwin, 1978.

Medvedev, Roy. *Let History Judge,* rev. and expanded ed. New York: Columbia University Press, 1989.

Mirsky, D. S., Prince. *The Intelligentsia of Great Britain.* London: V. Gollancz, Ltd., 1935.

Moore, Barrington. *Social Origins of Dictatorship and Democracy.* Boston: Beacon Press, 1996.

Morris, John. *The Age of Arthur; A History of the British Isles from 350 to 650.* New York, Scribner, 1973.

Moynihan, Daniel P. *Pandaemonium: Ethnicity in International Politics.* Oxford; New York: Oxford University Press, 1993.

Naipaul, V. S. *India: A Million Mutinies Now.* London: Heinemann, 1990.

Newman, P. R. *The Old Service: Royalist Regimental Colonels and the Civil War, 1642–46.* Manchester, U.K.: Manchester University Press, 1993.

Oakeshott, Michael. *Rationalism in Politics and Other Essays.* London: Methuen, 1981.

Orwell, George. *Animal Farm.* New York: Harcourt, Brace & Company, 1946.

———. *The Collected Essays, Journalism, and Letters of George Orwell.* New York: Harcourt, Brace & World, 1968.

———. *England, Your England, and Other Essays.* London: Secker & Warburg, 1953.

———. *Homage to Catalonia.* London: Secker & Warburg, 1938.

———. *Nineteen Eighty-Four.* Harmondsworth, U.K.: Penguin Books, 1954.

Pipes, Richard. *A Concise History of the Russian Revolution.* New York: Knopf, 1995.

———. *Russia under the Bolshevik Regime.* New York: Knopf, 1993.

Plumb, J. H. *The Death of the Past.* Boston: Houghton Mifflin, 1970.

Powell, Anthony. *Messengers of Day.* New York: Holt, Rinehart, and Winston, 1978.

Pryce-Jones, David. *The Strange Death of the Soviet Empire.* New York: Metropolitan Books, 1995.

Putnam, Robert D. *Making Democracy Work: Civic Traditions in Modern Italy.* Princeton, N.J.: Princeton University Press, 1993.

Rauschning, Hermann. *Germany's Revolution of Destruction.* London: W. Heinemann, 1939.

Remnick, David. *Lenin's Tomb: The Last Days of the Soviet Empire.* New York: Random House, 1993.

————. *Resurrection: The Struggle for a New Russia.* New York: Random House, 1997.

Roberts, Paul Craig. *Alienation and the Soviet Economy.* Albuquerque: University of New Mexico Press, 1971.

Sakharov, Andrei. *Alarm and Hope.* New York: Knopf, 1978.

————. *Memoirs.* Translated by Richard Lourie. New York: Knopf, 1990.

Salway, Peter. *Roman Britain.* Oxford: Clarendon Press, 1981.

Sartori, Giovanni. *The Theory of Democracy Revisited.* Chatham, N.J.: Chatham House Publishers, 1987.

Schapiro, Leonard. *The Origin of the Communist Autocracy.* New York: Praeger, 1965.

————. *Totalitarianism.* New York: Praeger, 1972.

Schlesinger, Arthur, Sr. *The Birth of the Nation: A Portrait of the American People on the Eve of Independence.* New York: Knopf, 1968.

Scott, James C. *Seeing Like a State: How Certain Schemes to Improve the Human Condition Have Failed.* New Haven, Conn.: Yale University Press, 1998.

Seton-Watson, Hugh. *From Lenin to Khrushchev: The History of World Communism.* New York: Praeger, 1960.

————. *Neither War nor Peace: The Struggle for Power in the Postwar World.* New York: Praeger, 1966.

Simmons, David. *Ideals and Dogma.* Northolt, U.K.: Third Avenue Press, 1980.

Solzhenitsyn, Aleksandr Isaevich. *The Cancer Ward.* New York: Dial Press, 1968.

————. *The Gulag Archipelago.* New York: Harper & Row, 1973.

"The Spanish Civil War: The View from the Left." *Revolutionary History* 4, no. 1/2 (1998).

Spear, Percival. *The Nabobs,* rev. ed. London: Oxford University Press, 1963.

Squire, John. *If It Had Happened Otherwise.* London: Sidgwick and Jackson, 1972.

Strachey, Lytton. *Books and Characters.* London: Chatto & Windus, 1922.

Swianiewicz, Stanislaw. *Forced Labour and Economic Development.* London: Oxford University Press, 1965.

Symons, Julian. *The Thirties.* London: Cresset Press, 1960.

Szamuely, Tibor. *The Russian Tradition.* Edited by Robert Conquest. New York: McGraw-Hill, 1974.

Thompson, E. P. *The Making of the English Working Class.* Harmondsworth, U.K.: Penguin, 1968.

Tocqueville, Alexis de. *Democracy in America.* New York: Vintage Books, 1990.

Todd, Emmanuel. *The Final Fall* [*La chute finale*]. New York: Karz Publishers, 1979.

Trevelyan, G. M. *Clio, A Muse, And Other Essays.* London: Longmans, Green and Co., 1931.

Turgenev, Ivan. *Sobranie Sochinenii* [*Works*]. Moscow: Gosudarstvennoe izdvo khudozhestvennoi literatury, 1961–1962.

Ulam, Adam. *The Communists.* New York: Scribner's, 1992.

————. *In the Name of the People.* New York: Viking Press, 1977.

————. *Russia's Failed Revolutions.* New York: Basic Books, 1981.

Vaksberg, Arkady. *Stalin's Prosecutor: The Life of Andrei Vyshinsky.* New York: Grove Weidenfeld, 1991.

Vansittart, Peter. *In Memory of England: A Novelist's View of History.* London: John Murray, 1998.

Veliz, Claudio. *The New World of the Gothic Fox: Culture and Economy in English and Spanish America.* Berkeley: University of California Press, 1994.

Vishnevskaia, Galina. *Galina.* Translated by Guy Daniels. San Diego: Harcourt Brace Jovanovich, 1984.

Wazyk, Adam. "Poem For Adults," in *Back to Life: Poems from behind the Iron Curtain* ed. Robert Conquest. London: Hutchinson, 1958.

Webb, Sidney, and Beatrice Webb. *Soviet Communism: A New Civilisation.* London: V. Gollancz, 1937.

Weissberg, Alexander. *Conspiracy of Silence.* London: Hamilton, 1952.

Wheeler, Mortimer. *Alms for Oblivion.* London: Weidenfeld & Nicolson, 1966.

Wolin, Richard, ed. *The Heidegger Controversy: A Critical Reader.* Cambridge, Mass.: MIT Press, 1993.

Wright, Richard. *American Hunger.* New York: Harper & Row, 1977.

Yeats, W. B. *Collected Poems.* London: Arena, 1990.

————. *The Senate Speeches of W. B. Yeats.* London: Faber and Faber, 1961.

Zhelev, Zheliu. *Fashizmut.* Boulder, Colo.: Social Science Monographs, 1990.

Zirkle, Conway. *Death of a Science in Russia.* Philadelphia: University of Pennsylvania Press, 1949.

Zubok, Vladislav, and Constantine Pleshakov. *Inside the Kremlin's Cold War: From Stalin to Khrushchev.* Cambridge, Mass.: Harvard University Press, 1996.

Index

ROBERT CONQUEST was born in Great Malvern, England, in 1917, the son of an American father and a British mother. He was educated at Winchester College and the Universities of Grenoble and Oxford, receiving from the latter his M.A. in politics, philosophy, and economics and his D.Litt. in history. He served in the Oxford and Bucks Light Infantry 1939–46, the U.K. Foreign Service 1946–56, and then various appointments in academia and journalism, including literary editor of the London *Spectator*, posts at the London School of Economics, Columbia University, the Woodrow Wilson Center, and, at present, the Hoover Institution at Stanford University. His books include seven volumes of verse—the latest, *Demons Don't*, was recently published—together with fiction, translation, literary criticism, biography, and such historical works as *The Great Terror* and *The Harvest of Sorrow*. He is married to Elizabeth, daughter of the late Colonel Richard D. Neece, USAF, and has two sons by a previous marriage.